CONSTITUTION & CANONS

CONSTITUTION & CANONS

TOGETHER WITH THE RULES OF ORDER

FOR THE GOVERNMENT OF THE PROTESTANT EPISCOPAL CHURCH
IN THE UNITED STATES OF AMERICA
OTHERWISE KNOWN AS

THE EPISCOPAL CHURCH

ADOPTED AND REVISED IN GENERAL CONVENTION, 1789–2003

2003

Edited by
The Archives of the Episcopal Church

General Convention Office
815 Second Avenue
New York, New York 10017

Church Publishing Incorporated

5 4 3 2 1

CONTENTS

CONSTITUTION OF THE GENERAL CONVENTION

CANONS OF THE GENERAL CONVENTION

Title III Ministry

Title IV Ecclesiastical Discipline

Title V General Provisions

Canon

RULES OF ORDER

House of Bishops

House of Deputies

INDEX

CONSTITUTION

PREAMBLE

The Protestant Episcopal Church in the United States of America, otherwise known as The Episcopal Church (which name is hereby recognized as also designating the Church), is a constituent member of the Anglican Communion, a Fellowship within the One, Holy, Catholic, and Apostolic Church, of those duly constituted Dioceses, Provinces, and regional Churches in communion with the See of Canterbury, upholding and propagating the historic Faith and Order as set forth in the Book of Common Prayer. This Constitution, adopted in General Convention in Philadelphia in October, 1789, as amended in subsequent General Conventions, sets forth the basic Articles for the government of this Church, and of its overseas missionary jurisdictions.

Name of Church.

Anglican Communion.

ARTICLE I

Sec. 1. There shall be a General Convention of this Church, consisting of the House of Bishops and the House of Deputies, which Houses shall sit and deliberate separately; and in all deliberations freedom of debate shall be allowed. Either House may originate and propose legislation, and all acts of the Convention shall be adopted and be authenticated by both Houses.

General Convention.

Sec. 2. Each Bishop of this Church having jurisdiction, every Bishop Coadjutor, every Suffragan Bishop, every Assistant Bishop, and every Bishop who by reason of advanced age or bodily infirmity, or who, under an election to an office created by the General Convention, or for reasons of mission strategy determined by action of the General Convention or the House of Bishops, has resigned a jurisdiction, shall have a seat and a vote in the House of Bishops. A majority of all Bishops entitled to vote, exclusive of Bishops who have resigned their jurisdiction or positions, shall be necessary to constitute a quorum for the transaction of business.

House of Bishops.

Quorum.

Sec. 3. At the General Convention next before the expiration of the term of office of the Presiding Bishop, it shall elect the Presiding Bishop of the Church. The House of Bishops shall choose one of the Bishops of this Church to be the Presiding Bishop of the Church by a vote of a majority of all Bishops, excluding retired Bishops not present, except that whenever two-thirds of the House of Bishops are present a majority vote shall suffice, such choice to be subject to confirmation by the House of Deputies. The term and tenure of office and duties and particulars of the election not inconsistent with the preceding provisions shall be prescribed by the Canons of the General Convention.

Election of Presiding Bishop.

Term and tenure of Office.

But if the Presiding Bishop of the Church shall resign the office as such, or if by reason of infirmity shall become disabled, or in case of death, the Bishop who, according to the Rules of the House of Bishops, becomes its Presiding Officer, shall (unless the date of the next General Convention is within three months) immediately call a special meeting of the House of Bishops, to elect a member thereof to be the Presiding Bishop. The certificate

Succession.

of election on the part of the House of Bishops shall be sent by the Presiding Officer to the Standing Committees of the several Dioceses, and if a majority of the Standing Committees of the Dioceses shall concur in the election, the Bishop elected shall become the Presiding Bishop of the Church.

House of Deputies.

Sec. 4. The Church in each Diocese which has been admitted to union with the General Convention, each area Mission established as provided by Article VI, and the Convocation of the American Churches in Europe, shall be entitled to representation in the House of Deputies by not more than four ordained persons, Presbyters or Deacons, canonically resident in the Diocese and not more than four Lay Persons, confirmed adult communicants of this Church, in good standing in the Diocese but not necessarily domiciled in the Diocese; but the General Convention by Canon may reduce the representation to not fewer than two Deputies in each order. Each Diocese, and the Convocation of the American Churches in Europe, shall prescribe the manner in which its Deputies shall be chosen.

Quorum.

To constitute a quorum for the transaction of business, the Clerical order shall be represented by at least one Deputy in each of a majority of the Dioceses entitled to representation, and the Lay order shall likewise be represented by at least one Deputy in each of a majority of the Dioceses entitled to representation.

Majority Vote.

Sec. 5. The vote on all questions which come before the House of Deputies shall be governed by the following provisions, supplemented by such procedural provisions as the House of Deputies may adopt in its Rules of Order:

Vote by Orders.

Unless a greater vote on any question is required by this Constitution or by the Canons in cases not specifically dealt with by this Constitution or unless a vote by orders on a question is required, the affirmative vote of a majority of all of the Deputies present and voting shall suffice to carry any question. A vote by orders on any question shall be taken if required for that question by this Constitution or by the Canons or if the Clerical or Lay representation from three or more separate Dioceses shall so request at the time of the call for the vote on that question. In all cases of a vote by orders, the vote of each order, Clerical and Lay, shall be counted separately, each order in each Diocese shall have one vote, and a vote in the affirmative by an order in a Diocese shall require the affirmative vote of a majority of the Deputies present in that order in that Diocese. To carry in the affirmative any question being voted on by orders requires concurrence in the affirmative by both orders and, unless a greater vote is required by this Constitution or by the Canons in cases not specifically dealt with by this Constitution, concurrence in the affirmative by an order requires the affirmative vote in that order by a majority of the Dioceses present in that order.

Adjournment.

Sec. 6. In either House any number less than a quorum may adjourn from day to day. Neither House, without the consent of the other, shall adjourn for more than three days, or to any place other than that in which the Convention shall be sitting.

Sec. 7. The General Convention shall meet not less than once in each three years, at a time and place appointed by a preceding Convention; but if there shall appear to the Presiding Bishop, acting with the advice and consent of the Executive Council of the Church or of a successor canonical body having substantially the powers now vested in the Executive Council, sufficient cause for changing the place or date so appointed, the Presiding Bishop, with the advice and consent of such body, shall appoint another place or date, or both, for such meeting. Special meetings may be provided for by Canon.

Time and place of meeting.

ARTICLE II

Sec. 1. In every Diocese the Bishop or the Bishop Coadjutor shall be chosen agreeably to rules prescribed by the Convention of that Diocese, *provided* that the retirement date of the Bishop Diocesan shall not be more than thirty-six months after the consecration of the Bishop Coadjutor. Bishops of Missionary Dioceses shall be chosen in accordance with the Canons of the General Convention.

Election of Bishops.

Sec. 2. No one shall be ordained and consecrated Bishop until the attainment of thirty years of age; nor without the consent of a majority of the Standing Committees of all the Dioceses, and the consent of a majority of the Bishops of this Church exercising jurisdiction. But if the election shall have taken place within three months next before the meeting of the General Convention, the consent of the House of Deputies shall be required in place of that of a majority of the Standing Committees. No one shall be ordained and consecrated Bishop by fewer than three Bishops.

Required age.

Consent to election.

Consecration.

Sec. 3. A Bishop shall confine the exercise of such office to the Diocese in which elected, unless requested to perform episcopal acts in another Diocese by the Ecclesiastical Authority thereof, or unless authorized by the House of Bishops, or by the Presiding Bishop by its direction, to act temporarily in case of need within any territory not yet organized into Dioceses of this Church.

Jurisdiction of Bishops.

Sec. 4. It shall be lawful for a Diocese, at the request of the Bishop of that Diocese, to elect not more than two Suffragan Bishops, without right of succession, and with seat and vote in the House of Bishops. A Suffragan Bishop shall be consecrated and hold office under such conditions and limitations other than those provided in this Article as may be provided by Canons of the General Convention. A Suffragan Bishop shall be eligible for election as Bishop or Bishop Coadjutor of a Diocese, or as a Suffragan in another Diocese.

Bishops Suffragan.

Sec. 5. It shall be lawful for a Diocese to prescribe by the Constitution and Canons of such Diocese that upon the death of the Bishop, a Suffragan Bishop of that Diocese may be placed in charge of such Diocese and become temporarily the Ecclesiastical Authority thereof until such time as a new Bishop shall be chosen and consecrated; or that during the disability

May become Ecclesiastical Authority.

or absence of the Bishop, a Bishop Suffragan of that Diocese may be placed in charge of such diocese and become temporarily the Ecclesiastical Authority thereof.

Resignation.

Sec. 6. A Bishop may not resign jurisdiction without the consent of the House of Bishops.

Bishop Suffragan for Armed Forces.

Sec. 7. It shall be lawful for the House of Bishops to elect a Suffragan Bishop who, under the direction of the Presiding Bishop, shall be in charge of the work of those chaplains in the Armed Forces of the United States, Veterans' Administration Medical Centers, and Federal Correctional Institutions who are ordained Ministers of this Church. The Suffragan Bishop so elected shall be consecrated and hold office under such conditions and limitations other than those provided in this Article as may be provided by Canons of the General Convention. The Suffragan Bishop shall be eligible for election as Bishop or Bishop Coadjutor or Suffragan Bishop of a Diocese.

Election of Bishops to other jurisdictions.

Sec. 8. A Bishop who has for at least five years next preceding, exercised jurisdiction as the Ordinary, or as the Bishop Coadjutor, of a Diocese, may be elected as Bishop, Bishop Coadjutor, or Suffragan Bishop of another Diocese. Before acceptance of such election a resignation of jurisdiction in the Diocese in which the Bishop is then serving, conditioned on the required consents of the Bishops and Standing Committees of the Church to such election, shall be submitted to the House of Bishops, and also, if the Bishop be a Bishop Coadjutor, a renunciation of the right of succession. Such resignation, and renunciation of the right of succession in the case of a Bishop Coadjutor, shall require the consent of the House of Bishops.

Resignation procedure must be followed.

Compulsory retirement age.

Sec. 9. Upon attaining the age of seventy-two years a Bishop shall resign from all jurisdiction.

ARTICLE III

Bishops consecrated for foreign lands.

Bishops may be consecrated for foreign lands upon due application therefrom, with the approbation of a majority of the Bishops of this Church entitled to vote in the House of Bishops, certified to the Presiding Bishop; under such conditions as may be prescribed by Canons of the General Convention. Bishops so consecrated shall not be eligible to the office of Diocesan or of Bishop Coadjutor of any Diocese in the United States or be entitled to vote in the House of Bishops, nor shall they perform any act of the episcopal office in any Diocese or Missionary Diocese of this Church, unless requested so to do by the Ecclesiastical Authority thereof. If a Bishop so consecrated shall be subsequently duly elected as a Bishop of a Missionary Diocese of this Church, such election shall then confer all the rights and privileges given in the Canon to such Bishops.

ARTICLE IV

Standing Committees.

In every Diocese a Standing Committee shall be elected by the Convention thereof, except that provision for filling vacancies between meetings of the Convention may be prescribed by the Canons of the respective Dioceses. When there is a Bishop in charge of the Diocese, the Standing Committee shall be the Bishop's Council of Advice. If there be no Bishop or Bishop Coadjutor or Suffragan Bishop canonically authorized to act, the Standing Committee shall be the Ecclesiastical Authority of the Diocese for all purposes declared by the General Convention. The rights and duties of the Standing Committee, except as provided in the Constitution and Canons of the General Convention, may be prescribed by the Canons of the respective Dioceses.

ARTICLE V

Admission of new Dioceses.

Sec. 1. A new Diocese may be formed, with the consent of the General Convention and under such conditions as the General Convention shall prescribe by General Canon or Canons, (1) by the division of an existing Diocese; (2) by the junction of two or more Dioceses or of parts of two or more Dioceses; or (3) by the erection into a Diocese of an unorganized area evangelized as provided in Article VI. The proceedings shall originate in a Convocation of the Clergy and Laity of the unorganized area called by the Bishop for that purpose; or, with the approval of the Bishop, in the Convention of the Diocese to be divided; or (when it is proposed to form a new Diocese by the junction of two or more existing Dioceses or of parts of two or more Dioceses) by mutual agreement of the Conventions of the Dioceses concerned, with the approval of the Bishop of each Diocese. In case the Episcopate of a Diocese be vacant, no proceedings toward its division shall be taken until the vacancy is filled. After consent of the General Convention, when a certified copy of the duly adopted Constitution of the new Diocese, including an unqualified accession to the Constitution and Canons of this Church, shall have been filed with the Secretary of the General Convention and approved by the Executive Council of this Church, such new Diocese shall thereupon be in union with the General Convention.

Rights of Bishops when Diocese divides.

Sec. 2. In case one Diocese shall be divided into two or more Dioceses, the Bishop of the Diocese divided, at least thirty days before such division, shall select the Diocese in which the Bishop will continue in jurisdiction. The Bishop Coadjutor, if there be one, subsequently and before the effective date of the division shall select the Diocese in which the Bishop Coadjutor shall continue in jurisdiction, and if it not be the Diocese selected by the Bishop shall become the Bishop thereof.

Rights of Bishops when new Diocese formed from parts of two or more Dioceses.

Sec. 3. In case a Diocese shall be formed out of parts of two or more Dioceses, each of the Bishops and Bishops Coadjutor of the several Dioceses out of which the new Diocese has been formed shall be entitled, in order of seniority of consecration, to the choice between the Bishop's Diocese and the new Diocese so formed. In the case the new Diocese shall not be so chosen, it shall have the right to choose its own Bishop.

Constitution and Canons of new Dioceses.

Sec. 4. Whenever a new Diocese is formed and erected out of an existing Diocese, it shall be subject to the Constitution and Canons of the Diocese out of which it was formed, except as local circumstances may prevent,until the same be altered in accordance with such Constitution and Canons by the Convention of the new Diocese.

Whenever a Diocese is formed out of two or more existing Dioceses, it shall be subject to the Constitution and Canons of that one of the said existing Dioceses to which the greater number of Members of the Clergy shall have belonged prior to the erection of such new Diocese, except as local circumstances may prevent, until the same be altered in accordance with such Constitution and Canons by the Convention of the new Diocese.

Number of Presbyters and Parishes.

Sec. 5. No new Diocese shall be formed unless it shall contain at least six Parishes and at least six Presbyters who have been for at least one year canonically resident within the bounds of such new Diocese, regularly settled in a Parish or Congregation and qualified to vote for a Bishop. Nor shall such new Diocese be formed if thereby any existing Diocese shall be so reduced as to contain fewer than twelve Parishes and twelve Presbyters who have been residing therein and settled and qualified as above provided.

Cession of diocesan territory.

General Convention to approve.

Rights of Bishops.

Sec. 6. By mutual agreement between the Conventions of two adjoining Dioceses, consented to by the Ecclesiastical Authority of each Diocese, a portion of the territory of one of said Dioceses may be ceded to the other Diocese, such cession to be considered complete upon approval thereof by the General Convention or by a majority of Bishops having jurisdiction in the United States, and of the Standing Committees of the Dioceses, in accordance with the Canons of this Church. Thereupon the part of the territory so ceded shall become a part of the Diocese accepting the same. The provisions of Section 3 of this Article V shall not apply in such case, and the Bishop and Bishop Coadjutor, if any, of the Diocese ceding such territory shall continue in their jurisdiction over the remainder of such Diocese, and the Bishop and Bishop Coadjutor, if any, of the Diocese accepting cession of such territory shall continue in jurisdiction over such Diocese and shall have jurisdiction in that part of the territory of the other Diocese that has been so ceded and accepted.

ARTICLE VI

Area Missions may be established.

Sec. 1. The House of Bishops may establish a Mission in any area not included within the boundaries of any Diocese of this Church or of any Church in communion with this Church, and elect or appoint a Bishop therefor.

Cession of jurisdiction.

Sec. 2. The General Convention may accept a cession of the territorial jurisdiction of a part of a Diocese when such cession shall have been proposed by the Bishop and the Convention of such Diocese, and consent thereto shall have been given by three-fourths of the Parishes in the ceded territory, and also by the same ratio of the Parishes within the remaining territory.

Retrocession of such jurisdiction.

Any territorial jurisdiction or any part of the same, which may have been ceded by a Diocese under the foregoing provision, may be retroceded to the said Diocese by such joint action of all the several parties as is herein required for its cession, save that in the case of retrocession of territory the consent of Parishes within the territory retroceded shall not be necessary; *Provided*, that such action of the General Convention, whether of cession or retrocession, shall be by a vote of two-thirds of all the Bishops present and voting and by a vote by orders in the House of Deputies in accordance with Article I, Section 5, except that concurrence by the orders shall require the affirmative vote in each order by two-thirds of the Dioceses.

Sec. 3. Missionary Dioceses shall be organized as may be prescribed by Canon of the General Convention.

Missionary Dioceses.

ARTICLE VII

Dioceses may be united into Provinces in such manner, under such conditions, and with such powers, as shall be provided by Canon of the General Convention; *Provided, however,* that no Diocese shall be included in a Province without its own consent.

Provinces.

ARTICLE VIII

No person shall be ordered Priest or Deacon to minister in this Church until the person shall have been examined by the Bishop and two Priests and shall have exhibited such testimonials and other requisites as the Canons in that case provided may direct. No person shall be ordained and consecrated Bishop, or ordered Priest or Deacon to minister in this Church, unless at the time, in the presence of the ordaining Bishop or Bishops, the person shall subscribe and make the following declaration:

Requisites for ordination.

I do believe the Holy Scriptures of the Old and New Testaments to be the Word of God, and to contain all things necessary to salvation; and I do solemnly engage to conform to the Doctrine, Discipline, and Worship of the Episcopal Church.

Declaration.

Provided, however, that any person consecrated a Bishop to minister in any Diocese of an autonomous Church or Province of a Church in communion with this Church may, instead of the foregoing declaration, make the promises of Conformity required by the Church in which the Bishop is to minister.

Proviso.

If any Bishop ordains a Priest or Deacon to minister elsewhere than in this Church, or confers ordination as Priest or Deacon upon a Christian minister who has not received Episcopal ordination, the Bishop shall do so only in accordance with such provisions as shall be set forth in the Canons of this Church.

No person ordained by a foreign Bishop, or by a Bishop not in communion with this Church, shall be permitted to officiate as a Minister of this Church until the person shall have complied with the Canon or Canons in that case provided and also shall have subscribed the aforesaid declaration.

Admission of foreign clergy.

A bishop may permit a minister ordained in the Evangelical Lutheran Church in America or its predecessor bodies who has made the promise of conformity required by that Church in place of the foregoing declaration to officiate on a temporary basis as an ordained minister of this church.

Lutheran exception.

ARTICLE IX

Court for trial of Bishops.

The General Convention may, by Canon, establish one or more Courts for the Trial of Bishops.

For trial of Presbyters and Deacons.

Presbyters and Deacons canonically resident in a Diocese shall be tried by a Court instituted by the Convention thereof; Presbyters and Deacons canonically resident in a Missionary Diocese shall be tried according to Canons adopted by the Bishop and Convocation thereof, with the approval of the House of Bishops; *Provided,* that the General Convention in each case may prescribe by Canon for a change of venue.

Courts of Review.

The General Convention, in like manner, may establish or may provide for the establishment of Courts of Review of the determination of diocesan or other trial Courts.

Court composed of Bishops.

The Court for the review of the determination of the trial Court, on the trial of a Bishop, shall be composed of Bishops only.

Court of Appeal.

The General Convention, in like manner, may establish an ultimate Court of Appeal, solely for the review of the determination of any Court of Review on questions of Doctrine, Faith, or Worship.

Bishop to pronounce sentence.

None but a Bishop shall pronounce sentence of suspension, or removal, or deposition from the Ministry, on any Bishop, Presbyter, or Deacon; and none but a Bishop shall admonish any Bishop, Presbyter, or Deacon.

Suspension.

A sentence of suspension shall specify on what terms or conditions and at what time the suspension shall cease. A sentence of suspension may be remitted in such manner as may be provided by Canon.

ARTICLE X

The Book of Common Prayer.

Alterations or additions.

The Book of Common Prayer, as now established or hereafter amended by the authority of this Church, shall be in use in all the Dioceses of this Church. No alteration thereof or addition thereto shall be made unless the same shall be first proposed in one regular meeting of the General Convention and by a resolve thereof be sent within six months to the Secretary of the Convention of every Diocese, to be made known to the Diocesan Convention at its next meeting, and be adopted by the General Convention at its next succeeding regular meeting by a majority of all Bishops, excluding retired Bishops not present, of the whole number of Bishops entitled to vote in the House of Bishops, and by a vote by orders in the House of Deputies in accordance with Article I, Sec. 5, except that concurrence by the orders shall require the affirmative vote in each order by a majority of the Dioceses entitled to representation in the House of Deputies.

Exceptions.

But notwithstanding anything herein above contained, the General Convention may at any one meeting, by a majority of the whole number of the Bishops entitled to vote in the House of Bishops, and by a majority of the Clerical and Lay Deputies of all the Dioceses entitled to representation in the House of Deputies, voting by orders as previously set forth in this Article:

Lectionary.

(a) Amend the Table of Lessons and all Tables and Rubrics relating to the Psalms:

(b) Authorize for trial use throughout this Church, as an alternative at any time or times to the established Book of Common Prayer or to any section or Office thereof, a proposed revision of the whole Book or of any portion thereof, duly undertaken by the General Convention.

Trial use.

And *Provided*, that nothing in this Article shall be construed as restricting the authority of the Bishops of this Church to take such order as may be permitted by the Rubrics of the Book of Common Prayer or by the Canons of the General Convention for the use of special forms of worship.

Special forms of worship.

ARTICLE XI

Interpretation of "Diocese."

Whenever the term "Diocese" is used without qualification in this Constitution, it shall be understood to refer both to Dioceses and to Missionary Dioceses and also, wherever applicable, to all other jurisdictions entitled to representation in the House of Deputies of the General Convention.

ARTICLE XII

Alterations or amendments to Constitution.

No alteration or amendment of this Constitution shall be made unless the same shall be first proposed at one regular meeting of the General Convention and be sent to the Secretary of the Convention of every Diocese, to be made known to the Diocesan Convention at its next meeting, and be adopted by the General Convention at its next succeeding regular meeting by a majority of all Bishops, excluding retired Bishops not present, of the whole number of Bishops entitled to vote in the House of Bishops, and by an affirmative vote by orders in the House of Deputies in accordance with Article I, Section 5, except that concurrence by the orders shall require the affirmative vote in each order by a majority of the Dioceses entitled to representation in the House of Deputies.

Notwithstanding the provisions of the foregoing paragraph, the adoption of any alteration or amendment of this Constitution which inserts or repeals an Article, or a Section or Clause of an Article, shall effect the necessary change in numbers or letters of Articles or Sections or Clauses of an Article, that follow, and in references made in this Constitution to any other part, without the necessity of specific provision therefor in the alteration or amendment.

Effective date.

Each duly adopted alteration or amendment to this Constitution, unless otherwise expressly stated therein, shall take effect on the first day of January following the adjournment of the General Convention at which it is finally adopted.

TITLE I
ORGANIZATION AND ADMINISTRATION

CANON 1: Of the General Convention

Organizing the House of Deputies.

Sec. 1 (a) At the time and place appointed for the meeting of the General Convention, the President of the House of Deputies, or, if absent, the Vice-President of the House, or, if there be neither, a presiding officer *pro tempore* appointed by the members of the House of Deputies on the Joint Committee of Arrangements for the General Convention, shall call to order the members present. The Secretary, or, if absent, a Secretary *pro tempore* appointed by the presiding officer, shall record the names of those whose testimonials, in due form, shall have been presented, which record shall be *prima facie* evidence that the persons whose names are therein recorded are entitled to seats. In the event that testimonials are presented by or on behalf of persons from jurisdictions which have not previously been represented in a General Convention, then the Secretary, or one appointed instead as provided herein, shall proceed as provided in Clause (c). If there be a quorum present, the Secretary shall so certify, and the House shall proceed to organize by the election, by ballot, of a Secretary, and a majority of the votes cast shall be necessary to such election. Upon such election, the presiding officer shall declare the House organized. If there be a vacancy in the office of President or Vice-President, the vacancy or vacancies shall then be filled by election, by ballot, the term of any officer so elected to continue until the adjournment of the General Convention. As soon as such vacancies are filled, the President shall appoint a committee to wait upon the House of Bishops and inform it of the organization of the House of Deputies, and of its readiness to proceed to business.

Election of President and Vice-President.

(b) There shall be a President and a Vice-President of the House of Deputies, who shall perform the duties normally appropriate to their respective offices or specified in these Canons. They shall be elected not later than the seventh day of each regular meeting of the General Convention in the manner herein set forth. The House of Deputies shall elect from its membership, by a majority of separate ballots, a President and a Vice-President, who shall be of different orders. Such officers shall take office at the adjournment of the regular meeting at which they are elected, and shall continue in office until the adjournment of the following regular meeting of the General Convention. They shall be and remain *ex officio* members of the House during their term of office. No person elected President or Vice-President shall be eligible for more than three consecutive full terms in each respective office. In case of resignation, death, absence, or inability, of the President, the Vice-President shall perform the duties of the office until a new President is elected. The President shall be authorized to appoint an Advisory Council for consultation and advice in the performance of the duties of the office. The President may also appoint a Chancellor to the President, a confirmed adult communicant of the Church in good standing who is learned in both ecclesiastical and

Advisory Council.

President may appoint a Chancellor.

secular law, to serve so long as the President may desire, as counselor in matters relating to the discharge of the responsibilities of that office.

Diocesan Journals to be forwarded.

(c) In order to aid the Secretary in preparing the record specified in Clause (a), it shall be the duty of the Secretary of the Convention of every Diocese to forward to the Secretary of the House of Deputies, as soon as may be practicable, a copy of the latest Journal of the Diocesan Convention, together with a certified copy of the testimonials of members aforesaid, and a duplicate copy of such testimonials. Where testimonials are received for persons from jurisdictions which have not previously been represented in General Convention, the Secretary shall ascertain that the applicable provisions of Article V, Section 1, of the Constitution have been complied with prior to such persons being permitted to take their seats in the House.

Testimonials required.

Secretary to keep minutes and records.

(d) The Secretary shall keep full minutes of the proceedings of the House; record them, with all reports, in a book provided for that purpose; preserve the Journals and Records of the House; deliver them to the Registrar, as hereinafter provided; and perform such other duties as may be directed by the House. The Secretary may, with the approval of the House, appoint Assistant Secretaries, and the Secretary and Assistant Secretaries shall continue in office until the organization of the next General Convention, and until their successors be chosen.

Notices of Amendments to Constitution and Prayer Book.

(e) It shall be the duty of the Secretary of the House of Deputies, whenever any alteration of the Book of Common Prayer or of the Constitution is proposed, or any other subject submitted to the consideration of the several Diocesan Conventions, to give notice thereof to the Ecclesiastical Authority of the Church in every Diocese, as well as to the Secretary of the Convention of every Diocese, and written evidence that the foregoing requirement has been complied with shall be presented by the Secretary to the General Convention at its next session. All such notices shall be sent by certified or registered mail, with the Secretary's certificates to be returned. The Secretary shall notify all diocesan Secretaries that it is their duty to make known such proposed alterations of the Book of Common Prayer, and of the Constitution, and such other subjects, to the Conventions of their respective Dioceses at their next meeting, and to certify to the Secretary of the House of Deputies that such action has been taken.

Secretary and Treasurer to have seat and voice.

(f) The Secretary of the House of Deputies and the Treasurer of the General Convention shall be entitled to seats upon the floor of the House, and, with the consent of the President, they may speak on the subjects of their respective offices.

Rules and Orders of the House of Deputies.

(g) At the meetings of the House of Deputies the Rules and Orders of the previous meeting shall be in force until they are amended or repealed by the House.

(h) In case of the resignation, death, or total disability of the President and Vice-President during the recess of the General Convention, the Secretary of the House of Deputies shall perform such *ad interim* duties as may appertain to the office of President until the next meeting of the General Convention or until such disability is removed.

(i) If, during recess, a vacancy shall occur in the office of Secretary of the House of Deputies, the duties thereof shall devolve upon the First Assistant Secretary, or, if there be none such, upon a Secretary *pro tempore* appointed by the President of the House, or if the office of President be also vacant, then by the Vice-President, and if both offices be vacant, then by the members from the House of Deputies of the Joint Committee on Planning and Arrangements for the next General Convention, appointed by the preceding General Convention.

Secretary of House of Deputies to be Secretary of Convention.

(j) At every regular meeting of the General Convention, the Secretary elected by the House of Deputies shall, by concurrent action of the two Houses of the General Convention, also be made the Secretary of the General Convention, who shall have responsibility for assembling and printing of the Journal of the General Convention, and for other matters specifically referred to the Secretary.

Standing Commissions.

Sec. 2 (a) The General Convention by Canon may establish Standing Commissions, to study and make recommendations to the General Convention on major subjects considered to be of continuing concern to the Church. The Canon shall specify the size, composition and duties of each such Commission. Standing Commissions shall be composed of Bishops, Priests and/or Deacons of this Church and Lay Persons, who shall be confirmed adult communicants of this Church in good standing. Priests, Deacons and Lay Persons may but need not be members of the House of Deputies.

Terms of office.

(b) The terms of all members of Standing Commissions shall be equal to the interval between the regular meeting of the General Convention preceding their appointment and the adjournment of the second succeeding regular meeting of the General Convention, and such terms shall be rotated so that, as near as may be, the term of one half of the members shall expire at the conclusion of each regular meeting of the General Convention. The term of a member shall become vacant in the event of two absences from meetings of the Commission occurring in the interval between successive regular meetings of the General Convention unless excused by the Commission for good cause.

Appointment of members.

(c) The Presiding Bishop shall appoint the Episcopal members, and the President of the House of Deputies the Lay and other Clerical members, of such Commissions as soon as practicable after the adjournment of the General Convention. Episcopal members appointed after the adjournment of any General Convention at which a Presiding Bishop is elected shall be appointed by the Presiding Bishop-elect. Vacancies shall be filled in similar manner; *provided, however,* that vacancies occurring within one year of the next regular General Convention shall not be filled unless so requested by the Commission.

Consultants and coordinators.

(d) The Presiding Bishop and the President of the House of Deputies may jointly appoint members of the Executive Council as liaison persons to provide for communication between the Executive Council and any Commission. Notice of such appointments shall be given to the Secretaries of both Houses. Such appointed liaison persons shall not be members of the Commission and shall have voice but not vote. The reasonable expenses thereof shall be provided for by the Executive Council. Each such Commission shall have power to constitute committees and to request the services of Executive Council staff, and, subject to the Commission's budget, engage the services of consultants and coordinators necessary to the carrying on of its work.

Ex officiis members.

(e) The Presiding Bishop and the President of the House of Deputies shall be members *ex officiis* of every Commission with the right, but no obligation, to attend meetings, and with seat and vote in the deliberations thereof, and shall receive their minutes and an annual report of their activities; *Provided,* that the said presiding officers may appoint personal representatives to attend any meeting in their stead, but without vote.

Notification of duties.

(f) The Executive Officer of the General Convention shall, not later than the month of January following the meeting of the General Convention, notify the members of the respective Houses of their appointments upon Commissions and their duty to present Reports to the next Convention. One year prior to the opening day of the Convention, the Executive Officer of the General Convention shall remind the Chairs and Secretaries of all Commissions of this duty.

Convenor appointed and officers elected.

(g) Every Commission shall be convened by a member of the Commission appointed by the Presiding Bishop and the President of the House of Deputies, and when convened shall be organized by electing a chair, vice-chair and secretary. In the event that the Commission is not convened as above provided within six months from the date of adjournment of each Convention, one-third of the members may take such action as shall be necessary to convene the Commission. After the Commission shall have been convened, and its officers chosen, the Chair or, in the absence of the Chair or in the Chair's inability or refusal to act, the Vice-Chair shall be empowered to call a meeting and fix the time and place and shall do so upon signed request of one-third of the members.

Referrals.

(h) It shall be the privilege of either House to refer to a Commission any matter related to the subject for which it was appointed; but neither House shall have the power, without the consent of the other, to instruct the Commission as to any particular line of action.

Public notice of meeting.

(i) It shall be the duty of each Commission to give appropriate notice in the Church press of issues before it and the time and place of meetings at which such issues are to be considered, together with instructions as to the manner in which members of the Church may address their views to such Commission.

Reports due.

(j) Every Commission shall prepare a Report, which, together with any minority Report, shall be sent, not later than 150 days prior to the opening day of each Convention, to the Executive Officer of the General Convention, who shall print and distribute the same, as far as practicable, to all members of said Convention.

Contents of Reports.

(k) The Report of every Commission presented at the General Convention shall:

(1) Set forth the names of its original members, any changes in membership, the names of all those who concur in and all

those who dissent from its recommendation, and shall further state, if less than a majority of its entire membership sign the Report, their authority for presenting it.

(2) Summarize the work of the Commission, including the various matters studied, the recommendations for action by the General Convention and drafts of Resolutions proposed for adoption to implement the recommendations of the Commission.

(3) Include a detailed report of all receipts and expenditures, including moneys received from any source whatsoever, during the preceding interval since the last meeting of the General Convention, and if it recommends that it be continued, the estimated requirements for the ensuing interval until the next regular meeting of the General Convention.

Spokesperson to be present at General Convention.

(l) Every Commission, as a condition precedent to the presentation and reception of any Report in either House, in which such Commission proposes the adoption of any Resolution, shall, by vote, authorize a member or members of that House, who, if possible, shall be a member of the Commission, with such limitations as the Commission may impose, to accept or reject, on behalf of the Commission, any amendments proposed in such House to any such Resolution; *Provided, however,* that no such amendment may change the substance of the proposal, but shall be primarily for the purpose of correcting errors. The name of the member or members of the particular House upon whom such authority has been conferred, and the limitations of authority, shall be communicated in writing to the Presiding Officer of such House not later than the presentation of such Report in that House. The application of this Rule in either House may be suspended, in any particular case, by the majority vote of the members of such House.

Budget requirements.

(m) Every Commission whose Report requests expenditure out of the funds of the General Convention (except for the printing of the Report) shall present to the Joint Standing Committee on Program, Budget, and Finance its written request, on or before the first business day of the session, and all Resolutions providing for any such expenditures shall be immediately referred to the Joint Standing Committee on Program, Budget, and Finance. No proposition involving such expenditures shall be considered unless so presented and until after report of the Joint Standing Committee on Program, Budget, and Finance.

(n) There shall be the following Standing Commissions:

Standing Commission on Anglican and International Peace with Justice Concerns.

(1) A Standing Commission on Anglican and International Peace with Justice Concerns consisting of 14 members (4 Bishops, 4 Priests and/or Deacons and 6 Lay Persons). It shall be the duty of the Commission to develop recommendations and strategies regarding common ministry opportunities and concerns with other Provinces of the Anglican Communion as to the work of this Church and the Anglican Communion on issues of international peace with justice and to make recommendations pertaining thereto to the Presiding Bishop, the Executive Council and the General Convention.

Standing Commission for Small Congregations.

(2) A Standing Commission for Small Congregations, consisting of 10 members (3 Bishops, 2 Priests and/or Deacons, and 5 Lay Persons). It shall be the duty of the Commission to concern itself with plans for new directions for Small Congregations.

Standing Commission on Constitution and Canons.

(3) A Standing Commission on Constitution and Canons, consisting of 12 members (3 Bishops, 3 Priests and/or Deacons, and 6 Lay Persons). The Standing Commission shall:

(i) Review such proposed amendments to the Constitution and Canons as may be submitted to the Commission, placing each such proposed amendment in proper Constitutional or Canonical form including all amendments necessary to effect the proposed change. The Commission shall express its views with respect to the substance of any such proposal only to the proponent thereof; *Provided, however,* that no member of the Commission shall, by reason of membership, be deemed to be disabled from expressing, before a Legislative Committee or on the floor of the House of membership, personal views with respect to the substance of any such proposed amendment.

(ii) Conduct a continuing comprehensive review of the Constitution and Canons with respect to their internal consistency and clarity, and on the basis of such a review propose to the General Convention such technical amendments to the Constitution and Canons as in the opinion of the Commission are necessary or desirable in order to achieve such consistency and clarity without altering the substance of any Constitutional and Canonical provisions; *Provided, however,* that the Commission shall propose, for the consideration of the appropriate Legislative Committees of the two Houses, such amendments to the Constitution and Canons as in the opinion of the Commission are technically desirable but involve a substantive alteration of a Constitutional or Canonical provision..

(iii) On the basis of such review suggest to the Executive Council and the Domestic and Foreign Missionary Society such amendments to their respective By-laws as in the opinion of the Commission are necessary or desirable in order to conform the same to the Constitution and Canons.

(iv) Discharge such other duties as shall from time to time be assigned by the General Convention.

Standing Commission on Domestic Mission and Evangelism.

(4) A Standing Commission on Domestic Mission and Evangelism consisting of 16 members (2 Bishops, 6 Priests and/or Deacons and 8 Lay Persons). It shall be the duty of the Commission to identify, study and consider major general policies, priorities

and concerns as to the domestic mission of this Church. This shall include a review of the shaping of new patterns and directions for evangelism particularly in rural and metropolitan areas. The Commission shall develop and recommend to the General Convention comprehensive and coordinated policies and strategies to restore all people to unity with God and each other in Christ.

Standing Commission on Ecumenical and Interreligious Relations.

(5) A Standing Commission on Ecumenical and Interreligious Relations consisting of 18 members (6 Bishops, 6 Priests and/or Deacons and 6 Lay Persons). Its duties shall be to recommend to the General Convention a comprehensive and coordinated policy and strategy on relations between this Church and other Churches, and this Church and other religions, to make recommendations to General Convention concerning interchurch cooperation and unity, and interreligious dialogue and action, and to carry out such instructions on ecumenical and interreligious matters as may be given it from time to time by the General Convention. It shall also nominate for appointment by the Presiding Bishop, with the advice and consent of the Executive Council, persons to serve on the governing bodies of ecumenical and interreligious organizations to which this Church belongs by action of the General Convention, who shall report to the Presiding Bishop, Executive Council and the Standing Commission on Ecumenical and Interreligious Relations.

Standing Commission on Liturgy and Music.

(6) A Standing Commission on Liturgy and Music consisting of 16 members (4 Bishops, 4 Priests and/or Deacons and 8 Lay Persons). In addition, the Custodian of the Book of Common Prayer shall be a member *ex officio* with voice, but without vote. The Standing Commission shall:

(i) Discharge such duties as shall be assigned to it by the General Convention as to policies and strategies concerning the common worship of this Church.

(ii) Collect, collate and catalogue material bearing upon possible future revisions of the Book of Common Prayer.

(iii) Cause to be prepared and to present to the General Convention recommendations concerning the Lectionary, Psalter, and offices for special occasions as authorized or directed by the General Convention or House of Bishops.

(iv) Recommend to the General Convention authorized translations of the Holy Scripture from which the Lessons prescribed in the Book of Common Prayer are to be read.

(v) Receive and evaluate requests for consideration of individuals or groups to be included in the Calendar of the Church year and make recommendations thereon to the General Convention for acceptance or rejection.

(vi) Collect, collate, and catalogue material bearing upon possible future revisions of The Hymnal 1982 and other musical publications regularly in use in this Church and encourage the composition of new musical materials.

(vii) Cause to be prepared and present to the General Convention recommendations concerning the musical settings of liturgical texts and rubrics, and norms as to liturgical music and the manner of its rendition.

(viii) At the direction of the General Convention, serve the Church in matters pertaining to policies and strategies concerning Church music.

Standing Commission on Ministry Development.

(7) A Standing Commission on Ministry Development consisting of 24 members. Nine members shall be appointed on the nomination of the nine Provincial Presidents, one nomination from each Province. The remaining 15 shall include 3 bishops, 4 priests and/or deacons, provided that two shall be deacons, and 8 lay persons. It shall be the duty of the Commission:

(i) to recommend policies and strategies to the General Convention for the development, affirmation and exercise of the ministry of all the baptized;

(ii) to encourage and facilitate networks of individuals, institutions and agencies engaged in education, training, deployment and formation for ministry by all four orders;

(iii) to study the needs and trends of theological education for all four orders with this Church, including issues of recruitment, training, deployment, evaluation and continuing education; to make recommendation to the several seminaries, the Executive Council and the General Convention; and to aid the General Board of Examining Chaplains in the exercise of its function;

(iv) to discharge such other duties as shall be assigned by the General Convention.

Standing Commission on National Concerns.

(8) A Standing Commission on National Concerns consisting of 16 members (2 Bishops, 6 Priests and/or Deacons and 8 Lay Persons). It shall be the duty of the Commission to identify, study and consider general policies, priorities and concerns about the theological, ethical and pastoral issues and strategies as to the ministries of this Church serving Christ, to strive for justice and peace among all peoples through the proclamation of the Gospel and to develop and recommend to the General Convention comprehensive and coordinated policies and strategies applicable to the same.

Standing Commission on Stewardship and Development.

(9) A Standing Commission on Stewardship and Development, consisting of 12 members (2 Bishops, 2 Priests and/or Deacons, and 8 Lay Persons). It shall be the duty of the Commission to hold up before the Church the responsibility of

faithful stewardship of time, talent and treasure in grateful thanksgiving for God's gifts. It shall recommend strategies for stewardship education throughout the Church with special sensitivity to the cultural and linguistic diversity of our Church. It shall recommend programs for long-range planning and development, ensuring that other Church bodies, including the Executive Council, are part of the process. It shall assure that there is an official, periodic gathering, interpretation, evaluation and reporting of stewardship from throughout the Church. It shall help coordinate all church-wide fund-raising activities.

(10) A Standing Commission on the Structure of the Church, consisting of 12 members (3 Bishops, 3 Presbyters and/or Deacons, and 6 Lay Persons). It shall be the duty of the Commission to study and make recommendations concerning the structure of the General Convention and of the Church. It shall, from time to time, review the operation of the several Committees and Commissions to determine the necessity for their continuance and the effectiveness of their functions and to bring about a coordination of their efforts. Whenever a proposal is made for the creation of a new Committee or Commission, it shall, wherever feasible, be referred to the Standing Commission on the Structure of the Church for its consideration and advice.

Standing Commission on Structure.

(11) A Standing Commission on World Mission, consisting of 12 members (3 Bishops, 3 Priests or Deacons, and 6 Lay Persons), whose members shall include persons broadly representative of jurisdictions outside the United States of America, as well as persons having direct engagement with and experience in world mission. It shall be the duty of the Commission, as to all mission outside the United States, to review and evaluate existing policies, priorities and strategies, and to promote partnership for global mission among the various groups within the church, to plan and propose policy on overseas mission, and to make recommendations pertaining to the Executive Council and the General Convention.

Standing Commission on World Mission.

(12) A Standing Commission on Episcopal Church Communication consisting of 14 members (4 Bishops, 4 Priests and/or Deacons, and 6 Lay Persons). It shall be the duty of the Commission to guide the policies, participate in the strategic planning, and share in the oversight of implementing a comprehensive communication strategy for the Episcopal Church.

Standing Commission on Communication.

(13) A Standing Commission on Health consisting of 11 members (3 Bishops, 3 Priests and/or Deacons, and 5 Lay Persons). It shall be the duty of the Commission to:

Standing Commission on Health

(i) Articulate and communicate positions adopted by the Episcopal Church on health care policy to Episcopalians, the public, and public policy makers;

(ii) Advocate, in cooperation with the Office of Government Relations, for a health care system in which all may be guaranteed decent and appropriate primary health care during their lives and as they approach death;
(iii) Bring together those within the Episcopal Church who develop, provide and/or teach health care and health policy to continue to develop a Christian approach to pressing issues that affect the health care system of this nation;
(iv) Understand and keep abreast of the rapidly changing health care market and developments in biomedical research that affect health policy;
(v) Collect and develop resources and teaching materials related to access to health care for the use of dioceses, congregations, and individuals;
(vi) Advocate health ministry in and through local Episcopal congregations; and
(vii) Discharge such other duties as shall be assigned by the General Convention.

Special meetings.

Sec. 3 (a) The right of calling special meetings of the General Convention shall be vested in the Bishops. The Presiding Bishop shall issue the summons for such meetings, designating the time and place thereof, with the consent, or on the requisition, of a majority of the Bishops, expressed to the Presiding Bishop in writing.

Deputies to special meetings.

(b) The Deputies elected to the preceding General Convention shall be the Deputies at such special meetings of the General Convention, except in those cases in which other Deputies shall have been chosen in the meantime by any of the Diocesan Conventions, and then such other Deputies shall represent in the special meeting of the General Convention the Church of the Diocese in which they have been chosen.

Vacancy.

(c) Any vacancy in the representation of any Diocese caused by the death, absence, or inability of any Deputy, shall be supplied either temporarily or permanently in such manner as shall be prescribed by the Diocese, or, in the absence of any such provision, by appointment by the Ecclesiastical Authority of the Diocese. During such periods as shall be stated in the certificate issued to such person by the appointing power, the Provisional Deputy so appointed shall possess and shall be entitled to exercise the power and authority of the Deputy in place of whom he or she shall have been designated.

Deputies to be elected twelve months prior to Convention.

Sec. 4 (a) All jurisdictions of this Church entitled by the Constitution or Canons to choose Deputies to the General Convention shall be required to do so not later than twelve months preceding the opening date of the General Convention for which they are chosen. Deputies of jurisdictions failing so to elect may not be seated unless permitted by ruling of the Presiding Officer.

(b) It shall be the duty of each seated Deputy to communicate to the electing jurisdiction the actions taken and the positions established by the General Convention.

(c) It shall be the responsibility of each Diocese to provide a forum in which the Deputies to the General Convention from that jurisdiction have opportunity to report.

Registrar.

Sec. 5 (a) The House of Deputies, upon the nomination of the House of Bishops, shall elect a Presbyter, to be known as the Registrar of the General Convention, whose duty it shall be to receive all Journals, files, papers, reports, and other documents or articles that are, or shall become, the property of either House of the General Convention, and to transmit the same to the Archives of the Church as prescribed by the Archivist.

To keep records of consecrations.

(b) It shall also be the duty of the said Registrar to maintain suitable records of the ordinations and consecrations of all the Bishops of this Church, designating accurately the time and place of the same, with the names of the consecrating Bishops, and of others present and assisting; to have the same authenticated in the fullest manner practicable; and to take care for the similar record and authentication of all future ordinations and consecrations of Bishops in this Church. Due notice of the time and place of such ordinations and consecrations shall be given by the Presiding Bishop to the Registrar; and thereupon it shall be the duty of the Registrar to attend such ordinations and consecrations, either in person or by deputy.

To prepare Letters of Consecration.

(c) The Registrar shall prepare, in such form as the House of Bishops shall prescribe, the Letters of Ordination and Consecration in duplicate, shall have the same immediately signed and sealed by the ordaining and consecrating Bishops, and by such other Bishops assisting as may be practicable, shall deliver to the newly consecrated Bishop one of the said Letters, shall carefully file and retain the other, and shall make a minute thereof in the official records.

Registrar as Historiographer.

(d) The Registrar shall also be Historiographer, unless in any case the House of Bishops shall make a separate nomination; and in this event the House of Deputies shall confirm the nomination.

Expenses.

(e) The necessary expenses incurred under this Section shall be paid by the Treasurer of the General Convention.

Journals and papers to be delivered to Registrar.

(f) It shall be the duty of the secretaries of both Houses, within thirty days after the adjournment of the General Convention, to deliver to the Registrar the manuscript minutes of both Houses, together with the Journals, files, papers, reports, and all other documents of either House. The manuscript minutes of both Houses shall remain filed until after the adjournment of the second Convention following that at which such minutes shall have been taken; *Provided, however,* that any part of such minutes, for any reason unpublished in the Journal, shall remain filed in the Archives. The Secretary of the House of Deputies shall also deliver to the Registrar, when not otherwise expressly directed, all the Journals, files, papers, reports, and other documents specified in Canon I.6. The Secretaries shall require the Registrar to give them receipts for the Journals and other papers.

Vacancy.

(g) In the case of a vacancy in the office of Registrar, the Presiding Bishop shall appoint a Registrar, who shall hold office until the next General Convention.

Recorder.

Sec. 6 (a) The House of Deputies, upon nomination of the House of Bishops, shall elect a Recorder (who may be a natural person or an incorporated organization of this Church), whose duty is/shall be to continue the List of Ordinations and to keep a list of the Clergy in regular standing.

Information to be sent to Recorder.

(b) It shall be the duty of the Bishop, or, if there be no Bishop, of the President of the Standing Committee of every jurisdiction to forward to the Recorder on or before the first day of March in each and every year a report certifying the following information as of the thirty-first day of December in the preceding year: (1) the names of the Clergy canonically resident therein with their several charges; (2) the names of the Clergy licensed by the Bishop to officiate, but not yet transferred; (3) the names of all persons connected with the jurisdiction who have been ordered Deacons or Priests during the preceding twelve months, with the date and place of ordination and the name of the Bishop ordaining; (4) the names of the Clergy of the jurisdiction who have died during the preceding twelve months, with the date and place of death; (5) the names of the Clergy who have been received during the preceding twelve months, with the date of their reception and the name of the jurisdiction from which received, and, in the case of Clergy not received from a jurisdiction of this Church, the date and place of ordination and the name of the Bishop ordaining; (6) the names of the Clergy who have been transferred during the preceding twelve months, with the dates of the Letters Dimissory and of their acceptance, and the name of the jurisdiction to which transferred; (7) the names of the Clergy who have been suspended during the preceding twelve months, with the date and ground of suspension; (8) the names of the Clergy who have been removed or deposed during the preceding twelve months, with the date, place, and ground of removal or deposition; (9) the names of the Clergy who have been restored during the preceding twelve months, with the date; (10) the names of Deaconesses canonically resident therein.

Recorder to furnish information.

(c) It shall be the duty of the Recorder to furnish, upon proper authority and at the expense of the applicant, such information as may be in the possession of the Recorder, based upon the reports required under Clause (b) hereof; but in no case shall the Recorder publish, or furnish for publication, the ground of any suspension, removal, or deposition.

Report to the General Convention.

(d) The Recorder shall prepare and present to each session of the General Convention a list of all Clergy ordained, received, suspended, removed, deposed, or restored, and of all Bishops consecrated, and of all Bishops and other Clergy who have died; such list to cover the period from the last preceding similar report of the Recorder through the thirty-first day of December immediately preceding each session of the General Convention.

Expenses.

(e) The necessary expenses incurred under this Section by the Recorder shall be paid by the Treasurer of the General Convention.

Vacancy.

(f) In case of a vacancy in the office of Recorder, the Presiding Bishop shall appoint a Recorder, who shall hold office until the next General Convention.

Treasurer.

Sec. 7 (a) At every regular meeting of the General Convention a Treasurer (who may also be Treasurer of the Domestic & Foreign Missionary Society and the Executive Council) shall be elected by concurrent action of the two

Houses, and shall remain in office until a successor shall be elected. It shall be the Treasurer's duty to receive and disburse all moneys collected under the authority of the Convention, and of which the collection and disbursement shall not otherwise be prescribed; and, with the advice and approval of the Presiding Bishop and the Treasurer of the Executive Council, to invest, from time to time, such surplus funds as may be on hand. The Treasurer's account shall be rendered to the Convention at each regular meeting, and shall be audited at the direction of a committee acting under its authority.

(b) In case of a vacancy, by death, resignation, or otherwise, in the office of Treasurer of the General Convention, the Presiding Bishop and the President of the House of Deputies shall appoint a Treasurer, who shall hold office until a successor is elected. In case of temporary inability of the Treasurer to act, from illness or other cause, the same officials shall appoint an Acting Treasurer who shall perform all duties of the Treasurer until the Treasurer is able to resume them.

Vacancy.

Sec. 8. The General Convention shall adopt, at each regular meeting, a budget to provide for the contingent expenses of the General Convention, the stipend of the Presiding Bishop together with the necessary expenses of that office, the necessary expenses of the President of the House of Deputies including the staff and Advisory Council required to assist in the performance of the duties and matters related to the President's office, and the applicable Church Pension Fund assessments. To defray the expense of this budget, an assessment shall be levied upon the Dioceses of the Church in accordance with a formula which the Convention shall adopt as part of this Expense Budget. It shall be the duty of each Diocesan Convention to forward to the Treasurer of the General Convention annually, on the first Monday of January, the amount of the assessment levied upon that Diocese.

Assessment for General Convention Expense Budget.

Sec. 9. The Treasurer of the General Convention shall have authority to borrow, in behalf and in the name of the General Convention, such a sum as may be judged by the Treasurer to be necessary to help defray the expenses of the General Convention, with the approval of the Presiding Bishop and the Executive Council.

Treasurer may borrow.

Sec. 10. The Treasurer shall give a bond conditioned on the faithful performance of assigned duties. The amount thereof and the terms on which the same shall be given shall be subject to the approval of the Presiding Bishop, the expense of such bond to be paid by the General Convention.

Shall give bond.

Sec. 11. The Treasurer shall submit to the General Convention at each regular meeting thereof a detailed budget in which the Treasurer proposes to request appropriations for the ensuing budgetary period and shall have power to expend all sums of money covered by this budget, subject to such provisions of the Canons as shall be applicable.

Shall submit budget.

Sec. 12. The Treasurer may appoint, subject to the approval of the Presiding Bishop, an Assistant Treasurer, who shall hold office during the pleasure of the Treasurer and shall perform such duties as shall be assigned

May appoint Assistant Treasurer.

by the Treasurer. The Assistant Treasurer shall give bond conditioned on the faithful performance of assigned duties. The amount thereof and the terms on which the same shall be given shall be subject to the approval of the Presiding Bishop, the expense of such bond to be paid by the General Convention.

General Convention Executive Office.

Sec. 13. There shall be an Executive Office of the General Convention, to be headed by a General Convention Executive Officer to be appointed jointly by the Presiding Bishop and the President of the House of Deputies. The Executive Office of the General Convention shall include the functions of the Secretary and the Treasurer of the General Convention and those of the Manager of the General Convention and, if the several positions are filled by different persons, such officers shall serve under the general supervision of the General Convention Executive Officer, who shall also coordinate the work of the Committees, Commissions, Boards and Agencies funded by the General Convention Expense Budget.

Site selection.

Sec. 14 (a) At each meeting of the General Convention the Joint Standing Committee on Planning and Arrangements shall submit to the General Convention its recommendations for sites for the meeting of the General Convention to be held as the third succeeding General Convention following the General Convention at which the report is made. In making such recommendations, the Committee shall certify to the Convention the willingness of the Dioceses within which recommended sites are located to have the General Convention meet within their jurisdictions.

Approval of sites.

(b) From the sites recommended by the Joint Committee, the General Convention shall approve no fewer than three nor more than five sites as possible for such meeting of the General Convention.

Determination of site.

(c) From the sites approved by the General Convention, the Joint Committee, with the advice and consent of a majority vote of the following: The Presidents and the Vice-Presidents of both Houses of Convention, the Presidents of the Provinces and the Executive Council, shall determine the site for such General Convention and proceed to make all reasonable and necessary arrangements and commitments for that meeting of the General Convention. The site and date thus selected shall be deemed to have been appointed by the General Convention, as provided in the Constitution.

Notice to Dioceses.

(d) Upon the final selection of and the arrangements for the site for that General Convention, the Joint Committee shall advise the Secretary of the General Convention, who shall communicate the determination to the Dioceses.

Changes in the date and length of General Convention.

(e) Within such guidelines as may have been established by the General Convention regarding the date and length of future General Conventions, and pursuant to the reasonable and necessary arrangements and commitments with the Dioceses and operators of facilities within the Diocese in which the next General Convention will be held, the Joint Committee shall fix the date and the length of the next succeeding Convention, report the same to the Secretary of the General Convention and include the same in its report to the Convention. In the event of a change of circumstances indicating the necessity or advisability of changing the date or length previously fixed, the Joint Committee shall investigate and make recommendations to the Presiding Bishop and the President of the House of Deputies, who, with the advice and consent of the Executive Council, may fix a different date or length or both.

CANON 2: Of the Presiding Bishop

Clerical and Lay members of Nominating Committee.

Sec. 1 (a) At each General Convention the House of Deputies shall elect one Clerical and one Lay Deputy from each Province as members of the Joint Nominating Committee for the Election of the Presiding Bishop. A Deputy from a particular Province may be nominated only by another Deputy from the same Province, but the election of each member of the Committee shall be by the entire membership of the House of Deputies, with a majority of those voting necessary for election. Prior to the election, the Clerical and Lay Deputies from each Province shall hold a caucus, at which two Clerical Deputies and two Lay Deputies as nominees shall be selected by the caucus, and these shall be the only nominees upon which the House of Deputies shall vote in electing the members of the Joint Nominating Committee. The President of the House of Deputies, after consultation with representatives of youth, shall appoint two persons, age 16-21, as members of the Joint Nominating Committee for the Election of the Presiding Bishop.

Episcopal members of Nominating Committee.

(b) At each General Convention the House of Bishops shall elect one Bishop from each Province as a member of the Joint Nominating Committee for the Election of the Presiding Bishop. A Bishop from a particular Province may be nominated only by another Bishop from the same Province, but the election of each member of the Committee shall be by the entire membership of the House of Bishops, with a majority of those voting necessary for election. Prior to the election, the Bishops from each Province shall hold a caucus, at which two Bishops as nominees shall be selected by the caucus, and these shall be the only nominees upon which the House of Bishops shall vote in electing the members of the Joint Nominating Committee.

Vacancies in Nominating Committee.

(c) In the event vacancies shall occur in the Joint Nominating Committee after the election of its members due to death, disability, resignation, or other cause within one year of the next General Convention, the vacancies shall not be filled and the remaining members shall constitute the Joint Nominating Committee. In the event such vacancies shall occur more than one year prior to the next General Convention, the Presiding Officer of the House of Bishops shall appoint Bishops and the President of the House of Deputies shall appoint Clerical and Lay Deputies, in all cases from the same Provinces as those Bishops or Deputies whose positions are being filled. An elected or appointed member who shall not be a Deputy to the next General Convention shall continue as a member of the Joint Nominating Committee until the adjournment of such next General Convention. A member of the Committee who transfers from one Province to another or a Lay Deputy who is ordained Presbyter or Deacon, or a Presbyter or Deacon who is consecrated a Bishop, shall not thereby become ineligible to continue to serve on the Joint Nominating Committee through the next succeeding General Convention.

Term of Nominating Committee.

(d) The Joint Nominating Committee shall remain in office until the adjournment of the next General Convention, at which a new Joint Nominating Committee shall be elected. Members of the Committee are eligible for reelection.

Election to follow Joint Session.

(e) At the General Convention at which a Presiding Bishop is to be elected, the Joint Nominating Committee shall present to the House of Bishops and the House of Deputies in Joint Session the names of not fewer than three members of the House of Bishops for the consideration of the two Houses in the choice of a Presiding Bishop. At the Joint Session to which the Joint Nominating Committee shall report, any Bishop or Deputy may nominate any other member of the House of Bishops for the consideration of the two Houses in the choice of a Presiding Bishop, and there may be discussion of all nominees. Commencing on the day following the Joint Session, election shall be by the House of Bishops from among such nominees. If the House of Bishops shall find itself unable to elect a Presiding Bishop from among such nominees, another Joint Session shall be held, at which additional nominations may be received, and on the following day, election shall be by the House of Bishops from among all of the nominees. After the election by the House of Bishops, report of the result thereof, including the number of votes cast for each nominee on each ballot, shall be made to the House of Deputies which shall vote to confirm or not to confirm such choice of Presiding Bishop.

Vacancy between meetings of the General Convention.

(f) In the event a vacancy in the office of Presiding Bishop shall occur in the interim between meetings of the General Convention, as specified in the second paragraph of Article I, Section 3 of the Constitution, the Joint Nominating Committee, subject to the said Article, shall submit to the Secretary of the House of Bishops the names of not fewer than three members of the House of Bishops for the consideration by that House in the choice of a Presiding Bishop to fill the vacancy, and simultaneously therewith shall transmit a copy of such report to the Secretary of the House of Deputies for mailing to all Deputies. Such report shall also be released to the Church and secular press. Thereafter, the House of Bishops shall hold a special meeting for the purpose of electing a Presiding Bishop to fill the vacancy, and, in such election, the vote shall be upon the nominees of the Joint Nominating Committee and any further nominations made by any voting member of the House of Bishops. Immediately following the election by the House of Bishops, the Secretary of the House of Bishops shall inform the President and Secretary of each Diocesan Standing Committee, requesting a meeting at the earliest possible date to consider approval. Upon receipt of the approval of a majority of the Standing Committees of the Dioceses, the Presiding Bishop Elect shall be declared elected.

Term of office.

Sec. 2. The term of office of the Presiding Bishop, when elected according to the provisions of Article I, Section 3 of the Constitution, shall be nine years, beginning the first day of the month of November following the close of the Convention at which the Presiding Bishop is elected, unless attaining the age of seventy years before the term shall have been completed; in that case the Presiding Bishop shall resign the office to the General Convention which occurs nearest to the date of attaining such age. At that Convention a successor shall be elected, and shall assume office on the first day of the month of November following the close of that Convention or immediately upon the death, retirement, or disability of the Presiding Bishop; except that when a Presiding Bishop has been elected by the House of Bishops to fill a vacancy, as provided for in the second paragraph of Article I., Section 3 of the Constitution, the Presiding Bishop so elected shall take office immediately.

To resign previous jurisdiction.

Sec. 3 (a) Upon the expiration of the term of office of the Presiding Bishop, the Bishop who is elected successor shall tender to the House of Bishops a resignation from the Bishop's previous jurisdiction to take effect upon the date of assuming the office of Presiding Bishop, or, upon good cause with the advice and consent of the Advisory Committee established under the Rules of Order of the House of Bishops, not later than six months thereafter.

(b) Such resignation shall be acted upon immediately by the House of Bishops.

Chief Pastor and Primate.

Sec. 4 (a) The Presiding Bishop shall be the Chief Pastor and Primate of the Church, and shall:

Policy and Strategy.

(1) Be charged with responsibility for leadership in initiating and developing the policy and strategy in the Church and speaking for the Church as to the policies, strategies and programs authorized by the General Convention;

Representative of Church and episcopate.

(2) Speak God's words to the Church and to the world, as the representative of this Church and its episcopate in its corporate capacity;

Provide for interim in a Diocese.

(3) In the event of an Episcopal vacancy within a Diocese, consult with the Ecclesiastical Authority to ensure that adequate interim Episcopal Services are provided;

Convene Bishops.

(4) Take order for the consecration of Bishops, when duly elected; and, from time to time, assemble the Bishops of this Church to meet, either as the House of Bishops or as a Council of Bishops, and set the time and place of such meetings;

Presiding Officer.

(5) Preside over meetings of the House of Bishops; and, when the two Houses of the General Convention meet in Joint Session, have the right of presiding over such Session, of calling for such Joint Session, of recommending legislation to either House and, upon due notification, of appearing before and addressing the House of Deputies; and whenever addressing the General Convention upon the state of the Church, it shall be incumbent upon both Houses thereof to consider and act upon any recommendations contained in such address;

Visitations.

(6) Visit every Diocese of this Church for the purpose of: (i) Holding pastoral consultations with the Bishop or Bishops thereof and, with their advice, with the Lay and Clerical leaders of the jurisdiction; (ii) Preaching the Word; and (iii) Celebrating the Holy Eucharist.

Reports and Pastoral Letters.

(b) The Presiding Bishop shall report annually to the Church, and may, from time to time, issue Pastoral Letters.

May delegate authority.

(c) The Presiding Bishop shall perform such other functions as shall be prescribed in these Canons; and, to be enabled better to perform such duties and responsibilities, the Presiding Bishop may appoint, to positions established by the Executive Council of General Convention, officers, responsible to the Presiding Bishop, who may delegate such authority as shall seem appropriate.

May appoint Chancellor.

Sec. 5. The Presiding Bishop may appoint, as Chancellor to the Presiding Bishop, a confirmed adult communicant of the Church in good standing who is learned in both ecclesiastical and secular law, to serve so long as the Presiding Bishop may desire, as counselor in matters relating to the office and the discharge of the responsibilities of that office.

Stipends.

Sec. 6. The stipends of the Presiding Bishop and such personal assistants as may be necessary during the Presiding Bishop's term of office for the effective performance of the duties, and the necessary expenses of that office, shall be fixed by the General Convention and shall be provided for in the budget to be submitted by the Treasurer, as provided in the Canon entitled, "Of the General Convention."

If disabled.

Sec. 7. In the event of the disability of the Presiding Bishop, the Bishop who, according to the Rules of the House of Bishops, becomes its Presiding Officer, shall be substituted for the Presiding Bishop for all the purposes of these Canons, except the Canons entitled, "Of the Domestic and Foreign Missionary Society," and "Of the Executive Council."

Disability allowance.

Sec. 8. Upon the acceptance of the Presiding Bishop's resignation for reasons of disability prior to the expiration of the term of office, the Presiding Bishop may be granted, in addition to whatever allowance may be received from The Church Pension Fund, a disability allowance to be paid by the Treasurer of the General Convention in an amount to be fixed by the Joint Standing Committee on Program, Budget, and Finance, and ratified at the next regular meeting of the General Convention.

CANON 3: Of the Domestic and Foreign Missionary Society

The Constitution of the said Society, which was incorporated by an act of the Legislature of the State of New York, as from time to time amended, is hereby amended and established so as to read as follows: *Constitution of The Domestic and Foreign Missionary Society of the Protestant Episcopal Church in the United States of America as established in 1821, and since amended at various times.*

Name of organization.

ARTICLE I This organization shall be called The Domestic and Foreign Missionary Society of the Protestant Episcopal Church in the United States of America, and shall be considered as comprehending all persons who are members of the Church.

Board of Directors.

ARTICLE II The Executive Council, as constituted by Canon, shall be its Board of Directors, and shall adopt By-laws for its government not inconsistent with the Constitution and Canons.

ARTICLE III The officers of the Society shall be a President, Vice Presidents, a Secretary, a Treasurer, and such other officers as may be appointed in accordance with the Canons or By-Laws. The Presiding Bishop of the Church shall be the President of the Society; one Vice President shall be the person who is the President of the House of Deputies; and one Vice President shall be the person who is the executive director; the Treasurer shall be the person who is the Financial Officer of the Executive Council; and the Secretary shall be the person who is the Secretary of the Executive Council, and shall have such powers and perform such duties as may be assigned by the By-Laws. The other officers of the Society shall be such as are provided for by the By-Laws of the Society. The tenure of office, compensation, powers, and duties of the officers of the Society shall be such as are prescribed by the Canons and by the By-laws of the Society not inconsistent therewith.

Officers.

ARTICLE IV This Constitution of the Society may be altered or amended at any time by the General Convention of the Church.

Amendment.

CANON 4: Of the Executive Council

Sec. 1 (a) There shall be an Executive Council of the General Convention (which Council shall generally be called simply the Executive Council)whose duty it shall be to carry out the program and policies adopted by the General Convention. The Executive Council shall have charge of the coordination, development, and implementation of the ministry and mission of the Church.

Function.

(b) The Executive Council shall be accountable to the General Convention and shall render a full published report concerning the work with which it is charged to each meeting of the said Convention. The report shall also include information on the implementation of all concurred resolutions of the previous General Convention calling for action by the Executive Council, by its officers and staff, and by the jurisdictions of the Church.

Accountability.

(c) Except as its membership may include additional persons elected prior to the adjournment of the meeting of the General Convention in 1976 for terms which have not expired, the Executive Council shall be composed (a) of twenty members elected by the General Convention, of whom four shall be Bishops, four shall be Presbyters or Deacons, and twelve shall be Lay Persons (two Bishops, two Presbyters or Deacons, and six Lay Persons to be elected by each subsequent regular meeting of the General Convention); (b) of eighteen members elected by the Provincial Synods; (c) of the following *ex officiis* members: the Presiding Bishop and the President of the House of Deputies; and (d) the Vice-President, the Secretary, and the Treasurer of the Executive Council, who shall have seat and voice but no vote. Each Province shall be entitled to be represented by one Bishop or Presbyter or Deacon canonically resident in a Diocese which is a constituent member of the Province and by one Lay Person who is a confirmed adult communicant in good standing of a Diocese which is a constituent member of the Province, and the terms of the representatives of each Province shall be so rotated that two persons shall not be simultaneously elected for equal terms.

How constituted.

How elected.

Sec. 2(a) Of the members to be elected by the General Convention, the Bishops shall be elected by the House of Bishops subject to confirmation by the House of Deputies, and the Presbyters or Deacons and Lay Persons shall be elected by the House of Deputies subject to confirmation by the House of Bishops.

Term of office.

(b) Except in the case of members initially elected for shorter terms in order to achieve rotation of terms, the terms of office of the members of the Council (other than *ex officiis* members) shall be equal to twice the interval between regular meetings of the General Convention. The terms of office of all members shall commence immediately upon the adjournment of the General Convention at which they were elected or, in the case of election by a Synod, upon the adjournment of the first regular meeting of General Convention following such election. The term of a member shall become vacant in the event of two absences from meetings of the Council in the interval between successive regular meetings of the General Convention unless excused by the Chair for good cause. Members shall remain in office until their successors are elected and qualified. No person who has served at least three consecutive years on the Executive Council shall be eligible for immediate re-election for a term of more than three years. After any person shall have served six consecutive years on the Executive Council, a period of three years shall elapse before such person shall be eligible for re-election to the Council.

Vacancy.

(c) Should any vacancy occur in the Council through the death or resignation of a member elected by the General Convention or through the change in status of any such member by consecration or ordination, the Council shall fill such vacancy by the election of a suitable person to serve until a successor is elected by the General Convention. The General Convention shall elect a suitable person to serve the portion of any term which will remain unexpired.

(d) Should any vacancy occur in the Council through the failure of any Provincial Synod to elect a member, or through the death, resignation, or removal from the Province of any such member, the President and Provincial Council of the Province shall appoint a suitable person, canonically resident in such Province, to serve until the Provincial Synod shall by election fill the vacancy.

Powers of Council.

(e) The Council shall exercise the powers conferred upon it by Canon, and such further powers as may be designated by the General Convention, and between sessions of the General Convention may initiate and develop such new work as it may deem necessary. It may, subject to the provision of this Canon, enact By-laws for its own government and the government of its several departments.

Serves as Board of Directors.

(f) In its capacity as the Board of Directors of The Domestic and Foreign Missionary Society, the Council shall have the power to direct the disposition of the moneys and other property of said Society in accordance with the provisions of this Canon and the orders and budgets adopted or approved by the General Convention.

Elects representatives.

(g) The Council shall elect representatives of this Church to the Anglican Consultative Council (ACC) and to other Anglican and ecumenical bodies for which no other procedure is provided.

Sec. 3 (a) The Presiding Bishop shall be *ex officio* the Chair and President. However, at the first meeting of the Executive Council following the adjournment of any General Convention at which a Presiding Bishop is elected if it occurs before the commencement of the term of the newly elected Presiding Bishop, the Presiding Bishop-elect shall be *ex officio* the Chair and President. The Chair and President shall be the chief executive officer of the Executive Council and as such the Chair and President shall have ultimate responsibility for the oversight of the work of the Executive Council in the implementation of the ministry and mission of the Church as may be committed to the Executive Council by the General Convention.

Officers.

Chair.

(b) The President of the House of Deputies shall be *ex officio* Vice Chair.

Vice Chair.

(c) The Secretary of the General Convention shall be the Secretary of the Executive Council *ex officio*.

Secretary.

(d) The Presiding Bishop shall appoint, with the advice and consent of a majority of the Executive Council, an executive director, who shall be an adult confirmed communicant in good standing or a member of the clergy of this Church in good standing who shall be the chief operating officer and who shall serve at the pleasure of the Presiding Bishop and be accountable to the Presiding Bishop. If a vacancy should occur in the office of the executive director, a successor shall be appointed in like manner.

Executive Director.

(e) Upon joint nomination of the Chair and Vice Chair, the Executive Council shall appoint a Financial Officer of the Executive Council, who may, but need not, be the same person as the Treasurer of the General Convention and who shall report and be accountable to the Chair of Executive Council and shall serve at the pleasure of the Chair of the Executive Council. If a vacancy should occur in that office, a successor shall be appointed in like manner.

Financial Officer.

(f) The Chair shall preside at meetings of the Council, shall perform such other duties as are customary for such office and shall perform such other duties as may be conferred by Canon and the By-laws of the Council. In the absence or at the request of the Chair, the Vice-Chair shall preside at meetings of the Council and shall perform such other duties as may be conferred by Canon and by the By-laws of the Council.

Chair to preside.

(g) The Executive Council shall establish by its By-laws such committees of the Executive Council as shall be deemed appropriate and necessary by the Executive Council for the discharge of its duties, the members of which are to be nominated jointly by the Chair and Vice-Chair and appointed by the Council.

Council to establish Committees.

(h) The additional officers, agents and employees of the Council shall be such and shall perform such duties as the Council, upon the recommendation and under the authority and direction of the Chair and President, may from time to time designate.

Employees.

Sec. 4 (a) The Council shall meet at such place, and at such stated times, at least three times each year, as it shall appoint and at such other times as it may be convened. The Council shall be convened at the request of the President, or on the written request of any nine members thereof.

Meetings.

(b) A majority of the elected members of the Council shall be necessary to constitute a quorum at any meeting of the Council. No action shall be

Quorum.

taken in the name of the Council except when a quorum, so defined, is present and voting.

Salaries.

Sec. 5. With the exception of the salary of the President, the salaries of all officers of the Council and of all agents and employees of the Council shall be fixed by the Council and paid by the Treasurer.

Budget for the Episcopal Church.

Sec. 6 (a) The Executive Council shall submit to the General Convention at each regular session thereof the Budget for the Episcopal Church for the ensuing budgetary period, which budgetary period shall be equal to the interval between regular meetings of the General Convention.

Budget to provide for Canonical and corporate expenses.

(b) The budget proposed for adoption by General Convention shall include a Canonical and corporate portion which shall provide for the contingent expenses of the General Convention, the stipend of the Presiding Bishop together with the necessary expenses of that office, the necessary expenses of the President of the House of Deputies, including the staff and Advisory Council required to assist in the performance of the duties and matters related to the President's office, and the applicable Church Pension Fund assessments, and also the corporate requirements for the administrative support of the Domestic & Foreign Missionary Society offices.

Budget to support Program.

(c) The budget proposed for adoption by the General Convention shall include provision for support for the Program of the Episcopal Church. The program so submitted shall include a detailed budget of that part of the program for which it proposes to make appropriations for the ensuing year, and estimated budgets for the succeeding portion of the budgetary period.

Convention to set formula for single asking.

(d) Revenue to support the Budget for the Episcopal Church shall be generated primarily by a single asking of the Dioceses of the church based on a formula which the General Convention shall adopt as part of its Program, Budget and Finance process. If in any year the total anticipated income for budget support is less than the amount required to support the budget approved by the General Convention, the canonical portion of the Budget for the Episcopal Church shall have funding priority over any other budget areas subject to any decreases necessary to maintain a balanced budget.

Canonical funding to have priority.

Council to share proposed budget four months prior to Convention.

(e) After the preparation of the budget the Executive Council shall, at least four months before the sessions of the General Convention, transmit to the Bishop of each Diocese and to the President of each Province a statement of the existing and the proposed askings necessary to support the Budget for the Episcopal Church. The Executive Council shall also submit to the General Convention, with the budget, a plan for the askings of the respective Dioceses of the sum needed to execute the budget.

Joint Sessions for the presentation of the Budget.

(f) There shall be joint sessions of the two Houses for the presentation of the Budget for the Episcopal Church; and thereafter consideration shall be given and appropriate action taken thereon by the General Convention. The Council shall have the power to expend all sums of money covered by the budget and estimated budgets approved by the Convention, subject to such restrictions as may be imposed by the General Convention, including but not limited to the priority declaration set forth in Section 6(d) of this Canon. It shall also have power to undertake such other work provided for in the budget approved by the General Convention, or other work under the jurisdiction of the Council, the need for which may have arisen after the action of the General Convention, as in the judgment of the Council its income will warrant.

(g) Upon the adoption by the General Convention of a Budget for the Episcopal Church and the planned askings for the budgetary period, the Council shall formally advise each Diocese of its share of the total askings to support the Budget for the Episcopal Church.

Notice of allotted objectives to be given.

(h) Each Diocese shall thereupon notify each Parish and Mission of the amount of the askings of such Diocese. Each Diocese shall present to each Parish and Mission a total objective which shall include both its share of the proposed Diocesan Budget and its share of the asking of the Diocese by the Executive Council in accordance with the plan adopted by the General Convention.

Diocese to allot objectives to Parishes.

(i) Each diocese shall annually report to the Executive Council such financial information as may be required in a form authorized by Executive Council.

Report Form.

Sec. 7 (a) Every Missionary Bishop or, in case of a vacancy, the Bishop in charge of the jurisdiction, receiving aid from the Council, shall report at the close of each fiscal year to the Council, giving account of work performed, of money received from all sources and disbursed for all purposes, and of the state of the Church in the jurisdiction at the date of such report, all in such form as the Council may prescribe.

Bishops receiving aid to report to Council.

(b) Every Bishop of a Diocese receiving aid from the Council shall report at the close of each fiscal year to the Council, giving account of the work in the Diocese supported in whole or in part by the Council.

Sec. 8. The Council, as soon as practicable after the close of each fiscal year, shall make and publish a full report of its work to the Church. Such report shall contain an itemized statement of all receipts and disbursements and a statement of all trust funds and other property of The Domestic and Foreign Missionary Society, and of all other trust funds and property in its possession or under its control. The Council shall make a like report, including a detailed schedule of the salaries paid to all officers, agents, and principal employees, to each General Convention.

Reports of the Council.

Sec. 9 (a) Ordained Ministers and Lay Communicants of this Church, or of some Church in communion with this Church, in good standing, who qualify in accordance with the standards and procedures adopted from time to time by the Executive Council, shall be eligible for appointment as Missionaries of this Church.

Qualifications of Missionaries.

(b) Members in good standing of Churches not in communion with this Church, but otherwise qualified as above, may, at the request of the Ecclesiastical Authority of the jurisdiction in which the requirement exists, be employed and assigned to positions for which they are professionally prepared; and may receive the same stipends and other allowances as appointed Missionaries. The Ecclesiastical Authority of a jurisdiction may employ any qualified person for work in the jurisdiction.

Employment of non-communicants.

CANON 5: Of the Archives of the Episcopal Church

Purpose.

Sec. 1. There shall be an Archives of the Episcopal Church, the purpose of which shall be to preserve by safekeeping, to arrange and to make available the records of the General Convention, Executive Council, and the Domestic and Foreign Missionary Society, and other important records and memorabilia of the life and work of the Church, and to carry out a program of records management, so as to further the historical dimension of the mission of the Church.

Records defined.

Sec. 2 For purposes of this Canon, records are defined as all fixed evidential information regardless of method, media, format or characteristics of the recording process, which have been created, received or gathered by the Church, its officers, agents or employees in pursuance of the legal, business and administrative function and the programmatic mission of the Church. Records include all original materials used to capture information, informality of the characteristics of the record. The records and archives of the Church are not limited by the medium in which they are kept and include such formats as paper records, electronic records, printed records and publications, photo-reproduced images, and machine-readable tapes, film and disks.

Board of the Archives.

Sec. 3 (a) There shall be a Board of the Archives which shall consist of the Archivist (*ex officio*, with vote), the Dean of the Episcopal Theological Seminary of the Southwest (*ex officio*, with vote), and twelve (12) appointed persons, three (3) of whom shall be Bishops, three (3) of whom shall be Clergy, and six (6) of whom shall be Lay Persons. All appointed Members of the Board shall serve terms beginning with the close of the General Convention at which their appointments are confirmed and ending with the close of the second regular Convention thereafter.

(b) Members shall serve rotating terms for the purpose of continuity on the Board. In the first instance following the adoption of these provisions, one of the Bishops and one half of the Clerical and Lay Appointees shall have terms expiring after the next regular meeting of the General Convention as determined by lot.

Membership.

(c) Bishops shall be appointed by the Presiding Bishop, and other Clerical and all Lay Members shall be appointed by the President of the House of Deputies, all subject to the confirmation of General Convention. Consideration shall be given to assure that membership includes persons who possess knowledge either of history or archival administration, or are persons skilled in disciplines pertinent to the resolutions of the concerns of the Archives. Positions of Members of the Board which become vacant prior to the normal expiration of such Members' terms shall be filled by appointment by the Presiding Bishop or by the President of the House of Deputies, as appropriate. Such appointments shall be for the remaining unexpired portion of such Members' terms, and if a regular meeting of the General Convention intervenes, appointments for terms extending beyond such meeting shall be subject to confirmation of the General Convention. Because of the special skills and knowledge needed by this Board, a Member shall be eligible for appointment for two successive terms, after which the Member may not be reappointed prior to the next meeting of the

General Convention following the meeting at the close of which the second successive term of the Member expired. Members appointed to fill vacancies in unexpired terms shall not thereby be disqualified from appointment to two full terms immediately thereafter.

(d) The Board of the Archives shall have the duty to set policy for the Archives, to elect the Archivist of the Episcopal Church, and to set forth the terms and conditions with regard to the work of the Archivist. Duties.

(e) The Board of the Archives shall meet annually, or more often as required.

(f) The Board of the Archives shall elect its own officers and have the power to create committees necessary for the carrying on of its work.

(g) The Board of the Archives shall adopt procedures consistent with the Constitution and Canons of the Episcopal Church for its organization and functioning.

(h) The Board of the Archives shall report to the General Convention, and the Executive Council, through the office of the Executive Officer of the General Convention, and to the Church. Report to Convention.

Sec. 4. There shall be an Archivist of the Episcopal Church whose duty shall be to manage the Archives, records, and related information resources of the Church at the direction of the Board. Archivist.

Sec. 5. The expenses of the Archives of the Episcopal Church shall be shared by the General Convention and the Executive Council. Expenses to be shared.

CANON 6: Of the Mode of Securing an Accurate View of the State of This Church

Sec. 1. A report of every Parish and other Congregation of this Church shall be prepared annually for the year ending December 31 preceding, in the form authorized by the Executive Council and approved by the Committee on the State of the Church, and shall be filed not later than March 1 with the Bishop of the Diocese, or, where there is no Bishop, with the ecclesiastical authority of the Diocese. The Bishop or the ecclesiastical authority, as the case may be, shall keep a copy and submit the report to the Executive Council not later than May 1. In every Parish and other Congregation the preparation and filing of this report shall be the joint duty of the Rector or Member of the Clergy in charge thereof and the lay leadership; and before the filing thereof the report shall be approved by the Vestry or bishop's committee or mission council. This report shall include the following information: Annual parish reports to Bishop.

(1) the number of baptisms, confirmations, marriages, and burials during the year; the total number of baptized members, the total number of communicants in good standing, and the total number of communicants in good standing under 16 years of age.

(2) a summary of all the receipts and expenditures, from whatever source derived and for whatever purpose used.

(3) such other relevant information as is needed to secure an accurate view of the state of this Church, as required by the approved form.

Sec. 2. Every Bishop, Presbyter, or Deacon whose report is not included in a parochial report shall also report on the exercise of such office, and if there has been none, the causes or reasons which have prevented the same. Non-parochial reports.

Sec. 3. These reports, or such parts of them as the Bishop may deem proper, shall be entered in the Journal of the convention.

Annual Diocesan Reports.

Sec. 4. Likewise, a report of every Diocese shall be prepared annually for the year ending December 31st preceding, in the form authorized by the Executive Council and approved by the Committee on the State of the Church, and shall be filed, not later than September 1, with the Executive Council. It shall include information concerning implementation by the Diocese of resolutions of the previous General Convention which have been specifically identified by the Secretary of General Convention under Joint Rule 13 as calling for Diocesan action.

Journals to be forwarded to Secretary and Archives.

Sec. 5 (a) It shall be the duty of the Secretary of the Convention of every jurisdiction to forward to the Secretary of the House of Deputies, immediately upon publication, two copies of the Journals of the Convention of the jurisdiction, together with episcopal charges, statements, and such other papers as may show the state of the Church in that jurisdiction, and one copy to the Archives of the Church.

Report to the House of Deputies.

(b) A Committee of the House of Deputies shall be appointed following the close of each General Convention, to serve *ad interim*, and to prepare and present to the next meeting of the House of Deputies a report on the State of the Church; which report, when agreed to by the said House, shall be sent to the House of Bishops.

CANON 7: Of Business Methods in Church Affairs

Standards observed.

Sec. 1. In every Province, Diocese, Parish, Mission and Institution connected with this Church, the following standard business methods shall be observed:

Provinces to be audited.

(a) All accounts of Provinces shall be audited annually by an independent certified public accountant, or independent licensed accountant, or such audit committee as shall be authorized by the Provincial Council. The Audit Report shall be filed with the Provincial Council not later than September 1 of each year, covering the preceding calendar year.

Deposit of funds.

(b) Funds held in trust, endowment and other permanent funds, and securities represented by physical evidence of ownership or indebtedness, shall be deposited with a National or State Bank, or a Diocesan Corporation, or with some other agency approved in writing by the Finance Committee or the Department of Finance of the Diocese, under a deed of trust, agency or other depository agreement providing for at least two signatures on any order of withdrawal of such funds or securities.

Proviso.

But this paragraph shall not apply to funds and securities refused by the depositories named as being too small for acceptance. Such small funds and securities shall be under the care of the persons or corporations properly responsible for them. This paragraph shall not be deemed to prohibit investments in securities issued in book entry form or other manner that dispenses with the delivery of a certificate evidencing the ownership of the securities or the indebtedness of the issuer.

Record of trust funds.

(c) Records shall be made and kept of all trust and permanent funds showing at least the following:

(i) Source and date.
(ii) Terms governing the use of principal and income.

(iii) To whom and how often reports of condition are to be made.

(iv) How the funds are invested.

(d) Treasurers and custodians, other than banking institutions, shall be adequately bonded; except treasurers of funds that do not exceed five hundred dollars at any one time during the fiscal year.

Treasurers to be bonded.

(e) Books of account shall be so kept as to provide the basis for satisfactory accounting.

Books of account.

(f) All accounts of the Diocese shall be audited annually by an independent Certified Public Accountant. All accounts of Parishes, Missions or other institutions shall be audited annually by an independent Certified Public Accountant, or independent Licensed Public Accountant, or such audit committee as shall be authorized by the Finance Committee, Department of Finance, or other appropriate diocesan authority.

Annual audit.

(g) All reports of such audits, including any memorandum issued by the auditors or audit committee regarding internal controls or other accounting matters, together with a summary of action taken or proposed to be taken to correct deficiencies or implement recommendations contained in any such memorandum, shall be filed with the Bishop or Ecclesiastical Authority not later than 30 days following the date of such report, and in no event, not later than September 1 of each year, covering the financial reports of the previous calendar year.

(h) All buildings and their contents shall be kept adequately insured.

Insurance.

(i) The Finance Committee or Department of Finance of the Diocese may require copies of any or all accounts described in this Section to be filed with it and shall report annually to the Convention of the Diocese upon its administration of this Canon.

Report to Convention.

(j) The fiscal year shall begin January 1.

Fiscal year.

Sec. 2 The several Dioceses shall give effect to the foregoing standard business methods by the enactment of Canons appropriate thereto, which Canons shall invariably provide for a Finance Committee, a Department of Finance of the Diocese, or other appropriate diocesan body with such authority.

Dioceses to enforce by Canon.

Sec. 3. No Vestry, Trustee, or other Body, authorized by Civil or Canon law to hold, manage, or administer real property for any Parish, Mission, Congregation, or Institution, shall encumber or alienate the same or any part thereof without the written consent of the Bishop and Standing Committee of the Diocese of which the Parish, Mission, Congregation, or Institution is a part, except under such regulations as may be prescribed by Canon of the Diocese.

Encumbrance of property requires consent.

Sec. 4 All real and personal property held by or for the benefit of any Parish, Mission or Congregation is held in trust for this Church and the Diocese thereof in which such Parish, Mission or Congregation is located. The existence of this trust, however, shall in no way limit the power and authority of the Parish, Mission or Congregation otherwise existing over such property so long as the particular Parish, Mission or Congregation remains a part of, and subject to, this Church and its Constitution and Canons.

Property held in trust.

Sec. 5 The several Dioceses may, at their election, further confirm the trust declared under the foregoing Section 4 by appropriate action, but no such action shall be necessary for the existence and validity of the trust.

CANON 8: Of The Church Pension Fund

Authorized to administer pension system.

Sec. 1. The Church Pension Fund, a corporation created by Chapter 97 of the Laws of 1914 of the State of New York as subsequently amended, is hereby authorized to establish and administer the clergy pension system, including life, accident and health benefits, of this Church, substantially in accordance with the principles adopted by the General Convention of 1913 and approved thereafter by the several Dioceses, with the view to providing pensions and related benefits for the Clergy who reach normal age of retirement, for the Clergy disabled by age or infirmity, and for the surviving spouses and minor children of deceased Clergy.

Election of Trustees.

Sec. 2. The General Convention at each regular meeting shall elect, on the nomination of a Joint Committee thereof, twelve persons to serve as Trustees of The Church Pension Fund for a term of six years and until their successors shall have been elected and have qualified, and shall also fill such vacancies as may exist on the Board of Trustees. Effective January 1, 1989, any person who has been elected as a Trustee by General Convention for twelve or more consecutive years shall not be eligible for reelection until the next regular General Convention following the one in which that person was not eligible for reelection to the Board of Trustees. Any vacancy which occurs at a time when the General Convention is not in session may be filled by the Board of Trustees by appointment, *ad interim*, of a Trustee who shall serve until the next session of the General Convention thereafter shall have elected a Trustee to serve for the remainder of the unexpired term pertaining to such vacancy.

Royalties.

Sec. 3. For the purpose of administering the pension system, The Church Pension Fund shall be entitled to receive and to use all net royalties from publications authorized by the General Convention, and to levy upon and to collect from all Parishes, Missions, and other ecclesiastical organizations or bodies subject to the authority of this Church, and any other societies, organizations, or bodies in the Church which under the regulations of The Church Pension Fund shall elect to come into the pension system, assessments based upon the salaries and other compensation paid to Clergy by such Parishes, Missions, and other ecclesiastical organizations or bodies for services rendered currently or in the past, prior to their becoming beneficiaries of the Fund.

Limit on allotment.

Sec. 4 The pension system shall be so administered that no pension shall be allotted before there shall be in the hands of The Church Pension Fund sufficient funds to meet such pension, except as directed by the General Convention in 1967.

Minimum retiring allowance.

Sec. 5. To every Member of the Clergy who shall have been ordained in this Church or received into this Church from another Church, and who shall have remained in service in the office and work of the Ministry in this Church for a period of at least twenty-five years, and in respect of whom the conditions of this Canon shall have been fulfilled in the payment of assessments on such reasonable basis as The Church Pension Fund may establish under its Rules of Administration, The Church Pension Fund shall provide a minimum retiring allowance the amount of which shall be determined by the Trustees of the Fund, and shall also provide surviving spouses' and minor children's allowances related thereto. In the case of a

Member of the Clergy in whose behalf assessments shall not have been fully paid for a period of at least twenty-five years, The Church Pension Fund shall be empowered to recompute the aforesaid minimum retiring allowance and the other allowances related thereto at a rate or rates consistent with the proper actuarial practice. The Trustees of The Church Pension Fund are hereby empowered to establish such Rules and Regulations as will fulfill the intention of this Canon and are consistent with sound actuarial practice. Subject to the provisions of this Canon, the general principle shall be observed that there shall be an actuarial relation between the several benefits; *Provided, however,* that the Board of Trustees shall have power to establish such maximum of annuities greater than two thousand dollars as shall be in the best interest of the Church, within the limits of sound actuarial practice.

Sec. 6. An Initial Reserve Fund, derived from voluntary gifts, shall be administered by The Church Pension Fund so as to assure to clergy ordained prior to March 1, 1917, and their families, such addition to the support to which they may become entitled on the basis of assessments authorized by this Canon as may bring their several allowances up to the scale herein established.

Initial Reserve Fund.

Sec. 7. The action of the Trustees of the General Clergy Relief Fund, in accepting the provisions of Chapter 239 of the Laws of 1915 of the State of New York authorizing a merger with The Church Pension Fund, upon terms agreed upon between said two Funds, is hereby approved. Any corporation, society, or other organization, which hitherto has administered clergy relief funds, may to such extent as may be compatible with its corporate powers and its existing obligations, and in so far as may be sanctioned in the case of diocesan societies by the respective Dioceses, merge with The Church Pension Fund, or if merger be impracticable, may establish by agreement with The Church Pension Fund the closest practicable system of co-operation with that fund. Nothing herein contained shall be construed to the prejudice of existing corporations or societies whose funds are derived from payments made by members thereof.

Merger of General Clergy Relief Fund with Church Pension Fund.

Sec. 8. Women ordained to the Diaconate prior to January 1, 1971, who are not employed in active service on January 1, 1977, shall continue to have the benefit of their present provisions for pension protection at the expense of their employers, through the Pension Plan for Deaconesses provided by the Church Life Insurance Corporation, or through some other pension plan providing equivalent or better guarantees of a dependable retirement income, approved by proper authority. Women ordained to the Diaconate prior to January 1, 1971, and who are employed in active service on or after January 1, 1977, shall be entitled to the same provisions for pension protection as other Deacons based on prospective service on or after January 1, 1977. Women ordained to the Diaconate on or after January 1, 1971, shall be entitled to the same pension protection as other Deacons.

Pensions for women.

Sec. 9. The General Convention reserves the power to alter or amend this Canon, but no such alteration or amendment shall be made until after the same shall have been communicated to the Trustees of The Church Pension Fund and such Trustees shall have had ample opportunity to be heard with respect thereto.

General Convention reserves right to amend this Canon.

CANON 9: Of Provinces

How constituted.

Sec. 1. Subject to the proviso in Article VII of the Constitution, the Dioceses of this Church shall be and are hereby united into Provinces as follows:

The First Province shall consist of the Dioceses within the States of Maine, New Hampshire, Vermont, Massachusetts, Rhode Island, and Connecticut.

The Second Province shall consist of the Dioceses within the States of New York and New Jersey, the Dioceses of Haiti and the Virgin Islands, and the Convocation of American Churches in Europe.

The Third Province shall consist of the Dioceses within the States of Pennsylvania, Delaware, Maryland, Virginia, West Virginia, and the District of Columbia.

The Fourth Province shall consist of the Dioceses within the States of North Carolina, South Carolina, Georgia, Florida, Alabama, Mississippi, Tennessee, Kentucky, and Louisiana, except for the portion thereof consisting of the Diocese of Western Louisiana.

The Fifth Province shall consist of the Diocese of Missouri, and of the Dioceses within the States of Ohio, Indiana, Illinois, Michigan, and Wisconsin.

The Sixth Province shall consist of the Dioceses within the States of Minnesota, Iowa, North Dakota, South Dakota, Nebraska, Montana, Wyoming, and Colorado.

The Seventh Province shall consist of the Dioceses of Western Louisiana and of West Missouri, and of the Dioceses within the States of Arkansas, Texas, Kansas, Oklahoma, and New Mexico.

The Eighth Province shall consist of the Dioceses within the States of Idaho, Utah, Washington, Oregon, Nevada, California, Arizona, Alaska, and Hawaii, the Diocese of Taiwan and the Area Mission of Navajoland.

The Ninth Province shall consist of the Dioceses of this Church in Colombia, the Dominican Republic, Ecuador, Honduras, and Puerto Rico.

New Dioceses.

Sec. 2 (a) When a new Diocese or Area Mission shall be created wholly within any Province, such new Diocese or Area Mission shall be included in such Province. In case a new Diocese or Area Mission shall embrace territory in two or more Provinces, it shall be included in and form part of the Province wherein the greater number of Presbyters and Deacons in such new Diocese or Area Mission shall, at the time of its creation, be canonically resident. Whenever a new Diocese or Area Mission shall be formed of territory not before included in any Province, the General Convention shall designate the Province to which it shall be annexed.

Transfer of Dioceses.

(b) By mutual agreement between the Synods of two adjoining Provinces, a Diocese or Area Mission may transfer itself from one of such Provinces to the other, such transfer to be considered complete upon approval thereof by the General Convention. Following such approval, Canon I.9.1 shall be appropriately amended.

Synodical rights and privileges.

Sec. 3. For the purpose of the Province the Synodical rights and privileges of the several Dioceses within the Province shall be such as from time to time shall be determined by the Synod of the Province.

Sec. 4. There shall be in each Province a Synod consisting of a House of Bishops and a House of Deputies, which Houses shall sit and deliberate either separately or together. The Synod shall meet on a regular basis as determined by each Province for the purpose of organizing and carrying out the responsibilities of the Province as provided in the Canons.

Provincial Synod.

Sec. 5. Every Bishop Diocesan of this Church, having jurisdiction within the Province, every Bishop Coadjutor, Bishop Suffragan, and Assistant Bishop, and every Bishop whose episcopal work has been within the Province, but who by reason of advanced age or bodily infirmity has resigned, shall have a seat and vote in the House of Bishops of the Province.

All bishops have seat and vote.

Sec. 6 (a) The President of each Province may be one of the Bishops, Presbyters, Deacons, or Lay Persons of the Province, elected by the Synod. The method of election and term of office shall be determined by the rules of the Synod.

President of Province.

(b) When the person elected is not a Bishop, a Vice-President shall be elected who shall be a Bishop member of the Province. In this event the Bishop so elected shall serve, *ex officio,* as President of the House of Bishops of the Synod, and shall represent the Province in all matters requiring the participation of a Bishop.

Sec. 7. Each Diocese and Area Mission within the Province shall be entitled to representation in the Provincial House of Deputies by Presbyters or Deacons canonically resident in the Diocese or Area Mission, and Lay Persons, confirmed adult communicants of this Church in good standing but not necessarily domiciled in the Diocese or Area Mission, in such number as the Provincial Synod, by Ordinance, may provide. Each Diocese and Area Mission shall determine the manner in which its Deputies shall be chosen.

Representatives of Dioceses.

Sec. 8. The Provincial Synod shall have power: (a) to enact Ordinances for its own regulation and government; (b) to elect judges of the Provincial Court of Review; (c) to perform such duties as many be committed to it by the General Convention; (d) to deal with all matters within the Province; *Provided, however,* that no Provincial Synod shall have power to regulate or control the internal policy or affairs of any constituent Diocese; and *Provided, further,* that all actions and proceedings of the Synod shall be subject to and in conformity with the provisions of the Constitution and the Canons for the government of this Church; (e) to adopt a budget for the maintenance of any Provincial work undertaken by the Synod, such budget to be raised in such manner as the Synod may determine; (f) to create by Ordinance a provincial Council with power to administer and carry on such work as may be committed to it by the General Convention, or by the Presiding Bishop and the Executive Council, or by the Synod of the Province.

Powers of Provincial Synod.

Sec. 9. The Synod of a Province may take over from the Executive Council, with its consent, and during its pleasure, the administration of any given work within the Province. If the Province shall provide the funds for such work, the constituent Dioceses then members of, and supporting, such

May take over administration of work.

Province shall receive proportional credit therefor upon the quotas assigned to them for the support of the Program of the Church, provided that the total amount of such credits shall not exceed the sum appropriated in the budget of the Executive Council for the maintenance of the work so taken over.

To consider subjects referred by General Convention.

Sec. 10. Within sixty days after each session of the General Convention, the Presidents of the two Houses thereof shall refer to the Provincial Synods, or any of them, such subjects as the General Convention may direct, or as they may deem advisable, for consideration thereof by the Synods, and it shall be the duty of such Synods to consider the subject or subjects so referred to them at the first meeting of the Synod held after the adjournment of the General Convention, and to report their action and judgment in the matter to the Secretary of the House of Bishops and to the Secretary of the House of Deputies at least six months before the date of the meeting of the next General Convention.

CANON 10: Of New Dioceses

Primary Convention.

Sec. 1. Whenever a new Diocese shall be formed within the limits of any Diocese, or by the junction of two or more Dioceses, or parts of Dioceses, and such action shall have been ratified by the General Convention, the Bishop of the Diocese within the limits of which a Diocese is formed, or in case of the junction of two or more Dioceses, or parts of Dioceses, the senior Bishop by consecration, shall thereupon call the Primary Convention of the new Diocese, for the purpose of enabling it to organize, and shall fix the time and place of holding the same, such place being within the territorial limits of the new Diocese.

How called with no Bishop.

Sec. 2. In case there should be no Bishop who can call such Primary Convention, pursuant to the foregoing provision, then the duty of calling such Convention for the purpose of organizing and of fixing the time and place of its meeting, shall be vested in the Standing Committee of the Diocese within the limits of which the new one is erected, or in the Standing Committee of the oldest of the Dioceses by the junction of which, or of parts of which, the new Diocese may be formed. And such Standing Committee shall make the call immediately after ratification of the General Convention.

Division of existing Diocese.

Sec. 3. Whenever one Diocese is about to be divided into two Dioceses, the Convention of such Diocese shall declare which portion thereof is to be in the new Diocese, and shall make the same known to the General Convention before the ratification of such division.

How admitted into union with General Convention.

Sec. 4. Whenever a new Diocese shall have organized in Primary Convention in accordance with the provisions of the Constitution and Canons in such case made and provided, and in the manner prescribed in the previous Sections of this Canon, and shall have chosen a name and acceded to the Constitution of the General Convention in accordance with Article V, Section 1 of the Constitution, and shall have laid before the Executive Council certified copies of the Constitution adopted at its

Primary Convention, and the proceedings preparatory to the formation of the proposed new Diocese, such new Diocese shall thereupon be admitted into union with the General Convention.

Sec. 5. In the event of the erection of an Area Mission into a Diocese of this Church, as provided in Article V, Sec. 1, the Convocation of the said Area Mission shall be entitled to elect Deputies to the succeeding General Convention, and also to elect a Bishop. The jurisdiction previously assigned to the Bishop in the Area Mission shall be terminated upon the admission of the new Diocese.

Convocation may elect Deputies and Bishop.

Sec. 6 (a) When a Diocese, and another Diocese which has been formed either by division therefrom or by erection into a Diocese or a Missionary Diocese formed by division therefrom, shall desire to be reunited into one Diocese, the proposed reunion must be initiated by a mutual agreement between the Conventions of the two Dioceses, consented to by the Ecclesiastical Authority of each Diocese. If the said agreement is made and the consents given more than three months before the next meeting of the General Convention, the fact of the agreement and consents shall be certified by the Ecclesiastical Authority and the Secretary of the Convention of each Diocese to all the Bishops of the Church having jurisdiction and to the Standing Committees of all the Dioceses; and when the consents of a majority of such Bishops and of a majority of the Standing Committees to the proposed reunion shall have been received, the facts shall be similarly certified to the Secretary of the House of Deputies of the General Convention, and thereupon the reunion shall be considered complete. But if the agreement is made and the consents given within three months of the next meeting of the General Convention, the facts shall be certified instead to the Secretary of the House of Deputies, who shall lay them before the two Houses; and the reunion shall be deemed to be complete when it shall have been sanctioned by a majority vote in the House of Bishops, and in the House of Deputies voting by orders.

Provision for reunion of Dioceses.

(b) The Bishop of the parent Diocese shall be the Bishop, and the Bishop of the junior Diocese shall be the Bishop Coadjutor, of the reunited Diocese; but if there be a vacancy in the Episcopate of either Diocese, the Bishop of the other Diocese shall be the Bishop, and the Bishop Coadjutor if there be one shall be the Bishop Coadjutor, of the reunited Diocese.

Rights and jurisdictions of Bishops.

(c) When the reunion of the two Dioceses shall have been completed, the facts shall be certified to the Presiding Bishop and to the Secretary of the House of Deputies. Thereupon the Presiding Bishop shall notify the Secretary of the House of Bishops of any alteration in the status or style of the Bishop or Bishops concerned, and the Secretary of the House of Deputies shall strike the name of the junior Diocese from the roll of Dioceses in union with the General Convention.

Dioceses in union with the General Convention.

CANON 11: Of Missionary Jurisdictions

Sec. 1. Area Missions established in accordance with Article VI, Sec. 1 and Missionary Dioceses organized in accordance with Article VI, Sec. 3 shall constitute jurisdictions for which this Church as a whole assumes a special responsibility.

Responsibility of the whole Church.

House of Bishops may establish Area Missions.

Sec. 2 (a) The House of Bishops may establish a Mission in any Area not included within the boundaries of a Diocese of this Church, or of a Church in communion with this Church, under such conditions and agreements, not inconsistent with the Constitution and Canons of this Church, as shall be approved by the House of Bishops from time to time.

May be ecumenical.

(b) Such Area Mission may be undertaken under the sole auspices of this Church, or it may be undertaken jointly with another Christian body or bodies, on such terms as shall not compromise the doctrines of the Christian faith as this Church has received the same.

Bishops to be assigned to oversee Area Missions.

(c) For every such Area Mission, a Bishop of this Church, or of a Church in communion with this Church, shall be assigned by the House of Bishops to give episcopal oversight. The person so assigned, if a Bishop of this Church, shall, for the duration of such assignment, exercise jurisdiction as a Missionary Bishop under these Canons, so far as they are applicable to the Area Mission; and should occasion arise for the function of a Standing Committee or a Commission on Ministry, the Bishop shall appoint a board or boards of Clergy and Lay Persons resident in the area, to fulfill such functions as may be required.

(d) Except as may be expressly provided otherwise in the agreements referred to in paragraph (a) of this Section, the Bishop having jurisdiction in an Area Mission may authorize the use of such forms of worship as the Bishop may judge appropriate to the circumstances.

May be terminated by House of Bishops.

(e) An Area Mission may be terminated by the House of Bishops as a mission of this Church; or it may be transferred by them to become a mission of another Church, or to become a constituent part of an autonomous Province in communion with this Church; or it may organize itself as an extra-provincial Diocese.

Representation in its Province.

(f) An Area Mission which shall have been undertaken under the sole auspices of this Church, with a Bishop of this Church assigned to give episcopal oversight, shall be entitled to representation in the Provincial House of Bishops and the Provincial House of Deputies in the Province of which it is a part.

May be organized as Missionary Diocese.

Sec. 3 (a) An Area not previously organized as a Diocese, and not under the permanent jurisdiction of a Bishop in communion with this Church, may, upon application for admission, in accordance with the procedures of Article V, Section 1, be admitted as a Diocese, and may be accepted as a Missionary Diocese within the meaning of Sec. 1 of this Canon. Such Missionary Diocese, and every present Missionary Diocese organized by the House of Bishops under previously existing Canons and admitted into union with the General Convention, shall be governed by a Constitution and Canons, adopted by the Convention of the said Diocese, which acknowledge the authority of the Constitution and Canons of the General Convention, and incorporate the provisions set forth in the subsequent paragraphs of this section.

To adopt a Constitution and Canons.

Transfer to another Province.

(b) In the event a Missionary Diocese beyond the territory of the United States of America is incapable of functioning as a jurisdiction in union with the Episcopal Church, and the Bishop, or if there be none the Ecclesiastical Authority, of such Diocese, after consultation with appropriate diocesan authorities and the Presiding Bishop agree that continuation in union with this Church is no longer feasible, the Presiding Bishop is authorized, after consultation with the appropriate authorities in the Anglican Communion, to take such action as needed for such Diocese to become a constituent part of another Province or Regional Council in communion with this Church.

(c) In every Missionary Diocese there shall be an annual Convention, composed of the Bishop or Bishops, the other Clergy of the Diocese, and Lay Delegates from the organized Congregations. Such Convention shall elect a Standing Committee, in accordance with the diocesan Canons, which shall have the powers and duties set forth for Standing Committees in Canon I.12 and in other Canons of the General Convention. It shall also elect Clerical and Lay Deputies and alternate Deputies to the General Convention, in accordance with its diocesan Canons, and the provisions of Article I.4 of the Constitution. If the Missionary Diocese is a member of a Province of this Church, it shall also provide for Clerical and Lay Deputies and alternate Deputies to the Synod, in accordance with the diocesan Canons and the provisions of the Ordinances of the Province.

Convention to elect Standing Committee and representatives.

(d) The Convention of a Missionary Diocese shall also adopt an annual budget and program for the Diocese, and provide for the means of its administration throughout the year; and shall make provision for the review and approval of requests for grants in aid from the Executive Council or other sources of funds, both toward current operations and for capital needs.

Missionary Diocese to adopt a budget.

(e) The election of the Bishop of a Missionary Diocese, in the event of a vacancy, or, when canonical consent is given, the election of a person to be Bishop Coadjutor or Bishop Suffragan, shall be made by a Diocesan Convention in accordance with its own Canons, and the provisions of Canons III.16 and III.17 of the General Convention.

Election of Bishop.

(f) At the request of the Convention of a Missionary Diocese, supported by the presentation of relevant facts and a reasonable plan, the General Convention may by joint Resolution (1) permit the Diocese seeking autonomy to unite with another Province, or Regional Council having metropolitical authority, of the Anglican Communion, or (2) permit the Diocese seeking autonomy but not planning to unite with another Province or Regional Council, to unite with no less than three (3) other viable Dioceses at the same time which are geographically contiguous, or so located geographically as to be considered of the same region, for the purpose of establishing a new Province, or new Regional Council having metropolitical authority, of the Anglican Communion.

General Convention may grant autonomy.

May transfer to another Province or Regional Council.

(g) At the request of the Convention of a Missionary Diocese, accompanied by the Bishop's written resignation of permanent jurisdiction therein, the General Convention may alter the status of a Missionary Diocese to that of an Area Mission, under such terms and conditions as may be stipulated by the House of Bishops in accordance with Canon I.11.2(a); and in such case, its right to representation by Deputies in the General Convention shall cease.

Status of Missionary Diocese may be altered to Area Mission.

Sec. 4. Notice shall be sent to all Archbishops and Metropolitans, and all Presiding Bishops, of Churches in communion with this Church, of the establishment of any Area Mission, or of the organization or change of status of any Missionary Diocese outside the United States; and of the consecration, or assignment, of a Missionary Bishop therefor.

Notices to be sent to Primates.

Two Bishops not to exercise jurisdiction in same place.

It is hereby declared as the judgment of this Church that no two Bishops of Churches in communion with each other should exercise jurisdiction in the same place; except as may be defined by a concordat adopted jointly by the competent authority of each of the said Churches, after consultation with the appropriate inter-Anglican body.

CANON 12: Of Standing Committees

Meetings.

Sec. 1. In every Diocese the Standing Committee shall elect from their own body a President and a Secretary. They may meet in conformity with their own rules from time to time, and shall keep a record of their proceedings; and they may be summoned to a special meeting whenever the President may deem it necessary. They may be summoned on the requisition of the Bishop, whenever the Bishop shall desire their advice; and they may meet of their own accord and agreeably to their own rules when they may be disposed to advise the Bishop.

Quorum.

Sec. 2. In all cases in which a Canon of the General Convention directs a duty to be performed, or a power to be exercised, by a Standing Committee, or by the Clerical members thereof, or by any other body consisting of several members, a majority of said members, the whole having been duly cited to meet, shall be a quorum; and a majority of the quorum so convened shall be competent to act, unless the contrary is expressly required by the Canon.

CANON 13: Of Parishes and Congregations

Congregation to belong to Diocese where its place of worship is situated.

Clergy to have seat in one Convention.

Sec. 1. Every Congregation of this Church shall belong to the Church in the Diocese in which its place of worship is situated; a Member of the Clergy serving a Cure having Congregations in more than one jurisdiction shall have such rights, including vote, in the Convention of the jurisdiction in which the Member of the Clergy has canonical residence as may be provided in the canons of that diocese and may be granted seat and voice in the jurisdiction(s) in which the Member of the Clergy does not have canonical residence.

Parish Boundaries.

Sec. 2 (a) The ascertainment and defining of the boundaries of existing Parishes or Parochial Cures, as well as the establishment of a new Parish or Congregation, and the formation of a new Parish within the limits of any other Parish, is left to the action of the several Diocesan Conventions.

Formation of new Parish within limits of existing Parish.

(b) Until a Canon or other regulation of a Diocesan Convention shall have been adopted, the formation of new Parishes, or the establishment of new Parishes or Congregations within the limits of existing Parishes, shall be vested in the Bishop of the Diocese, acting by and with the advice and consent of the Standing Committee thereof, and, in case of there being no Bishop, of the Ecclesiastical Authority.

Boundaries of Parish when not defined by law.

Sec. 3 (a) Where Parish boundaries are not defined by law, or settled by Diocesan Authority under Section 2 of this Canon, or are not otherwise settled, they shall be defined by the civil divisions of the State as follows:

Parochial boundaries shall be the limits as fixed by law, of a village, town, township, incorporated borough, city, or of some division of any such civil district, which may be recognized by the Bishop, acting with the advice and consent of the Standing Committee, as constituting the boundaries of a Parish.

Parochial Cure.

(b) If there be but one Church or Congregation within the limits of such village, town, township, borough, city, or such division of a civil district, as herein provided, the same shall be deemed the Parochial Cure of the Member of the Clergy having charge thereof. If there be two or more Churches or Congregations therein, it shall be deemed the Cure of the Members of the Clergy thereof.

Not to affect legal rights.

(c) This Canon shall not affect the legal rights of property of any Parish or Congregation.

CANON 14: Of Parish Vestries

Regulations left to State or Diocesan law.

Sec. 1. In every Parish of this Church the number, mode of selection, and term of office of Wardens and Members of the Vestry, with the qualifications of voters, shall be such as the State or Diocesan law may permit or require, and the Wardens and Members of the Vestry selected under such law shall hold office until their successors are selected and have qualified.

As agents and legal representatives.

Sec. 2. Except as provided by the law of the State or of the Diocese, the Vestry shall be agents and legal representatives of the Parish in all matters concerning its corporate property and the relations of the Parish to its Clergy.

Rector to preside.

Sec. 3. Unless it conflict with the law as aforesaid, the Rector, or such other member of the Vestry designated by the Rector, shall preside in all the meetings of the Vestry.

CANON 15: Of Congregations in Foreign Lands

Congregations in foreign lands.

Sec. 1. It shall be lawful, under the conditions hereinafter stated, to organize a Congregation in any foreign land and not within the jurisdiction of any Missionary Bishop of this Church nor within any Diocese, Province, or Regional Church of the Anglican Communion.

Who may officiate temporarily.

Sec. 2. The Bishop in charge of such Congregations, and the Council of Advice hereinafter provided for, may authorize any Presbyter of this Church to officiate temporarily at any place to be named by them within any such foreign land, upon being satisfied that it is expedient to establish at such place a Congregation of this Church.

Organization.

Sec. 3. Such Presbyter, after having publicly officiated at such place on four consecutive Sundays, may give notice, in the time of Divine Service, that a meeting of the persons of full age and attending the services, will be held, at a time and place to be named by the Presbyter in charge, to organize the Congregation. The said meeting may proceed to effect an organization subject to the approval of the said Bishop and Council of Advice and in conformity to such regulations as the said Council of Advice may provide.

To recognize Constitution and Canons.

Sec. 4. Before being taken under the direction of the General Convention of this Church, such Congregation shall be required, in its Constitution, or Plan, or Articles of Organization, to recognize and accede to the Constitution,

Canons, Doctrine, Discipline, and Worship of this Church, and to agree to submit to and obey such directions as may be, from time to time, received from the Bishop in charge and Council of Advice.

Sec. 5. The desire of such Congregation to be taken under the direction of the General Convention shall be duly certified by the Member of the Clergy, one Warden, and two Vestry members or Trustees of said Congregation, duly elected.

To be received by General Convention.

Sec. 6. Such certificate, and the Constitution, Plan, or Articles of Organization, shall be submitted to the General Convention, if it be in session, or to the Presiding Bishop at any other time; and in case the same are found satisfactory, the Secretary of the House of Deputies of the General Convention, under written instruction from the Presiding Bishop, shall thereupon place the name of the Congregation on the list of Congregations in foreign lands under the direction of the General Convention; and a certificate of the said official action shall be forwarded to and filed by the Registrar of this Church. Such Congregations are placed under the government and jurisdiction of the Presiding Bishop.

How accepted.

Sec. 7. The Presiding Bishop may, from time to time, by written commission under the episcopal signature and seal, assign to a Bishop or Bishops of this Church, or of a Church in communion with this Church, the care of, and responsibility for, one or more of such Congregations and the Clergy officiating therein, for such period of time as the Presiding Bishop may deem expedient; *Provided,* that, should such term expire in a year during which a General Convention is to be held, prior to said Convention, the commission may be extended until the adjournment of the Convention.

Presiding Bishop may assign jurisdiction.

Sec. 8. Nothing in this Canon is to be construed as preventing the election of a Bishop to have charge of such Congregations under the provision of Canon III.18.

Sec. 9. To aid the Presiding Bishop or the Bishop in charge of these foreign Churches in administering the affairs of the same, and in settling such questions as may, by means of their peculiar situation, arise, a Council of Advice, consisting of four Clergy and four Lay Persons, shall be constituted as follows, and shall act as a Council of Advice to the Bishop in charge of the foreign Churches. They shall be chosen to serve for two years and until their successors are elected and have accepted election, by a Convocation duly convened, of all the Clergy of the foreign Churches or Chapels, and of two Lay representatives of each Church or Chapel, chosen by its Vestry or Committee. The Council of Advice shall be convened on the requisition of the Bishop whenever the Bishop may desire their advice, and they may meet of their own accord and agreeably to their own rules when they may wish to advise the Bishop. When a meeting is not practicable, the Bishop may ascertain their mind by letter.

Council of Advice and its function.

It shall be lawful for the Presiding Bishop at any time to authorize by writing under the episcopal hand and seal the Council of Advice to act as the Ecclesiastical Authority.

Members of the Clergy charged with canonical offense.

Sec. 10. In case a Member of the Clergy in charge of a Congregation in a foreign land shall be accused of any offense under the Canons of this Church, it shall be the duty of the Bishop in charge of such Congregations to summon the Council of Advice, and cause an inquiry to be instituted as to the truth of such accusation; and should there be reasonable grounds for believing the same to be true, the said Bishop and the Council of Advice shall appoint a Commission, consisting of three Clergy and two Lay Persons, whose duty it shall be to meet in the place where the accused resides, and to obtain all the evidence in the case from the parties interested; they shall give to the accused all rights under the Canons of this Church which can be exercised in a foreign land. The judgment of the said Commission, solemnly made, shall then be sent to the Bishop in charge, and to the Presiding Bishop, and, if approved by them, shall be carried into effect;

Proviso.

Provided, that no such Commission shall recommend any other discipline than admonition or removal of the Member of the Clergy from charge of said Congregation.

Should the result of the inquiry of the aforesaid Commission reveal evidence tending, in their judgment, to show that said Member of the Clergy deserves a more severe discipline, all the documents in the case shall be placed in the hands of the Presiding Bishop, who may proceed against the Member of the Clergy, as far as possible, according to the Canons of the General Convention.

Formation of new Congregations.

Sec. 11. If there be a Congregation within the limits of any city in a foreign land, no new Congregation shall be established in that city, except with the consent of the Bishop in charge and the Council of Advice.

Differences between Member of the Clergy and Congregation.

Sec. 12. In case of a difference between the Member of the Clergy and a Congregation in a foreign land, the Bishop in charge shall duly examine the same, and the said Bishop shall, with the Council of Advice, have full power to settle and adjust such difference upon principles recognized in the Canons of the General Convention.

Appointment of Clergy.

Sec. 13. No Member of the Clergy shall be allowed to take charge of a Congregation in a foreign land, organized under this Canon, until nominated by the Vestry thereof, or, if there be no Vestry, by the Council of Advice, and approved by the Bishop in charge; and once having accepted such appointment, the Member of the Clergy shall be transferred to the jurisdiction of the Presiding Bishop.

CANON 16: Of Clergy and Congregations Seeking Affiliation with This Church

Congregation seeking affiliation with this Church.

Sec. 1. Whenever a Congregation of Christian people, holding the Christian faith as set forth in the Catholic creeds and recognizing the Scriptures as containing all things necessary to salvation, but using a rite other than that set forth by this Church, shall desire affiliation with this Church, while retaining the use of its own rite, such congregation shall, with the consent of the Bishop in whose Diocese it is situate, make application through the Bishop to the Presiding Bishop for status.

Sec. 2. Any person who has not received episcopal ordination, and desires to serve such a Congregation as a Member of the Clergy, shall conform to the provisions of Canon III.10.

Non-episcopally ordained Clergy.

Sec. 3. A Member of the Clergy of such Congregation who shall have been ordained by a Bishop not in communion with this Church, but the regularity of whose ordination is approved by the Presiding Bishop, shall be admitted in the appropriate Order under the provision of Canon III.11.

Clergy regularly ordained.

Sec. 4. Clergy and delegates of such Congregations may have seats but no vote in the Diocesan Convention unless by formal action of such Convention they are so admitted.

To have seats but no vote.

Sec. 5. The oversight of Congregations so admitted shall rest with the Bishop of the Diocese unless the Bishop delegates this authority to another Bishop who may be commissioned by the Presiding Bishop to have oversight of such Congregations.

Oversight with Bishop of Diocese.

CANON 17: Of Regulations Respecting the Laity

Sec. 1 (a) All persons who have received the Sacrament of Holy Baptism with water in the Name of the Father, and of the Son, and of the Holy Spirit, whether in this Church or in another Christian Church, and whose Baptisms have been duly recorded in this Church, are members thereof.

Baptized members.

(b) Members sixteen years of age and over are to be considered adult members.

Adult members.

(c) It is expected that all adult members of this Church, after appropriate instruction, will have made a mature public affirmation of their faith and commitment to the responsibilities of their Baptism and will have been confirmed or received by the laying on of hands by a Bishop of this Church or by a Bishop of a Church in communion with this Church. Those who have previously made a mature public commitment in another Church may be received by the laying on of hands by a Bishop of this Church, rather than confirmed.

Members confirmed or received.

(d) Any person who is baptized in this Church as an adult and receives the laying on of hands by the Bishop at Baptism is to be considered, for the purpose of this and all other Canons, as both baptized and confirmed; also,

Adult baptism.

Any person who is baptized in this Church as an adult and at some time after the Baptism receives the laying on of hands by the Bishop in Reaffirmation of Baptismal Vows is to be considered, for the purpose of this and all other Canons, as both baptized and confirmed; also,

Any baptized person who received the laying on of hands at Confirmation (by any Bishop in apostolic succession) and is received into the Episcopal Church by a Bishop of this Church is to be considered, for the purpose of this and all other Canons, as both baptized and confirmed; and also,

Any baptized person who received the laying on of hands by a Bishop of this Church at Confirmation or Reception is to be considered, for the purpose of this and all other Canons, as both baptized and confirmed.

Sec. 2 (a) All members of this Church who have received Holy Communion in this Church at least three times during the preceding year are to be considered communicants of this Church.

Communicants.

Adult communicants.

(b) For the purposes of statistical consistency throughout the Church, communicants sixteen years of age and over are to be considered adult communicants.

Communicants in good standing.

Sec. 3. All communicants of this Church who for the previous year have been faithful in corporate worship, unless for good cause prevented, and have been faithful in working, praying, and giving for the spread of the Kingdom of God, are to be considered communicants in good standing.

Removing to another congregation.

Sec. 4 (a) A member of this Church removing from the congregation in which that person's membership is recorded shall procure a certificate of membership indicating that that person is recorded as a member (or adult member) of this Church and whether or not such a member:

(1) is a communicant;
(2) is recorded as being in good standing;
(3) has been confirmed or received by a Bishop of this Church or a Bishop in communion with this Church.

Upon acknowledgment that a member who has received such a certificate has been enrolled in another congregation of this or another Church, the Member of the Clergy in charge or Warden issuing the certificate shall remove the name of the person from the parish register.

(b) The Member of the Clergy in charge or Warden of the congregation to which such certificate is surrendered shall record in the parish register the information contained on the presented certificate of membership, and then notify the Member of the Clergy in charge or Warden of the congregation which issued the certificate that the person has been duly recorded as a member of the new congregation. Whereupon the person's removal shall be noted in the parish register of the congregation which issued the certificate.

(c) If a member of this Church, not having such a certificate, desires to become a member of a congregation in the place to which he or she has removed, that person shall be directed by the Member of the Clergy in charge of the said congregation to procure a certificate from the former congregation, although on failure to produce such a certificate through no fault of the person applying, appropriate entry may be made in the parish register upon the evidence of membership status sufficient in the judgment of the Member of the Clergy in charge or Warden.

(d) Any communicant of any Church in communion with this Church shall be entitled to the benefit of this section so far as the same can be made applicable.

Rights of Laity.

Sec. 5. No one shall be denied rights, status or access to an equal place in the life, worship, and governance of this Church because of race, color, ethnic origin, national origin, marital status, sex, sexual orientation, disabilities or age, except as otherwise specified by Canons.

Refusal of Holy Communion.

Sec. 6. A person to whom the Sacraments of the Church shall have been refused, or who has been repelled from the Holy Communion under the rubrics, or who has been informed of an intention to refuse or repel him or her from the Holy Communion under the rubrics, may appeal to the Bishop or Ecclesiastical Authority. A Priest who refuses or repels a person from the Holy Communion, or who communicates to a person an intent to repel that person from the Holy Communion shall inform that person, in writing, within fourteen days thereof of (i) the reasons therefor and (ii) his or her right to appeal to the Bishop or Ecclesiastical Authority. No Member of the Clergy of this Church shall be required to admit to the Sacraments a person so refused or repelled without the written direction of the Bishop or Ecclesiastical Authority. The Bishop or Ecclesiastical Authority may in certain circumstances see fit to require the person to be admitted or restored because of the insufficiency of the cause assigned by the member of the Clergy. If it shall appear to the Bishop or Ecclesiastical Authority that there is sufficient cause to justify refusal of the Holy Communion, however, appropriate steps shall be taken to institute such inquiry as may be directed by the Canons of the Diocese; and should no such Canon exist, the Bishop or Ecclesiastical Authority shall proceed according to such principles of law and equity as will ensure an impartial investigation and judgment, which judgment shall be made in writing within sixty days of the appeal and which shall also specify the steps required for readmission to Holy Communion.

Sec. 7. No unbaptized person shall be eligible to receive Holy Communion in this Church.

Eligibility for Communion.

Sec. 8. Any person accepting any office in this Church shall well and faithfully perform the duties of that office in accordance with the Constitution and Canons of this Church and of the Diocese in which the office is being exercised.

Fiduciary responsibility.

CANON 18: Of the Solemnization of Holy Matrimony

Sec. 1. Every Member of the Clergy of this Church shall conform to the laws of the State governing the creation of the civil status of marriage, and also to the laws of this Church governing the solemnization of Holy Matrimony.

Legal and canonical requirements.

Sec. 2. Before solemnizing a marriage the Member of the Clergy shall have ascertained:

Conditions.

- **(a)** That both parties have the right to contract a marriage according to the laws of the State. *Laws of State.*
- **(b)** That both parties understand that Holy Matrimony is a physical and spiritual union of a man and a woman, entered into within the community of faith, by mutual consent of heart, mind, and will, and with intent that it be lifelong. *Understanding Holy Matrimony.*
- **(c)** That both parties freely and knowingly consent to such marriage, without fraud, coercion, mistake as to identity of a partner, or mental reservation. *Free consent.*
- **(d)** That at least one of the parties has received Holy Baptism. *One party baptized.*
- **(e)** That both parties have been instructed as to the nature, meaning, and purpose of Holy Matrimony by the Member of the Clergy, or that they have both received such instruction from persons known by the Member of the Clergy to be competent and responsible. *Instruction.*

Procedures.

Sec. 3. No Member of the Clergy of this Church shall solemnize any marriage unless the following procedures are complied with:

Thirty days' notice.

(a) The intention of the parties to contract marriage shall have been signified to the Member of the Clergy at least thirty days before the service of solemnization; *Provided,* that for weighty cause, this requirement may be dispensed with if one of the parties is a member of the Congregation of the Member of the Clergy, or can furnish satisfactory evidence of responsibility.

In case the thirty days' notice is waived, the Member of the Clergy shall report such action in writing to the Bishop immediately.

Witnesses.

(b) There shall be present at least two witnesses to the solemnization of marriage.

Recorded in Register.

(c) The Member of the Clergy shall record in the proper register the date and place of the marriage, the names of the parties and their parents, the age of the parties, their residences, and their Church status; the witnesses and the Member of the Clergy shall sign the record.

Declaration of Intention.

(d) The Member of the Clergy shall have required that the parties sign the following declaration:

(e) "We, A.B. and C.D., desiring to receive the blessing of Holy Matrimony in the Church, do solemnly declare that we hold marriage to be a lifelong union of husband and wife as it is set forth in the Book of Common Prayer.

(f) "We believe that the union of husband and wife, in heart, body, and mind, is intended by God for their mutual joy; for the help and comfort given one another in prosperity and adversity; and, when it is God's will, for the procreation of children and their nurture in the knowledge and love of the Lord.

(g) "And we do engage ourselves, so far as in us lies, to make our utmost effort to establish this relationship and to seek God's help thereto."

Sec. 4. It shall be within the discretion of any Member of the Clergy of this Church to decline to solemnize any marriage.

CANON 19: Of Regulations Respecting Holy Matrimony: Concerning Preservation of Marriage, Dissolution of Marriage, and Remarriage

When marriage is imperiled.

Sec. 1. When marital unity is imperiled by dissension, it shall be the duty, if possible, of either or both parties, before taking legal action, to lay the matter before a Member of the Clergy; it shall be the duty of such Member of the Clergy to act first to protect and promote the physical and emotional safety of those involved and only then, if it be possible, to labor that the parties may be reconciled.

Application for judgment on marital status.

Sec. 2 (a) Any member of this Church whose marriage has been annulled or dissolved by a civil court may apply to the Bishop or Ecclesiastical Authority of the Diocese in which such person is legally or canonically resident for a judgment as to his or her marital status in the eyes of the Church. Such judgment may be a recognition of the nullity, or of the termination of the said marriage; *Provided,* that no such judgment shall be construed as affecting in any way the legitimacy of children or the civil validity of the former relationship.

(b) Every judgment rendered under this Section shall be in writing and shall be made a matter of permanent record in the Archives of the Diocese.

Judgment in writing.

Sec. 3. No Member of the Clergy of this Church shall solemnize the marriage of any person who has been the husband or wife of any other person then living, nor shall any member of this Church enter into a marriage when either of the contracting parties has been the husband or the wife of any other person then living, except as hereinafter provided:

Conditions for re-marriage.

(a) The Member of the Clergy shall be satisfied by appropriate evidence that the prior marriage has been annulled or dissolved by a final judgment or decree of a civil court of competent jurisdiction.

Decree that former marriage is dissolved.

(b) The Member of the Clergy shall have instructed the parties that continuing concern must be shown for the well-being of the former spouse, and of any children of the prior marriage.

Responsibility to former spouse and children.

(c) The Member of the Clergy shall consult with and obtain the consent of the Bishop of the Diocese wherein the Member of the Clergy is canonically resident or the Bishop of the Diocese in which the Member of the Clergy is licensed to officiate prior to, and shall report to that Bishop, the solemnization of any marriage under this Section.

Consent of Bishop and report given.

(d) If the proposed marriage is to be solemnized in a jurisdiction other than the one in which the consent has been given, the consent shall be affirmed by the Bishop of that jurisdiction.

Consent of Bishop of other jurisdiction.

Sec. 4. All provisions of Canon I.18 shall, in all cases, apply.

TITLE II
WORSHIP

CANON 1: Of the Due Celebration of Sundays

All persons within this Church shall celebrate and keep the Lord's Day, commonly called Sunday, by regular participation in the public worship of the Church, by hearing the Word of God read and taught, and by other acts of devotion and works of charity, using all godly and sober conversation.

The Lord's Day to be observed.

CANON 2: Of Translations of the Bible

The Lessons prescribed in the Book of Common Prayer shall be read from the translation of the Holy Scriptures commonly known as the King James or Authorized Version (which is the historic Bible of this Church) together with the Marginal Readings authorized for use by the General Convention of 1901; or from one of the three translations known as Revised Versions, including the English Revision of 1881, the American Revision of 1901, and the Revised Standard Version of 1952; from the Jerusalem Bible of 1966; from the New English Bible with the Apocrypha of 1970; or from The 1976 Good News Bible (Today's English Version); or from The New American Bible (1970); or from The Revised Standard Version, an Ecumenical Edition, commonly known as the "R.S.V. Common Bible" (1973); or from The New International Version (1978); or from The New Jerusalem Bible (1987); or from the Revised English Bible (1989); or from the New Revised Standard Version (1990); or from translations, authorized by the diocesan bishop, of those approved versions published in any other language; or from other versions of the Bible, including those in languages other than English, which shall be authorized by diocesan bishops for specific use in congregations or ministries within their dioceses.

Authorized versions.

CANON 3: Of the Standard Book of Common Prayer

Sec. 1. The copy of the Book of Common Prayer accepted by the General Convention of this Church, in the year of our Lord 1979, and authenticated by the signatures of the Presiding Officers and Secretaries of the two Houses of the General Convention, is hereby declared to be the Standard Book of Common Prayer of this Church.

Standard Book of Common Prayer.

Sec. 2. All copies of the Book of Common Prayer to be hereafter made and published shall conform to this Standard, and shall agree therewith in paging, and, as far as it is possible, in all other matters of typographical arrangement, except that the Rubrics may be printed either in red or black, and that page numbers shall be set against the several headings in the Table of Contents. The requirement of uniformity in paging shall apply to the entire book but shall not extend to editions smaller than those known as 32mo, or to editions noted for music.

All copies to conform.

Sec. 3. In case any typographical inaccuracy shall be found in the Standard Book of Common Prayer, its correction may be ordered by a joint Resolution of any General Convention, and notice of such corrections shall

Correcting inaccuracies.

be communicated by the Custodian to the Ecclesiastical Authority of each Diocese of this Church, and to actual publishers of the Book of Common Prayer.

Copies of Standard to be sent to Dioceses.

Sec. 4 Folio copies of the Standard Book of Common Prayer, duly authenticated, as in the case of the Standard Book, shall be sent to the Ecclesiastical Authority of each Diocese in trust for the use thereof, and for reference and appeal in questions as to the authorized formularies of this Church.

All editions must be authorized.

Sec. 5. No copy, translation, or edition of the Book of Common Prayer, or a part or parts thereof, shall be made, printed, published, or used as of authority in this Church, unless it contains the authorization of the Custodian of the Standard Book of Common Prayer, certifying that the Custodian or some person appointed by the Custodian has compared the said copy, translation, or edition with the said Standard, or a certified copy thereof, and that it conforms thereto. And no copy, translation, or edition of the Book of Common Prayer, or a part or parts thereof, shall be made, printed, published, or used as of authority in this Church, or certified as aforesaid, which contains or is bound up with any alterations or additions thereto, or with any other matter, except the Holy Scriptures or the authorized Hymnal of this Church, or with material set forth in the Book of Occasional Services and The Proper for the Lesser Feasts and Fasts, as those books are authorized from time to time by the General Convention.

Trial use.

Sec. 6 (a) Whenever the General Convention, pursuant to Article X of the Constitution, shall authorize for trial use a proposed revision of the Book of Common Prayer, or of a portion or portions thereof, the enabling Resolution shall specify the period of such trial use, the precise text thereof, and any special terms or conditions under which such trial use shall be carried out.

Duties of Custodian.

(b) It shall be the duty of the Custodian of the Standard Book of Common Prayer:

(1) To arrange for the publication of such proposed revision;

(2) To protect, by copyright, the authorized text of such revision, on behalf of the General Convention; which copyright shall be relinquished when such proposed revision or revisions shall have been adopted by the General Convention as an alteration of, or addition to, the Book of Common Prayer;

(3) To certify that printed copies of such revision or revisions have been duly authorized by the General Convention, and that the printed text conforms to that approved by the General Convention.

Authorized variations in trial use texts.

(c) During the said period of trial use and under the modifying conditions specified, only the material so authorized, and in the exact form in which it has been so authorized, shall be available as an alternative for the said Book of Common Prayer or the said portion or portions thereof; *Provided, however*, that it shall be competent for the Presiding Bishop and the President of the House of Deputies, jointly, on recommendation by a resolution duly adopted at a meeting of the Standing Commission on Liturgy and Music communicated to the said presiding officers in writing, to authorize variations and adjustments to, or substitutions for, or alterations in, any portion of the texts under trial, which seem desirable as a result of such trial use, and which do not change the substance of a rite.

(d) In the event of the authorization of such variations, adjustments, substitutions, or alternatives, as aforesaid, it shall be the duty of the Custodian of the Standard Book of Common Prayer to notify the Ecclesiastical Authority of every Diocese, and the Convocation of the American Churches in Europe, of such action, and to give notice thereof through the media of public information.

Appointment of Custodian.

Sec. 7. The appointment of the Custodian of the Standard Book of Common Prayer shall be made by nomination of the House of Bishops and confirmed by the House of Deputies at a meeting of the General Convention. The Custodian shall hold office until the second General Convention following the General Convention at which the Custodian was nominated and confirmed. A vacancy occurring in the office of Custodian when General Convention is not meeting may be filled until the next General Convention by appointment by the Presiding Bishop upon the confirmation of the Executive Council.

Action on unauthorized editions.

Sec. 8. It shall be the duty of the Ecclesiastical Authority of any Diocese in which any unauthorized edition of the Book of Common Prayer, or any part or parts thereof, shall be published or circulated, to give public notice that the said edition is not of authority in this Church.

CANON 4: Of the Authorization of Special Forms of Service

Authorized forms of worship in a foreign language.

In any Congregation, worshipping in other than the English language, which shall have placed itself under the oversight of a Bishop of this Church, it shall be lawful to use a form of service in such language; *Provided*, that such form of service shall have previously been approved by the Bishop of the Diocese, until such time as an authorized edition of the Book of Common Prayer in such language shall be set forth by the authority of the General Convention; and *Provided further*, that no Bishop shall license any such form of service until first satisfied that the same is in accordance with the Doctrine and Worship of this Church; nor in any case shall such form of service be used for the ordination or consecration of Bishops, Priests, or Deacons.

CANON 5: Of the Music of the Church

Clergy responsible for music used in the Congregation.

It shall be the duty of every Member of the Clergy to see that music is used as an offering for the glory of God and as a help to the people in their worship in accordance with the Book of Common Prayer and as authorized by the rubrics or by the General Convention of this Church. To this end the Member of the Clergy shall have final authority in the administration of matters pertaining to music. In fulfilling this responsibility the Member of the Clergy shall seek assistance from persons skilled in music. Together they shall see that music is appropriate to the context in which it is used.

CANON 6: Of Dedicated and Consecrated Churches

Evidence of affiliation.

Sec. 1. No Church or Chapel shall be consecrated until the Bishop shall have been sufficiently satisfied that the building and the ground on which it is erected are secured for ownership and use by a Parish, Mission, Congregation, or Institution affiliated with this Church and subject to its Constitution and Canons.

Consent required to encumber or alienate consecrated property.

Sec. 2. It shall not be lawful for any Vestry, Trustees, or other body authorized by laws of any State or Territory to hold property for any Diocese, Parish or Congregation, to encumber or alienate any dedicated and consecrated Church or Chapel, or any Church or Chapel which has been used solely for Divine Service, belonging to the Parish or Congregation which they represent, without the previous consent of the Bishop, acting with the advice and consent of the Standing Committee of the Diocese.

Consent to deconsecrate Churches.

Sec. 3. No dedicated and consecrated Church or Chapel shall be removed, taken down, or otherwise disposed of for any worldly or common use, without the previous consent of the Standing Committee of the Diocese.

All Churches to be held in trust.

Sec. 4. Any dedicated and consecrated Church or Chapel shall be subject to the trust declared with respect to real and personal property held by any Parish, Mission, or Congregation as set forth in Canon I.7.4.

TITLE III
MINISTRY

CANON 1: Of the Ministry of All Baptized Persons

Sec. 1. Each Diocese shall make provision for the affirmation and development of the ministry of all baptized persons, including:

Responsibility of Diocese.

(a) Assistance in understanding that all baptized persons are called to minister in Christ's name, to identify their gifts with the help of the Church and to serve Christ's mission at all times and in all places.

(b) Assistance in understanding that all baptized persons are called to sustain their ministries through commitment to life-long Christian formation.

Sec. 2. No person shall be denied access to the discernment process for any ministry, lay or ordained, in this Church because of race, color, ethnic origin, national origin, sex, marital status, sexual orientation, disabilities or age, except as otherwise provided by these Canons. No right to licensing, ordination, or election is hereby established.

Access to discernment process.

CANON 2: Of Commissions on Ministry

Sec. 1. In each Diocese there shall be a Commission on Ministry ("Commission") consisting of Priests, Deacons, if any, and Lay Persons. The Canons of each Diocese shall provide for the number of members, terms of office, and manner of selection to the Commission.

Each Diocese to have a Commission.

Sec. 2. The Commission shall advise and assist the Bishop:

To assist the Bishop.

(a) In the implementation of Title III of these Canons.

(b) In the determination of present and future opportunities and needs for the ministry of all baptized persons.

(c) In the design and oversight of the ongoing process for recruitment, discernment, formation for ministry, and assessment of readiness therefor.

Sec. 3. The Commission may adopt rules for its work, subject to the approval of the Bishop; *Provided* that they are not inconsistent with the Constitution and Canons of this Church and of the Diocese.

May adopt rules.

Sec. 4. The Commission may establish committees consisting of members and other persons to report to the Commission or to act on its behalf.

Sec. 5. The Bishop and Commission shall ensure that the members of the Commission and its committees receive ongoing education and training for their work.

Education and training.

CANON 3: Of Discernment

Sec. 1. The Bishop and Commission shall provide encouragement, training, and necessary resources to assist each congregation in developing an ongoing process of community discernment appropriate to the cultural background, age, and life experiences of all persons seeking direction in their call to ministry.

Community discernment in the call to ministry.

Sec. 2. The Bishop, in consultation with the Commission, may utilize college and university campus ministry centers and other communities of

Discernment communities.

faith as additional communities where discernment takes place. In cases where these discernment communities are located in another jurisdiction, the Bishop will consult with the Bishop where the discernment community is located.

Recruiting leadership.

Sec. 3. The Bishop and Commission shall actively solicit from congregations, schools and other youth organizations, college and university campus ministry centers, seminaries, and other communities of faith names of persons whose demonstrated qualities of Christian commitment and potential for leadership and vision mark them as desirable candidates for positions of leadership in the Church.

Support for discernment process.

Sec. 4. The Bishop, Commission, and the discernment community shall assist persons engaged in a process of ministry discernment to determine appropriate avenues for the expression and support of their ministries, either lay or ordained.

CANON 4: Of Licensed Ministries

Selection and license.

Sec. 1. **(a)** A confirmed communicant in good standing or, in extraordinary circumstances, subject to guidelines established by the Bishop, a communicant in good standing, may be licensed by the Ecclesiastical Authority to serve as Pastoral Leader, Worship Leader, Preacher, Eucharistic Minister, Eucharistic Visitor, or Catechist. Requirements and guidelines for the selection, training, continuing education, and deployment of such persons, and the duration of licenses shall be established by the Bishop in consultation with the Commission on Ministry.

Member of the Armed Forces.

(b) The Presiding Bishop or the Bishop Suffragan for the Armed Forces may authorize a member of the Armed Forces to exercise one or more of these ministries in the Armed Forces in accordance with the provisions of this Canon. Requirements and guidelines for the selection, training, continuing education, and deployment of such persons shall be established by the Bishop granting the license.

Terms.

Sec. 2. **(a)** The Member of the Clergy or other leader exercising oversight of the congregation or other community of faith may request the Ecclesiastical Authority with jurisdiction to license persons within that congregation or other community of faith to exercise such ministries. The license shall be issued for a period of time to be determined under Canon III.4.1(a) and may be renewed. The license may be revoked by the Ecclesiastical Authority upon request of or upon notice to the Member of the Clergy or other leader exercising oversight of the congregation or other community of faith.

Renewal.

(b) In renewing the license, the Ecclesiastical Authority shall consider the performance of the ministry by the person licensed, continuing education in the licensed area, and the endorsement of the Member of the Clergy or other leader exercising oversight of the congregation or other community of faith in which the person is serving.

(c) A person licensed in any Diocese under the provisions of this Canon may serve in another congregation or other community of faith in the same or another Diocese only at the invitation of the Member of the Clergy or other leader exercising oversight, and with the consent of the Ecclesiastical Authority in whose jurisdiction the service will occur.

Sec. 3. A Pastoral Leader is a lay person authorized to exercise pastoral or administrative responsibility in a congregation under special circumstances, as defined by the Bishop.

Pastoral Leader.

Sec. 4. A Worship Leader is a lay person who regularly leads public worship under the direction of the Member of the Clergy or other leader exercising oversight of the congregation or other community of faith.

Worship Leader.

Sec. 5. A Preacher is a lay person authorized to preach. Persons so authorized shall only preach in congregations under the direction of the Member of the Clergy or other leader exercising oversight of the congregation or other community of faith.

Preacher.

Sec. 6. A Eucharistic Minister is a lay person authorized to administer the Consecrated Elements at a Celebration of Holy Eucharist. A Eucharistic Minister should normally act under the direction of a Deacon, if any, or otherwise, the Member of the Clergy or other leader exercising oversight of the congregation or other community of faith.

Eucharistic Minister.

Sec. 7. A Eucharistic Visitor is a lay person authorized to take the Consecrated Elements in a timely manner following a Celebration of Holy Eucharist to members of the congregation who, by reason of illness or infirmity, were unable to be present at the Celebration. A Eucharistic Visitor should normally act under the direction of a Deacon, if any, or otherwise, the Member of the Clergy or other leader exercising oversight of the congregation or other community of faith.

Eucharistic Visitor.

Sec. 8. A Catechist is a lay person authorized to prepare persons for Baptism, Confirmation, Reception, and the Reaffirmation of Baptismal Vows, and shall function under the direction of the Member of the Clergy or other leader exercising oversight of the congregation or other community of faith.

Catechist.

CANON 5: Of General Provisions Respecting Ordination

Sec. 1. **(a)** The canonical authority assigned to the Bishop Diocesan by this Title may be exercised by a Bishop Coadjutor, when so empowered under Canon III.19, by a Bishop Suffragan when requested by the Bishop Diocesan, or by any other Bishop of the Anglican Communion canonically in charge of a Diocese, at the request of the ordinand's Bishop.

Canonical authority.

(b) The Council of Advice of the Convocation of American Churches in Europe, and the board appointed by a Bishop having jurisdiction in an Area Mission in accordance with the provisions of Canon I.11.2(c), shall, for the purpose of this and other Canons of Title III have the same powers as the Standing Committee of a Diocese.

(c) In case of a vacancy in the episcopate in a Diocese, the Ecclesiastical Authority may authorize and request the President of the House of Bishops of the Province to take order for an ordination.

Sec. 2. **(a)** No Nominee, Applicant, Postulant, or Candidate for ordination shall sign any of the certificates required by this Title.

Testimonials.

(b) Testimonials required of the Standing Committee by this Title must be signed by a majority of the whole Committee, at a meeting duly convened, except that testimonials may be executed in counterparts, each of which shall be deemed an original.

Letter of support.

(c) Whenever the letter of support of a Vestry is required, the letter must be signed and dated by at least two-thirds of all of the members of the Vestry, at a meeting duly convened, and by the Rector or Priest-in-Charge of the Parish, and attested by the Clerk of the Vestry. Should there be no Rector or Priest-in-Charge, the letter shall be signed by a Priest of the Diocese acquainted with the nominee and the Parish, the reason for the substitution being stated in the attesting clause.

(d) If the congregation or other discernment community of which the nominee is a member is not a Parish, the letter of support required by Canon III.6 or Canon III.8 shall be signed and dated by the Member of the Clergy and the council of the congregation or other community of faith, and shall be attested by the secretary of the meeting at which the letter was approved. Should there be no Member of the Clergy, the letter shall be signed and dated by a Priest of the Diocese acquainted with the nominee and the congregation or other community of faith, the reason for the substitution being stated in the attesting clause.

Member of a Religious Order or Community.

(e) If the applicant is a member of a Religious Order or Christian Community recognized by Canon III.24, the letters of support referred to in Canon III.5 or Canon III.6 and any other requirements imposed on a congregation or Member of the Clergy may be given by the Superior or person in charge, and Chapter, or other comparable body of the Order or Community.

Dispensation.

Sec. 3. An application for any dispensation permitted by this Title from any of the requirements for ordination must first be made to the Bishop, and if approved, referred to the Standing Committee for its advice and consent.

CANON 6: Of the Ordination of Deacons

Procedures for selection.

Sec. 1. Selection

The Bishop, in consultation with the Commission, shall establish procedures to identify and select persons with evident gifts and fitness for ordination to the Diaconate.

(a) Nomination. A confirmed adult communicant in good standing, may be nominated for ordination to the diaconate by the person's congregation or other community of faith. The Nomination shall be in writing, and shall include:

Criteria for Nomination.

(1) Full name and date of birth.
(2) The length of time resident in the Diocese.
(3) Evidence of Baptism and Confirmation.
(4) Whether an application has been made previously for Postulancy or the person has been nominated in any diocese.
(5) A description of the process of discernment by which the applicant has been identified for ordination to the Diaconate.

(6) The level of education attained and, if any, the degrees earned and areas of specialization.

(7) A letter of support by the applicant's discernment community, including a statement committing the discernment community to involve itself in the applicant's preparation for ordination to the Diaconate. If it be a congregation, the letter shall be signed by a two-thirds majority of the Vestry or comparable body, and the Member of the Clergy or leader exercising oversight.

(8) An acceptance in writing by the nominated person.

The nomination shall be submitted to the Bishop, who may admit the person as a Postulant for ordination to the Diaconate.

Definition of Admission to Postulancy.

(b) Admission to Postulancy. Admission is the time between nomination and candidacy and includes a process of exploration of and decision on the Postulant's call to the Diaconate.

Investigation.

(1) There shall be a thorough investigation of the Postulant which shall include:

(i) a background check, and

(ii) medical and complete psychological evaluation by professionals approved by the Bishop, using forms prepared for the purpose by The Church Pension Fund, and if desired or necessary, psychiatric referral.

(iii) Reports of all investigations and examinations shall be kept on file by the Bishop.

Interview.

(2) The Bishop, or the Bishop's designee, may interview the Postulant. The Commission or a designated committee shall interview the Postulant, and the Commission or designated committee shall submit a recommendation to the Bishop.

(3) The Bishop may then admit the Postulant as a Candidate, informing the Candidate and the Member of the Clergy or other leader of the Candidate's discernment community in writing.

Sec. 2. Candidacy

Definition of Candidacy.

(a) Candidacy is a time, no less than one year in length, of formation in preparation for ordination to the Diaconate, established by a formal commitment by the Candidate, the Bishop, the Commission, and the congregation or other community of faith.

(b) The Bishop may assign the Candidate to any congregation of the diocese or other community of faith after consultation with the Member of the Clergy or other leader exercising oversight.

Removal.

(c) At the Bishop's sole discretion, any Candidate may be removed from the list of Candidates, with written notice of the removal being given to the Candidate and the Member of the Clergy or other leader exercising oversight of the nominating congregation or other community of faith and the Commission.

Sec. 3. Preparation for Ordination

Length and time of formation.

(a) The Bishop, in consultation with the Commission, shall determine the length of time and extent of formation needed to prepare each Candidate for ordination.

Areas of competence.

(b) Before ordination each Candidate shall be prepared in and demonstrate basic competence in five general areas:

(1) Academic studies including, The Holy Scriptures, theology, and the tradition of the Church.

(2) Diakonia and the diaconate.

(3) Human awareness and understanding.

(4) Spiritual development and discipline.

(5) Practical training and experience.

Training.

(c) The formation process shall include sexual misconduct prevention training, training regarding Title IV of these Canons, and anti-racism training.

Formation.

(d) Formation shall reflect the local culture and each Candidate's background, age, occupation, and ministry. Prior education and learning from life experience may be considered as part of the formation required for ordination.

(e) Wherever possible, formation shall take place in community, including persons in preparation for the diaconate, or others preparing for ministry.

Ember weeks.

(f) Each Candidate shall communicate with the Bishop in person or by letter, four times a year, in the Ember Weeks, reflecting on the Candidate's academic, diaconal, human, spiritual, and practical development.

Evaluation of progress.

(g) During Candidacy each Candidate's progress shall be evaluated from time to time, and there shall be a written report of the evaluation by those authorized by the Commission to be in charge of the evaluation program. Upon certification by those in charge of the Candidate's program of preparation that the Candidate has successfully completed preparation and is ready for ordination, a final written assessment of readiness for ordination to the Diaconate shall be prepared as determined by the Bishop in consultation with the Commission. This report shall include a recommendation from the Commission regarding the readiness of the Candidate for ordination. Records shall be kept of all evaluations, assessments, and the recommendation, and shall be made available to the Standing Committee.

Examinations and requirements.

(h) If the medical examination, psychological examination, or background check have taken place more than 36 months prior to ordination, they must be updated.

(i) Before ordination each Candidate must have reached the age of twenty-four, and made application for ordination.

(j) Upon certification in writing by the Standing Committee that all canonical requirements have been met and that there is no sufficient objection on medical, psychological, moral, doctrinal, or spiritual grounds and that they recommend ordination, the Bishop may ordain the Candidate a Deacon.

CANON 7: Of the Life and Work of Deacons

Sec. 1. Deacons serve directly under the authority of and are accountable to the Bishop.

Community of Deacons.

Sec. 2. Deacons canonically resident in each Diocese constitute a Community of Deacons, which shall meet from time to time. The Bishop may appoint one or more of such Deacons as Archdeacon(s) to assist the Bishop in the formation, deployment, supervision, and support of the Deacons or those in preparation to be Deacons, and in the implementation of this canon.

Council on Deacons.

Sec. 3. The Bishop may establish a Council on Deacons ("Council") to oversee, study, and promote the Diaconate.

Assignment and responsibilities.

Sec. 4. The Bishop, after consultation with the Deacon and the Member of the Clergy or other leader exercising oversight, may assign a Deacon to one or more congregations, other communities of faith or non-parochial ministries. Deacons assigned to a congregation or other community of faith act under the authority of the Member of the Clergy or other leader exercising oversight in all matters concerning the congregation.

(a) Deacons may have a letter of agreement, subject to the Bishop's approval, setting forth mutual responsibilities in the assignment.

(b) Deacons shall report annually to the Bishop or the Bishop's designee on their life and work.

(c) Deacons may serve as administrators of congregations or other communities of faith, but no Deacon shall be in charge of a congregation or other community of faith.

(d) Deacons may accept chaplaincies in any hospital, prison, or other institution.

Continuing education.

Sec. 5. The Bishop and Commission shall require and provide for the continuing education of Deacons and keep a record of such education.

License to serve in another Diocese.

Sec. 6. **(a)** A Deacon may not serve as Deacon for more than two months in any Diocese other than the Diocese in which the Deacon is canonically resident unless the Bishop of the other Diocese shall have granted a license to the Deacon to serve in that Diocese.

(b)

Letters Dimissory.

(1) A Deacon desiring to become canonically resident within a Diocese shall request a testimonial from the Ecclesiastical Authority of the Diocese in which the Deacon is canonically resident to present to the receiving Diocese, which testimonial, if granted, shall be given by the Ecclesiastical Authority to the applicant, and a duplicate thereof may be sent to the Ecclesiastical Authority of the Diocese to which transfer is proposed. The testimonial shall be in the following words:

I hereby certify that A.B., who has signified to me the desire to be transferred to the Ecclesiastical Authority of __________, is a Deacon of __________ in good standing, and has not, so far as I know or believe, been justly liable to evil report for error in religion or for viciousness of life, for the last three years.

(Date) __________ (Signed) _______________

(2) Such testimonial shall be called Letters Dimissory. If the Ecclesiastical Authority accepts the Letters Dimissory, the canonical residence of the Deacon so transferred shall date from the acceptance of the Letters Dimissory, of which prompt notice shall be given both to the applicant and to the Ecclesiastical Authority from which it came.

(3) Letters Dimissory not presented within six months from the date of transmission to the applicant shall become void.

(4) A statement of the record of payments to The Church Pension Fund by or on behalf of the Deacon concerned shall accompany Letters Dimissory.

Retirement.

Sec. 7. A Deacon may retire from active service for reasons of age or infirmity with the consent of the Bishop at any time and shall retire for reasons of age or infirmity at the request of the Bishop. The Bishop may, with the consent of the Deacon, assign a retired Deacon to any congregation, other community of faith or non-parochial ministry, for a period not to exceed twelve months, and this period may be renewed.

CANON 8: Of the Ordination of Priests

Sec. 1. The Bishop, in consultation with the Commission, shall establish procedures to identify and select persons with evident gifts and fitness for ordination to the Priesthood.

Sec. 2. Of General Provisions concerning Postulancy and Candidacy

Postulancy.

(a) Postulancy is a time, no less than six months in length, for the exploration of and decision on the Postulant's call to the Priesthood.

Candidacy.

(b) Candidacy is a time of formation in preparation for ordination to the Priesthood, established by a formal commitment by the Candidate, the Bishop, the Commission and the congregation or other community of faith. The period of Candidacy shall be no less than six months.

(c) The combined period for Postulancy, Candidacy, and Diaconate under this canon shall be no less than 18 months.

Responsibilities.

(d) The responsibilities for the formation and preparation of Postulants and Candidates shall include the following:

(1) Each Postulant or Candidate for ordination to the Priesthood shall communicate with the Bishop in person or by letter, four times a year, in the Ember Weeks, reflecting on the individual's academic experience and personal and spiritual development.

(2) The congregation or other community of faith shall nominate appropriate persons for the ordination process, nurture them in their faith, and provide continuing support for such persons through Postulancy, Candidacy, and ordination.

(3) The Bishop and the Commission shall work closely with the Postulant or Candidate to develop and monitor a program of preparation for ordination to the Priesthood in accordance with Canon III.8.4 and to ensure that pastoral guidance is provided throughout the period of preparation.

(4) The Standing Committee shall certify that all canonical requirements for ordination have been met and make a recommendation regarding ordination as prescribed in sections 6 and 7 of this canon.

(5) The seminary or other formation program shall provide for, monitor, and report on the academic performance and personal qualifications of the Candidate or Postulant for ordination. These reports will be made upon request of the Bishop and Commission, but at least once per year.

Criteria to be met.

(e) Prior to ordination as a deacon under this canon, the following must be accomplished:

(1) a thorough background check of the applicant,

(2) sexual misconduct prevention training, training regarding Title IV of these canons, and anti-racism training,

(3) thorough examinations, both medical and psychological, by professionals approved by the Bishop, using the forms prepared by The Church Pension Fund for this purpose, and if desired or necessary, psychiatric referral. These reports shall be kept on file by the Bishop.

(4) if the medical examination, psychological examination, or background check have taken place more than 36 months prior to ordination as a Deacon under this canon, they must be updated.

Sec. 3. Postulancy

Requirements for admission as Postulant.

(a) A person nominated for admission as a Postulant for ordination to the Priesthood shall provide to the Bishop the following:

(1) Full name and date of birth,

(2) The length of time resident in the Diocese,

(3) Evidence of Baptism and Confirmation,

(4) Whether an application or Nomination has been made previously for Postulancy in any diocese,

(5) A description of the process of discernment by which the nominee has been identified for ordination to the Priesthood,

(6) The level of education attained and, if any, the degrees earned and areas of specialization, including official transcripts,

(7) A letter of support by the nominee's congregation or other community of faith, including a statement committing the congregation or other community of faith to involve itself in the nominee's preparation for ordination to the Priesthood. If it be a congregation, the letter shall be signed and dated by a two-thirds majority of the Vestry, and the Member of the Clergy or leader exercising oversight,

(8) A written request from the nominee for admission to Postulancy.

Bishop to confirm qualifications.

(b) Before granting admission as a Postulant, the Bishop:

(1) shall determine that the person is a confirmed adult communicant in good standing of a congregation or other community of faith, and

(2) shall confer in person with the nominee,
(3) shall consult with the nominee regarding financial resources which will be available for the support of the Postulant throughout preparation for ordination. During Postulancy and later Candidacy, the Bishop or someone appointed by the Bishop shall review periodically the financial condition and plans of the Postulant.

(c) On the basis of the application and the personal interview, the Bishop shall notify the nominee and the Commission whether the application process may proceed.

Commission to review the application.

(d) If the Bishop approves proceeding, the Commission, or a committee of the Commission, shall meet with the nominee to review the application and prepare an evaluation of the nominee's qualifications to pursue a course of preparation for ordination to the Priesthood. The Commission shall present its evaluation and recommendations to the Bishop.

Process of admission.

(e) The Bishop may admit the nominee as a Postulant for ordination to the Priesthood. The Bishop shall record the Postulant's name and date of admission in a Register kept for that purpose. The Bishop shall inform the Postulant, the Member of the Clergy or other leader exercising oversight of the Postulant's congregation or other community of faith, the Commission, the Standing Committee, and the Dean of the seminary the Postulant may be attending or proposes to attend, or the director of Postulant's program of preparation, of the fact and date of such admission.

Removal.

(f) Any Postulant may be removed as a Postulant at the sole discretion of the Bishop. The Bishop shall give written notice of the removal to the Candidate and the Member of the Clergy or other leader exercising oversight of the Postulant's congregation or other community of faith, the Commission, the Standing Committee, and the Dean of the seminary the Postulant may be attending or the director of the program of preparation.

Prior refusal or cessation.

(g) No Bishop shall consider accepting as a Postulant any person who has been refused admission as a Candidate for ordination to the Priesthood in any other Diocese, or who, having been admitted, has afterwards ceased to be a Candidate, until receipt of a letter from the Bishop of the Diocese refusing admission, or in which the person has been a Candidate, declaring the cause of refusal or of cessation. If the Bishop decides to proceed the Bishop shall send the letter to the Commission.

Program of preparation.

Sec. 4. Formation. Postulants shall pursue the program of preparation for ordination to the Priesthood developed by the Bishop and Commission. The program shall include theological training, practical experience, emotional development, and spiritual formation.

Previous education.

(a) If the Postulant has not previously obtained a baccalaureate degree, the Commission, Bishop, and Postulant shall design a program of such additional academic work as may be necessary to prepare the Postulant to undertake a program of theological education.

(b) Prior education and learning from life experience may be considered as part of the formation required for the Priesthood.

(c) Whenever possible, formation for the Priesthood shall take place in community, including other persons in preparation for the Priesthood, a ministry team, or others preparing for ministry.

(d) Formation shall take into account the local culture and each Candidate's background, age, occupation, and ministry.

Formation and study.

(e) Subject areas for study during this program of preparation shall include:

(1) The Holy Scriptures;
(2) Church History, including the Ecumenical Movement;
(3) Christian Theology, including Missionary Theology and Missiology;
(4) Christian Ethics and Moral Theology;
(5) Studies in contemporary society, including racial and minority groups;
(6) Liturgics and Church Music; Christian Worship and Music according to the contents and use of the Book of Common Prayer and the Hymnal, and authorized supplemental texts; and
(7) Theory and practice of ministry.

Sec. 5. Candidacy

Application for Candidacy.

(a) A person desiring to be considered as a Candidate for ordination to the Priesthood shall apply to the Bishop. Such application shall include the following:

(1) the Postulant's date of admission to Postulancy, and
(2) letter of support by the Postulant's congregation or other community of faith. If it be a congregation, the letter shall be signed and dated by at least two-thirds of the Vestry and the Member of the Clergy or other leader exercising oversight.

Admission as a Candidate.

(b) Upon compliance with these requirements, and receipt of a statement from the Commission attesting to the continuing formation of the Postulant, the Bishop may admit the applicant as a Candidate for ordination to the Priesthood. The Bishop shall record the Candidate's name and date of admission in a Register kept for that purpose. The Bishop shall inform the Candidate, the Member of the Clergy or leader exercising oversight of the Candidate's congregation or other community of faith, the Commission, the Standing Committee, and the Dean of the seminary the Candidate may be attending or proposes to attend, or the director of the Candidate's program of preparation, of the fact and date of such admission.

(c) A Candidate must remain in canonical relationship with the Diocese in which admission has been granted until ordination to the Diaconate under this canon, except as provided in Canon III.8.5(d).

Transfer to another Diocese.

(d) For reasons satisfactory to the Bishop, the Candidate may be transferred to another Diocese upon request, provided that the Bishop of the receiving Diocese is willing to accept the Candidate.

Candidate may be removed.

(e) Any Candidate may be removed as a Candidate at the sole discretion of the Bishop. The Bishop shall give written notice of the removal to the Candidate and the Member of the Clergy or other leader exercising oversight of the Candidate's congregation or other community of faith, the Commission, the Standing Committee, and the Dean of the seminary the Candidate may be attending or the director of the program of preparation.

(f) If a Bishop has removed the Candidate's name from the list of Candidates, except by transfer, or the Candidate's application for ordination has been rejected, no other Bishop may ordain the person without readmission to Candidacy for a period of at least twelve months.

Sec. 6. Ordination to the Diaconate

Criteria for ordination.

(a) A Candidate must first be ordained Deacon before being ordained Priest.

(b) To be ordained Deacon under this canon, a person must be at least twenty-one years of age.

(c) No one shall be ordained Deacon under this canon within six months of admission as a Candidate nor within one year of admission as Postulant.

Papers required by the Bishop.

(d) The Bishop shall obtain in writing:

(1) an application from the Candidate requesting ordination as a Deacon under this canon, including the Candidate's dates of admission to Postulancy and Candidacy;

(2) a letter of support from the Candidate's congregation or other community of faith, signed and dated by at least two-thirds of the Vestry and the Member of the Clergy or other leader exercising oversight;

(3) a certificate from the seminary or other program of preparation, showing the Candidate's scholastic record in the subjects required by the canons, and giving an evaluation with recommendation as to the Candidate's other personal qualifications for ordination together with a recommendation regarding ordination to the Diaconate under this canon.

Papers required by the Standing Committee.

(e) The Standing Committee shall obtain:

(1) the application for ordination to the Diaconate under this canon specified in Canon III.8.6.(d)(1), including the accompanying letter of support by the Candidate's congregation or other community of faith specified in Canon III.8.6.(d)(2),

(2) certificates from the Bishop who admitted the Candidate to Postulancy and Candidacy, giving the dates of admission, and

(3) a certificate from the Commission giving a recommendation regarding ordination to the Diaconate under this canon.

Standing Committee to consent and certify candidates for Diaconate.

(f) On the receipt of such certificates, the Standing Committee, a majority of all the members consenting, shall certify that the canonical requirements for ordination to the Diaconate under this canon have been met and there is no sufficient objection on medical, psychological, moral, doctrinal, or spiritual grounds and that they recommend ordination, by a testimonial addressed to the Bishop in the form specified below and signed by the consenting members of the Standing Committee.

To the Right Reverend_______, Bishop of_______ We, the Standing Committee of________, having been duly convened at________, do testify that A.B., desiring to be ordained to the Diaconate and Priesthood under Canon III.8, has presented to us the certificates as required by the Canons indicating A.B.'s preparedness for ordination to the Diaconate under Canon III.8; and we certify that all canonical requirements for ordination to the Diaconate under Canon III.8 have been met; and we find no sufficient objection to ordination. Therefore, we recommend A. B. for ordination. In witness whereof, we have hereunto set our hands this ____ day of_____, in the year of our Lord_____.

(Signed)____________

(g) The testimonial having been presented to the Bishop, and there being no sufficient objection on medical, psychological, moral, doctrinal, or spiritual grounds, the Bishop may ordain the Candidate to the Diaconate under this canon; and at the time of ordination the Candidate shall subscribe publicly and make, in the presence of the Bishop, the declaration required in Article VIII of the Constitution.

Declaration of belief and conformity.

Sec. 7. Ordination to the Priesthood

(a) A person may be ordained Priest:

Criteria for ordination.

(1) after at least six months since ordination as a Deacon under this canon, and
(2) upon attainment of at least twenty-four years of age, and
(3) if the medical examination, psychological examination, and background check have taken place or been updated within 36 months prior to ordination as a Priest.

(b) The Bishop shall obtain in writing and provide to the Standing Committee:

Papers to be provided to Standing Committee.

(1) an application from the Deacon requesting ordination as a Priest, including the Deacon's dates of admission to Postulancy and Candidacy and ordination as a Deacon under this canon,
(2) a letter of support from the Deacon's congregation or other community of faith, signed by at least two-thirds of the Vestry and the Member of the Clergy or other leader exercising oversight,
(3) evidence of admission to Postulancy and Candidacy, including dates of admission, and ordination to the Diaconate,
(4) a certificate from the seminary or other program of preparation, showing the Deacon's scholastic record in the subjects required by the canons, and giving an evaluation with recommendation as to the Deacon's other personal qualifications for ordination together with a recommendation regarding ordination to the Priesthood, and
(5) a statement from the Commission attesting to the successful completion of the program of formation designed during Postulancy under Canon III.8.4, and recommending the Deacon for ordination to the Priesthood.

(c) On the receipt of such certificates, the Standing Committee, a majority of all the members consenting, shall certify that the canonical requirements for ordination to the Priesthood have been met and there is no sufficient objection on medical, psychological, moral, doctrinal, or spiritual grounds and that they recommend ordination, by a testimonial addressed to the Bishop in the form specified below and signed by the consenting members of the Standing Committee.

Standing Committee to consent and certify candidates for Priesthood.

To the Right Reverend_______, Bishop of_______ We, the Standing Committee of________, having been duly convened at________, do testify that A.B., desiring to be ordained to the Priesthood, has presented to us the certificates as required by the Canons indicating A.B.'s preparedness for ordination to the Priesthood have been met; and we certify that all canonical requirements for ordination to the Priesthood

have been met, and we find no sufficient objection to ordination. Therefore, we recommend A. B. for ordination. In witness whereof, we have hereunto set our hands this _____ day of _____, in the year of our Lord _____.
(Signed) ____________

Declaration of belief and conformity.

(d) The testimonial having been presented to the Bishop, and there being no sufficient objection on medical, psychological, moral, doctrinal, or spiritual grounds, the Bishop may ordain the Deacon to the Priesthood; and at the time of ordination the Deacon shall subscribe publicly and make, in the presence of the Bishop, the declaration required in Article VIII of the Constitution.

Evidence of appointment.

(e) No Deacon shall be ordained to the Priesthood until having been appointed to serve in a Parochial Cure within the jurisdiction of this Church, or as a Missionary under the Ecclesiastical Authority of a Diocese, or as an officer of a Missionary Society recognized by the General Convention, or as a Chaplain of the Armed Services of the United States, or as a Chaplain in a recognized hospital or other welfare institution, or as a Chaplain or instructor in a school, college, or other seminary, or with other opportunity for the exercise of the office of Priest within the Church judged appropriate by the Bishop.

Deacons subsequently called to the Priesthood.

(f) A person ordained to the Diaconate under Canon III.6 who is subsequently called to the Priesthood shall fulfill the Postulancy and Candidacy requirements set forth in this canon. Upon completion of these requirements, the Deacon may be ordained to the Priesthood.

CANON 9: Of the Life and Work of Priests

Continuing education.

Sec. 1. The Bishop and Commission shall require and provide for the continuing education of Priests and keep a record of such education.

Of Mentoring for Newly Ordained Priests

Sec. 2. Each newly ordained Priest, whether employed or not, shall be assigned a mentor Priest by the Bishop in consultation with the Commission on Ministry. The mentor and new Priest shall meet regularly for at least a year to provide guidance, information, and a sustained dialogue about priestly ministry.

Of the Appointment of Priests

Sec. 3.

(a) Rectors.

Parish without a Rector.

(1) When a Parish is without a Rector, the Wardens or other officers shall promptly notify the Ecclesiastical Authority in writing. If the Parish shall for thirty days fail to provide services of public worship, the Ecclesiastical Authority shall make provision for such worship.

Election.

(2) No Parish may elect a Rector until the names of the proposed nominees have been forwarded to the Ecclesiastical Authority and a time, not exceeding sixty days, given to the Ecclesiastical

Authority to communicate with the Vestry, nor until any such communication has been considered by the Vestry at a meeting duly called and held for that purpose.

(3) Written notice of the election of a Rector, signed by the Wardens, shall be forwarded to the Ecclesiastical Authority. If the Ecclesiastical Authority is satisfied that the person so elected is a duly qualified Priest and that such Priest has accepted the office to which elected, the notice shall be sent to the Secretary of the Convention, who shall record it. Race, color, ethnic origin, sex, national origin, marital status, sexual orientation, disabilities or age, except as otherwise specified by these canons, shall not be a factor in the determination of the Ecclesiastical Authority as to whether such person is a duly qualified Priest. The recorded notice shall be sufficient evidence of the relationship between the Priest and the Parish.

Written notice to Ecclesiastical Authority.

(4) Rectors may have a letter of agreement with the Parish setting forth mutual responsibilities, subject to the Bishop's approval.

Agreement.

(b) Priests-in-Charge. After consultation with the Vestry, the Bishop may appoint a Priest to serve as Priest-in-Charge of any congregation in which there is no Rector. In such congregations, the Priest-in-Charge shall exercise the duties of Rector outlined in Canon III.9.5 subject to the authority of the Bishop.

Priests-in-Charge.

(c) Assistants. A Priest serving as an assistant in a Parish, by whatever title designated, shall be selected by the Rector, and when required by the canons of the Diocese, subject to the approval of the Vestry, and shall serve under the authority and direction of the Rector. Before the selection of an assistant the name of the Priest proposed for selection shall be made known to the Bishop and a time, not exceeding sixty days, given for the Bishop to communicate with the Rector and Vestry on the proposed selection. Any assistant shall serve at the pleasure of the Rector and may not serve beyond the period of service of the Rector, except that pending the call of a new Rector, an assistant may continue in the service of the Parish if requested to do so by the Vestry under such conditions as the Bishop and Vestry shall determine. An assistant may continue to serve at the request of a new Rector. Assistants may have a letter of agreement with the Rector and the Vestry setting forth mutual responsibilities subject to the Bishop's approval.

Rector to select assistants.

In case of new Rector.

(d) Chaplains.

(1) A Priest may be given ecclesiastical endorsement for service as a Chaplain in the Armed Services of the United States of America or as a Chaplain for the Veterans' Administration, or in any Federal Correctional Institution, by the Office of the Bishop Suffragan for the Armed Forces subject to the approval of the Ecclesiastical Authority of the Diocese in which the Priest is canonically resident.

Endorsement of Chaplains.

(2) Any Priest serving on active duty with the Armed Services shall retain the Priest's canonical residence and shall be subject to the ecclesiastical supervision of the Bishop of the Diocese

Active duty Chaplains.

of which the Priest is canonically resident, even though the Priest's work as a Chaplain shall be subject to the general supervision of the Office of the Bishop Suffragan for the Armed Forces, or such other Bishop as the Presiding Bishop may designate.

Areas of service.

(3) Any Priest serving on a military installation or at a Veterans' Administration facility or Federal Correctional Institution shall not be subject to Canons III.9.3.(e)(1) or III.9.4.(a). When serving other than on a military installation or at a Veterans' Administration facility, or Federal Correctional Institution, a Chaplain shall be subject to these Sections.

(e) Non-ecclesiastical or Non-parochial Employment of Priests.

Non-parochial Priests.

(1) Any Priest who has left a position in this Church without having received a call to a new ecclesiastical position and who desires to continue the exercise of the office of Priest shall notify the Ecclesiastical Authority of the Diocese in which the Priest is canonically resident and shall advise the Bishop that reasonable opportunities for the exercise of the office of Priest exist and that use will be made of such opportunities. After having determined that the person will have and use opportunities for the exercise of the office of Priest, the Bishop, with the advice and consent of the Standing Committee, may approve the Priest's continued exercise of the office on condition that the Priest report annually in writing, in a manner prescribed by the Bishop, as provided in Canon I.6.2.

Release from the exercise of office.

(2) A Priest who would be permitted under Canon III.13 to renounce the exercise of ordained office, who desires to enter into other than ecclesiastical employment, may declare in writing to the Ecclesiastical Authority of the Diocese in which the Priest is canonically resident a desire to be released from the obligations of the office and a desire to be released from the exercise of the office of Priest. Upon receipt of such declaration, the Ecclesiastical Authority shall proceed in the same manner as if the declaration was one of renunciation of the ordained Priesthood under Canon III.13.

Moving to another jurisdiction.

(3)

(i) A Priest not in parochial employment moving to another jurisdiction shall report to the Bishop of that jurisdiction within sixty days of such move.

(ii) The Priest:

(a) May officiate or preach in that jurisdiction only under the terms of Canon III.9.5.(a).

(b) Shall provide notice of such move, in writing and within sixty days, to the Ecclesiastical Authority of the Diocese in which the Priest is canonically resident.

(c) Shall forward a copy of the report required by Canon I.6.2 to the Ecclesiastical Authority to whose jurisdiction the Priest has moved.

(iii) Upon receipt of the notice required by Canon III.9.3.(e)(3)(ii)(b), the Ecclesiastical Authority shall provide written notice thereof to the Ecclesiastical Authority into whose jurisdiction the person has moved.

(4) If the Priest fails to comply with the provisions of this canon, the Bishop of the Diocese in which the Priest is canonically resident may proceed in accordance with Canon IV.11.

Failure to comply.

Of Letters Dimissory

Sec. 4. (a) A Priest desiring to become canonically resident within a Diocese shall present to the Ecclesiastical Authority a testimonial from the Ecclesiastical Authority of the Diocese of current canonical residence, which testimonial shall be given by the Ecclesiastical Authority to the applicant, and a duplicate thereof may be sent to the Ecclesiastical Authority of the Diocese to which transfer is proposed. The testimonial shall be accompanied by a statement of the record of payments to The Church Pension Fund by or on behalf of the Priest concerned and shall be in the following words:

Testimonial for transfer.

I hereby certify that A.B., who has signified to me the desire to be transferred to the Ecclesiastical Authority of _______, is a Priest of _______ in good standing, and has not, so far as I know or believe, been justly liable to evil report, for error in religion or for viciousness of life, for the last three years.
(Date) _______ (Signed) ___________

(b) Such a testimonial shall be called Letters Dimissory. If the Ecclesiastical Authority accepts the Letters Dimissory, the canonical residence of the Priest transferred shall date from such acceptance, and prompt notice of acceptance shall be given to the applicant and to the Ecclesiastical Authority issuing the Letters Dimissory.

Acceptance.

(c) Letters Dimissory not presented within six months of their date of receipt by the applicant shall become void.

Void after six months.

(d) If a Priest has been called to a Cure in a congregation in another Diocese, the Priest shall present Letters Dimissory. The Ecclesiastical Authority of the Diocese shall accept Letters Dimissory within three months of their receipt unless the Bishop or Standing Committee has received credible information concerning the character or behavior of the Priest concerned which would form grounds for canonical inquiry and presentment. In such a case, the Ecclesiastical Authority shall notify the Ecclesiastical Authority of the Diocese in which the Priest is canonically resident and need not accept the Letters Dimissory unless and until the Priest shall be exculpated. The Ecclesiastical Authority shall not refuse to accept Letters Dimissory based on the applicant's race, color, ethnic origin, sex, national origin, marital status, sexual orientation, disabilities, or age.

Grounds for nonacceptance.

(e) A Priest shall not be in charge of any congregation in the Diocese to which the person moves until obtaining from the Ecclesiastical Authority of that Diocese a certificate in the following words:

Certificate of reception.

I hereby certify that A.B. has been canonically transferred to my jurisdiction and is a Priest in good standing.
(Date) __________ (Signed) ____________________

In case of prior refusal.

(f) No person who has been refused ordination or reception as a Candidate in any Diocese, and is thereafter ordained in another Diocese, shall be transferred to the Diocese in which such refusal has occurred without the consent of its Ecclesiastical Authority.

Of Priests and Their Duties

Sec. 5.

(a)

Authority and responsibility of Rector.

(1) The Rector shall have full authority and responsibility for the conduct of the worship and the spiritual jurisdiction of the Parish, subject to the Rubrics of the Book of Common Prayer, the Constitution and Canons of this Church, and the pastoral direction of the Bishop.

Control of buildings.

(2) For the purposes of the office and for the full and free discharge of all functions and duties pertaining thereto, the Rector shall at all times be entitled to the use and control of the Church and Parish buildings together with all appurtenances and furniture, and to access to all records and registers maintained by or on behalf of the congregation.

(b)

Instruction in faith and ministry.

(1) It shall be the duty of the Priest to ensure all persons in their charge receive Instruction in the Holy Scriptures; in the subjects contained in An Outline of the Faith, commonly called the Catechism; in the doctrine, discipline, and worship of this Church; and in the exercise of their ministry as baptized persons.

(2) It shall be the duty of Priests to ensure that all persons in their charge are instructed concerning Christian stewardship, including:

(i) reverence for the creation and the right use of God's gifts;

(ii) generous and consistent offering of time, talent, and treasure for the mission and ministry of the Church at home and abroad;

(iii) the biblical standard of the tithe for financial stewardship; and

(iv) the responsibility of all persons to make a will as prescribed in the Book of Common Prayer.

Preparing persons for Baptism.

(3) It shall be the duty of Priests to ensure that persons be prepared for Baptism. Before baptizing infants or children, Priests shall ensure that sponsors be prepared by instructing both the parents and the Godparents concerning the significance of Holy Baptism, the responsibilities of parents and Godparents for the Christian training of the baptized child, and how these obligations may properly be discharged.

(4) It shall be the duty of Priests to encourage and ensure the preparation of persons for Confirmation, Reception, and the Reaffirmation of Baptismal Vows, and to be ready to present them to the Bishop with a list of their names.

Confirmation, Reception, and Reaffirmation.

(5) On notice being received of the Bishop's intention to visit any congregation, the Rector shall announce the fact to the congregation. At every visitation it shall be the duty of the Rector and the Wardens, Vestry or other officers, to exhibit to the Bishop the Parish Register and to give information as to the state of the congregation, spiritual and temporal, in such categories as the Bishop shall have previously requested in writing.

Duty to announce and inform the Bishop.

(6) The Alms and Contributions, not otherwise specifically designated, at the Administration of the Holy Communion on one Sunday in each calendar month, and other offerings for the poor, shall be deposited with the Rector or with such Church officer as the Rector shall appoint to be applied to such pious and charitable uses as the Rector shall determine. When a Parish is without a Rector or Priest-in-Charge, the Vestry shall designate a member of the Parish to fulfill this function.

Alms and offerings.

(7) Whenever the House of Bishops shall publish a Pastoral Letter, it shall be the duty of the Rector to read it to the congregation on some occasion of public worship on a Lord's Day, or to cause copies of the same to be distributed to the members of the congregation, not later than thirty days after receipt.

Communicate a Pastoral Letter.

(8) Whenever the House of Bishops shall adopt a Position Paper, and require communication of the content of the Paper to the membership of the Church, the Rector shall so communicate the Paper in the manner set forth in the preceding section of this canon.

(c)

(1) It shall be the duty of the Rector to record in the Parish Register all Baptisms, Confirmations (including the canonical equivalents in Canon I.17.1(d)), Marriages and Burials.

The Parish Register.

(2) The registry of each Baptism shall be signed by the officiating Member of the Clergy.

(3) The Rector shall record in the Parish Register all persons who have received Holy Baptism, all communicants, all persons who have received Confirmation (including the canonical equivalents in Canon I.17.1(d)), all persons who have died, and all persons who have been received or removed by letter of transfer. The Rector shall also designate in the Parish Register the names of (1) those persons whose domicile is unknown, (2) those persons whose domicile is known but are inactive, and (3) those families and persons who are active within the congregation. The Parish Register shall remain with the congregation at all times.

Records to be entered in the Register.

Of Licenses

Sec. 6.

License to officiate in a Diocese.

(a) No Priest shall preach, minister the Sacraments, or hold any public service, within the limits of any Diocese other than the Diocese in which the Priest is canonically resident for more than two months without a license from the Ecclesiastical Authority of the Diocese in which the Priest desires to so officiate. No Priest shall be denied such a license on account of the Priest's race, color, ethnic origin, sex, national origin, marital status, sexual orientation, disabilities, or age, except as otherwise provided in these canons. Upon expiration or withdrawal of a license, a priest shall cease immediately to officiate.

Consent of Rector.

(b) No Priest shall preach, read prayers in public worship, or perform any similar function, in a congregation without the consent of the Rector or Priest-in-Charge of that congregation, except as follows:

Exceptions.

(1) In the absence or disability of the Rector or Priest-in-Charge, and if provision has not been made for the stated services of the congregation or other community of faith, a Warden may give such consent.

(2) If there be two or more congregations or Churches in one Cure, as provided by Canon I.13.3(b), consent may be given by the majority of the Priests-in-Charge of such congregations, or by the Bishop; *Provided*, that nothing in this Section shall prevent any Member of the Clergy of this Church from officiating, with the consent of the Rector or Priest-in-Charge, in the Church or place of public worship used by the congregation of the consenting Rector or Priest-in-Charge, or in private for members of the congregation; or in the absence of the Rector or Priest-in-Charge, with the consent of the Wardens or Trustees of the congregation; *Provided* further, that the license of the Ecclesiastical Authority provided in Canon III.9.5(a), if required, be obtained.

(3) This canon shall not apply to any Church, Chapel, or Oratory, which is part of the premises of an incorporated institution created by legislative authority, *Provided* that such place of worship is designated and set apart for the convenience and use of such institution, and not as a place for public or parochial worship.

Evidence required to officiate.

(c) No Rector or Priest-in-Charge of any congregation of this Church, or if there be none, no Wardens, Members of the Vestry, or Trustees of any congregation, shall permit any person to officiate in the congregation without sufficient evidence that such person is duly licensed and ordained and in good standing in this Church; *Provided*, nothing in these canons shall prevent:

Proviso.

(1) The General Convention, by canon or otherwise, from authorizing persons to officiate in congregations in accordance with such terms as it deems appropriate; or

(2) The Bishop of any Diocese from giving permission

(i) To a Member of the Clergy of this Church, to invite Clergy of another Church to assist in the Book of Common Prayer Offices of Holy Matrimony or of the Burial of the Dead, or to read Morning or Evening Prayer, in the manner specified in Canon III.9.5; or

Bishop may authorize other officiants.

(ii) To Clergy of any other Church to preach the Gospel, or in ecumenical settings to assist in the administration of the sacraments; or

(iii) To godly persons who are not Clergy of this Church to address the Church on special occasions.

(iv) To the Member of the Clergy or Priest-in-Charge of a congregation or if there be none, to the Wardens, to invite Clergy ordained in another Church in communion with this Church to officiate on an occasional basis, provided that such clergy are instructed to teach and act in a manner consistent with the Doctrine, Discipline, and Worship of this Church.

(d) If any Member of the Clergy or Priest-in-Charge, as a result of disability or any other cause, shall neglect to perform regular services in the congregation, and refuse, without good cause, to consent to any other duly qualified Member of the Clergy to perform such services, the Wardens, Vestry, or Trustees of the congregation shall, upon providing evidence to the Ecclesiastical Authority of the Diocese of such neglect or refusal and with the written consent of the Ecclesiastical Authority, have the authority to permit any duly qualified Member of the Clergy to officiate.

Neglect or refusal to officiate.

(e)

(1) Any Priest desiring to officiate temporarily outside the jurisdiction of this Church but in a Church in communion with this Church, shall obtain from the Ecclesiastical Authority of the Diocese in which the person is canonically resident, a testimonial which shall set forth the person's official standing, and which may be in the following words:

Officiating outside Church's jurisdiction.

I hereby certify that A.B., who has signified to me the desire to be permitted to officiate temporarily in churches not under the jurisdiction of The Episcopal Church, yet in communion with this Church, is a Priest of __________ in good standing, and as such is entitled to the rights and privileges of that Order.
(Date) __________ (Signed) ____________________

Such testimonial shall be valid for one year and shall be returned to the Ecclesiastical Authority at the end of that period.

(2) The Ecclesiastical Authority giving such testimonial shall record its issuance, the name of the Priest to whom issued, its date and the date of its return.

Record to be kept.

Of Retirement

Mandatory at age seventy-two.

Sec. 7. Upon attaining the age of seventy-two years, a Priest occupying any position in this Church shall resign that position and retire from active service, and the resignation shall be accepted. Thereafter, the Priest may accept any position in this Church, including, with the permission of the Ecclesiastical Authority, the position or positions from which resignation pursuant to this Section has occurred; *Provided*,

Proviso.

(a) tenure in the position shall be for a period of not more than one year, which period may be renewed from time to time,

(b) service in the position shall have the express approval of the Bishop of the Diocese in which the service is to be performed, acting in consultation with the Ecclesiastical Authority of the Diocese in which the Priest is canonically resident.

(c) Anything in this canon to the contrary notwithstanding, a Priest who has served in a non-stipendiary capacity in a position before retirement may, at the Bishop's request, serve in the same position for six months thereafter, and this period may be renewed from time to time.

CANON 10: Of Christian Clergy Previously Ordained or Licensed in Churches Not in the Historic Succession

Sec. 1. If a person ordained or licensed by other than a Bishop in the Historic Succession to minister in a Christian body not in communion with this Church, desires to be ordained,

Must be communicant.

(a) The person must first be a confirmed adult communicant in good standing in a Congregation of this Church;

Examination of applicant.

(b) The Commission shall examine the applicant and report to the Bishop with respect to:

(1) Whether the applicant has served in the previous Christian body with diligence and good reputation and the causes which have impelled the applicant to leave the body and seek ordination in this Church,

(2) The nature and extent of the applicant's education and theological training,

(3) The preparations necessary for ordination to the Order(s) to which the applicant feels called;

Exceptions to canonical requirements.

(c) The provisions of Canons III. 5, 6 and 8 shall be followed except that the minimum period of Candidacy need not apply, if the Bishop and the Standing Committee at the recommendation of the Commission judge the Candidate to be ready for ordination to the Diaconate earlier than eighteen months; and with the exception that if the person furnishes evidence of satisfactory theological training in the previous Christian body and has exercised a ministry therein with good repute and success for at least five years, the applicant shall be examined by the Commission and show proficiency in the following subjects:

Examination.

(1) Church History: the history of the Anglican Communion;

(2) Doctrine: the Church's teaching as set forth in the Creeds and in An Outline of the Faith, commonly called the Catechism;

(3) Liturgics: the principles and history of Christian worship; the contents of the Book of Common Prayer;
(4) Practical Theology:
  (i) The office and work of a Deacon and a Priest,
  (ii) The conduct of public worship,
  (iii) The Constitution and Canons of the General Convention, and of the Diocese in which the applicant is resident,
  (iv) The use of the voice in reading and speaking;
(5) The points of Doctrine, Discipline, Polity, and Worship in which the Communion from which the applicant has come differs from this Church. This portion of the examination shall be conducted, in part at least, by written questions and answers, and the replies kept on file for at least three years.

Special prefaces authorized.

(d) Having fulfilled all the requirements of this Canon, the Bishop may ordain the Candidate a Deacon, and, no sooner than six months thereafter, a Priest. At the time of such ordination the Bishop may read this preface to the service:

The Ecclesiastical Authority of this Diocese is satisfied that A.B. accepts the Doctrine, Discipline, and Worship of this Church and now desires to be ordained a Deacon (or ordained a Priest) in this Church. We are about to confer upon A.B. the grace and authority of Holy Orders as this Church has received them and requires them for the exercise of the ministry of a Deacon (or a Priest).

The letters of ordination in such cases may contain the words:

Acknowledging the ministry which A.B. has already received and hereby adding to that commission the grace and authority of Holy Orders as understood and required by this Church for the exercise of the ministry of a Deacon (or a Priest).

CANON 11: Of Priests and Deacons Ordained in Churches in the Historic Succession but Not in Communion with This Church

Procedures for making application.

Sec. 1 (a) When a Priest or Deacon ordained in a Church by a Bishop of the Historic Episcopate but not in communion with this Church desires to be received as a Member of the Clergy in this Church, the person shall apply in writing to a Bishop, attaching the following:
(1) Evidence that the person is a confirmed adult communicant in good standing in a Congregation of this Church;
(2) Evidence of previous Ministry and that all other credentials are valid and authentic;
(3) Evidence of moral and godly character; and that the person is free from any vows or other engagements inconsistent with the exercise of Holy Orders in this Church;
(4) Transcripts of all relevant academic and theological studies;
(5) A certificate from at least two Presbyters of this Church stating that, from personal examination or from satisfactory evidence

presented to them, they believe that the departure of the person from the Communion to which the person has belonged has not arisen from any circumstance unfavorable to moral or religious character, or on account of which it may not be expedient to admit the person to Holy Orders in this Church;

(6) Certificates in the forms provided in Canon III.8.6 and III.8.7 from the Rector or Member of the Clergy in charge and Vestry of a Parish of this Church; and

(7) A statement of the reasons for seeking to enter Holy Orders in this Church.

Examinations.

(b) With regard to the fulfillment of requirements as to pretheological education, the provisions of Canon III.6.3 and III.8.4 shall be applicable. The applicant shall also submit to the examinations required in Canon III.6.1, III.6.3, and III.8.2, the result of the examinations to be filed and submitted as therein required.

Evidence of proficiency.

Sec. 2(a) If the person furnishes evidence of satisfactory theological training in the previous Communion, and has exercised a ministry therein with good repute and success for at least five years, the applicant shall be examined by the Commission and show proficiency in the following subjects:

(1) Church History: the history of the Anglican Communion;

(2) Doctrine: the Church's teaching as set forth in the Creeds and in An Outline of the Faith, commonly called the Catechism;

(3) Liturgics: the principles and history of Christian worship; the contents and use of the Book of Common Prayer;

(4) Practical Theology:

(i) The office and work of a Deacon and a Priest,

(ii) The conduct of public worship,

(iii) The Constitution and Canons of the General Convention, and of the Diocese in which the applicant is resident,

(iv) The use of the voice in reading and speaking;

(5) The points of Doctrine, Discipline, Polity, and Worship in which the Communion from which the applicant has come differs from this Church. This portion of the examination shall be conducted, in part at least, by written questions and answers, and the replies kept on file for at least three years.

(b) The Commission may, with the consent of the Bishop, and with due notice to the applicant, examine the latter in any other subject required by Canon III.6.3 or III.8.4.

Candidate to undertake studies and training.

Sec. 3. Prior to being examined pursuant to Sec. 2(a) of this canon, the applicant shall have received certificates from the Bishop and from the Standing Committee that the applicant is acceptable as a Member of the Clergy of this Church, subject to the successful completion of the examination; but the applicant shall not be received until at least six months after the certificates have been received, during which period the applicant shall undertake such studies and training, in a theological school or otherwise, as shall be directed by the Bishop with the advice of the Commission.

Sec. 4. Before the person may be ordained or received into Holy Orders in this Church, the Bishop shall require a promise in writing to submit in all things to the Discipline of this Church without recourse to any other ecclesiastical jurisdiction or foreign civil jurisdiction, and shall further require the person to subscribe and make in the presence of the Bishop and two or more Presbyters the declaration required in Article VIII of the Constitution.

Declaration required.

Sec. 5 (a) Thereafter the Bishop, being satisfied of the person's theological qualifications and successful completion of the examination specified in Sec. 2 and soundness in the faith, may:

Bishop may receive, confirm, or ordain.

(1) Receive, with the advice and consent of the Standing Committee, the person into this Church in the Orders to which already ordained by a Bishop in the historic succession; or
(2) Confirm and make the person a Deacon and, no sooner than four months thereafter, ordain as Priest, if the person has not received such ordination; or
(3) Ordain as a Deacon and, no sooner than four months thereafter, ordain the person a Priest conditionally (having baptized and confirmed the person conditionally if necessary) if ordained by a Bishop whose authority to convey such orders has not been recognized by this Church.

(b) In the case of an ordination pursuant to Sec. 5(a)(2) of this Canon, the Bishop may, at the time of such ordination, read this preface to the service:

Special prefaces authorized.

The Ecclesiastical Authority of this Diocese is satisfied that A.B., who is already a minister of Christ, accepts the Doctrine, Discipline, and Worship of this Church and now desires to be ordained a Deacon (or ordained a Priest) in this Church. We are about to confer upon A.B. the grace and authority of Holy Orders as this Church has received them and requires them for the exercise of the ministry of a Deacon (or a Priest)

The letters of ordination in such cases may contain the words:

Acknowledging the ministry which A.B. has already received and hereby adding to that commission the grace and authority of Holy Orders as understood and required by this Church for the exercise of the ministry of a Deacon (or a Priest)

(c) In the case of a conditional ordination pursuant to Sec. 5(a)(3) of this Canon, the Bishop shall at the time of such ordination, read this preface to the service:

Conditional ordination.

The Ecclesiastical Authority of this Diocese has been satisfied that A.B., who has been ordained by a Bishop whose authority has not been recognized by this Church, accepts the Doctrine, Discipline, and Worship of this Church, and now desires conditional ordination. By this service of ordination, we propose to establish that A.B. is qualified to exercise the ministry of a Deacon (or a Priest).

Sec. 6. No one shall be ordained or received as a Deacon until age twenty-one. No one shall be ordained or received as a Priest until age twenty-four.

Age limits.

Deacon desiring ordination to Priesthood.

Sec. 7. A Deacon received under Sec. 5 of this Canon, desiring to be ordained to the Priesthood must satisfy all the requirements for ordination to the Priesthood as set forth in Canon III.8.

CANON 12: Of Clergy Ordained by Bishops of Other Churches in Communion with This Church

Certificate required to officiate.

Sec. 1 (a) A Member of the Clergy, ordained by a Bishop of another Church in communion with this Church, or by a Bishop consecrated for a foreign land by Bishops of this Church under Article III of the Constitution, shall, before being permitted to officiate in any Congregation of this Church, exhibit to the Member of the Clergy in charge, or, if there be no Member of the Clergy in charge, to the Vestry thereof, a certificate of recent date, signed by the Ecclesiastical Authority of the Diocese that the person's letters of Holy Orders and other credentials are valid and authentic, and given by a Bishop in communion with this Church, and whose authority is acknowledged by this Church; and also that the person has exhibited to the Ecclesiastical Authority satisfactory evidence of (i) moral and godly character and of (ii) theological qualifications.

Before taking charge of a Congregation.

(b) Before being permitted to take charge of any Congregation, or being received into any Diocese of this Church as a Member of its Clergy, the Ecclesiastical Authority shall receive Letters Dimissory or equivalent credentials under the hand and seal of the Bishop with whose Diocese the person has been last connected, which letters or credentials shall be delivered within six months from the date thereof. Before receiving the Member of the Clergy the Bishop shall require a promise in writing to submit in all things to the Discipline of this Church, without recourse to any foreign jurisdiction, civil or ecclesiastical; and shall further require the person to subscribe and make in the Bishop's presence, and in the presence of two or more Presbyters, the declaration required in Article VIII of the Constitution. The Bishop and at least one Presbyter shall examine the person as to knowledge of the history of this Church, its worship and government. The Bishop also being satisfied of the person's theological qualifications, may then receive the person into the Diocese as a Member of the Clergy of this Church.

Examination.

(c) A Member of the Clergy ordained by a Bishop of another Church in communion with this Church, or by a Bishop consecrated for a foreign land by Bishops of this Church, under Article III of the Constitution, shall not be accepted nor shall the Member of the Clergy be placed on the clergy list of this Church until having submitted to, and satisfactorily passed, a thorough examination, covering both medical and psychological condition by professionals appointed by the Bishop. The forms for medical and psychological and psychiatric reports prepared by The Church Pension Fund shall be used for these purposes.

Clergy of the Evangelical Lutheran Church.

(d) The provisions of this Section 1 shall be fully applicable to all Members of the Clergy ordained in the Evangelical Lutheran Church in America or its predecessor bodies before January 1, 2001, as well as those ordained after that date by Bishops of that Church.

Sec. 2. A Member of the Clergy who is a Deacon shall not be ordered Priest until having resided within the jurisdiction of this Church at least one year and all the requirements for ordination to the Priesthood as required by Canon III.8 have been satisfied.

Deacons to reside one year in jurisdiction.

CANON 13: Of Renunciation of the Ordained Ministry

Of Priests and Deacons

Sec. 1. If any Priest or Deacon of this Church not subject to the provisions of Canon IV.8 shall declare, in writing, to the Ecclesiastical Authority of the Diocese in which such Priest or Deacon is canonically resident, a renunciation of the ordained Ministry of this Church, and a desire to be removed therefrom, it shall be the duty of the Bishop to record the declaration and request so made. The Bishop, being satisfied that the person so declaring is not subject to the provision of Canon IV.8 but is acting voluntarily and for causes, assigned or known, which do not affect the Priest's or Deacon's moral character, shall lay the matter before the clerical members of the Standing Committee, and with the advice and consent of a majority of such members the Ecclesiastical Authority may pronounce that such renunciation is accepted, and that the Priest or Deacon is released from the obligations of the Ministerial office, and is deprived of the right to exercise the gifts and spiritual authority as a Minister of God's Word and Sacraments conferred in Ordination. The Bishop shall also declare in pronouncing and recording such action that it was for causes which do not affect the person's moral character, and shall, if desired, give a certificate to this effect to the person so removed from the ordained Ministry.

Notice of renunciation to Ecclesiastical Authority.

Sec. 2. If a Priest or Deacon making the aforesaid declaration of renunciation of the ordained Ministry be under Presentment for any canonical Offense, or shall have been placed on Trial for the same, the Ecclesiastical Authority to whom such declaration is made shall not consider or act upon such declaration until after the said Presentment shall have been dismissed or the said Trial shall have been concluded and the Priest or Deacon judged not to have committed an Offense.

Presentment to delay action by Ecclesiastical Authority.

Sec. 3. In the case of the renunciation of the ordained Ministry by a Priest or Deacon as provided in this Canon, a declaration of removal shall be pronounced by the Bishop in the presence of two or more Priests, and shall be entered in the official records of the Diocese in which the Priest or Deacon being removed is canonically resident. The Bishop who pronounces the declaration of removal as provided in this Canon shall give notice thereof in writing to every Member of the Clergy, each Vestry, the Secretary of the Convention and the Standing Committee of the Diocese in which the Member of the Clergy was canonically resident; and to all Bishops of this Church, the Ecclesiastical Authority of each Diocese of this Church, the Presiding Bishop, the Recorder, the Secretary of the House of Bishops, the Secretary of the House of Deputies, the Church Pension Fund, and the Church Deployment Board.

Declaration of removal by the Bishop.

Notice of removal to be given.

Of Bishops

Presiding Bishop to record declaration of renunciation by a Bishop.

Sec. 4. If any Bishop of this Church not subject to the provisions of Canon IV.8 shall declare, in writing, to the Presiding Bishop a renunciation of the ordained Ministry of this Church, and a desire to be removed therefrom, it shall be the duty of the Presiding Bishop to record the declaration and request so made. The Presiding Bishop, being satisfied that the person so declaring is not subject to the provisions of Canon IV.8 but is acting voluntarily and for causes, assigned or known, which do not affect the person's moral character, shall lay the matter before the Advisory Council to the Presiding Bishop, and with the advice and consent of a majority of the members of the Advisory Council the Presiding Bishop may pronounce that such renunciation is accepted, and that the Bishop is released from the obligations of all Ministerial offices, and is deprived of the right to exercise the gifts and spiritual authority as a Minister of God's Word and Sacraments conferred in Ordinations. The Presiding Bishop shall also declare in pronouncing and recording such action that it was for causes which do not affect the person's moral character, and shall, if desired, give a certificate to this effect to the person so removed.

If under Presentment, no action to be taken.

Sec 5. If a Bishop making the aforesaid declaration of the renunciation of the ordained Ministry be under Presentment for any canonical Offense, or shall have been placed on Trial for the same, the Presiding Bishop shall not consider or act upon such declaration until after the Presentment shall have been dismissed or the said Trial shall have been concluded and the Bishop judged not to have committed an Offense.

Presiding Bishop to give notice.

Sec 6. In the case of such renunciation by a Bishop as provided in this Canon, a declaration of removal shall be pronounced by the Presiding Bishop in the presence of two or more Bishops, and shall be entered in the official records of the House of Bishops and of the Diocese in which the Bishop being removed is canonically resident. The Presiding Bishop shall give notice thereof in writing to the Secretary of the Convention and the Ecclesiastical Authority and the Standing Committee of the Diocese in which the Bishop was canonically resident, to all Bishops of this Church, the Ecclesiastical Authority of each diocese of this Church, the Recorder, the Secretary of the House of Bishops, the Secretary of the General Convention, the Church Pension Fund, and the Church Deployment Board.

CANON 14: Of the Reconciliation of Disagreements Affecting the Pastoral Relation

Rector or Vestry may petition Ecclesiastical Authority.

When the pastoral relationship in a parish between a Rector and the Vestry or Congregation is imperiled by disagreement or dissension, and the issues are deemed serious by a majority vote of the Vestry or the Rector, either party may petition the Ecclesiastical Authority, in writing, to intervene and assist the parties in their efforts to resolve the disagreement. The Ecclesiastical Authority shall initiate such proceedings as are deemed appropriate under the circumstances for that purpose by the Ecclesiastical Authority, which may include the appointment of a consultant. The parties to the disagreement, following the recommendations of the Ecclesiastical Authority, shall labor in good faith that the parties may be reconciled. Whenever the Standing Committee is the Ecclesiastical Authority, it shall request the Bishop of a neighboring Diocese to perform the duties of the Ecclesiastical Authority under this Canon.

Consultant may be appointed.

CANON 15: Of the Dissolution of the Pastoral Relation

Resignation or removal of a Rector.

Sec. 1. Except upon mandatory resignation by reason of age, a Rector may not resign as Rector of a parish without the consent of its Vestry, nor may any Rector canonically or lawfully elected and in charge of a Parish be removed therefrom by the Vestry against the Rector's will, except as hereinafter provided.

Notice to Ecclesiastical Authority.

Sec. 2. If for any urgent reason a Rector or Vestry desires a dissolution of the pastoral relation, and the parties cannot agree, either party may give notice in writing to the Ecclesiastical Authority of the Diocese. Whenever the Standing Committee is the Ecclesiastical Authority of the Diocese, it shall request the Bishop of another Diocese to perform the duties of the Bishop under this Canon.

Bishop to mediate.

Sec. 3. Within sixty days of receipt of the written notice the Bishop, as chief pastor of the Diocese, shall mediate the differences between Rector and Vestry in every informal way which the Bishop deems proper and may appoint a committee of at least one Presbyter and one Lay Person, none of whom may be members of the Parish involved, to make a report to the Bishop.

Procedure for settling differences.

Sec. 4 . If the differences between the parties are not resolved after completion of the mediation, the Bishop shall proceed as follows:

(a) The Bishop shall give notice to the Rector and Vestry that a godly judgment will be rendered in the matter after consultation with the Standing Committee and that either party has the right within ten days to request in writing an opportunity to confer with the Standing Committee before it consults with the Bishop.

(b) If a timely request is made, the President of the Standing Committee shall set a date for the conference, which shall be held within thirty days.

(c) At the conference each party shall be entitled to representation and to present its position fully.

(d) Within thirty days after the conference or after the Bishop's notice if no conference is requested, the Bishop shall confer with and receive the recommendation of the Standing Committee; thereafter the Bishop, as final arbiter and judge, shall render a godly judgment.

(e) Upon the request of either party the Bishop shall explain the reasons for the judgment. If the explanation is in writing, copies shall be delivered to both parties.

(f) If the pastoral relation is to be continued, the Bishop shall require the parties to agree on definitions of responsibility and accountability for the Rector and the Vestry.

(g) If the relation is to be dissolved:

(1) The Bishop shall direct the Secretary of the Convention to record the dissolution.

(2) The judgment shall include such terms and conditions including financial settlements as shall seem to the Bishop just and compassionate.

Sec. 5. In either event the Bishop shall offer appropriate supportive services to the Priest and the Parish.

Failure or refusal to comply with judgment.

Sec. 6. In the event of the failure or refusal of either party to comply with the terms of the judgment, the Bishop may impose such penalties as may be set forth in the Constitution and Canons of the Diocese; and in default of any provisions for such penalties therein, the Bishop may act as follows:

(a) In the case of a Rector, suspend the Rector from the exercise of the priestly office until the Priest shall comply with the judgment.

(b) In the case of a Vestry, invoke any available sanctions including recommending to the Convention of the Diocese that the Parish be placed under the supervision of the Bishop as a Mission until it has complied with the judgment.

Time may be extended.

Sec. 7. For cause, the Bishop may extend the time periods specified in this Canon, provided that all be done to expedite these proceedings. All parties shall be notified in writing of the length of any extension.

Statements not discoverable or admissible under Title IV.

Sec. 8 (a) Statements made during the course of proceedings under this Canon are not discoverable nor admissible in any proceedings under Title IV provided that this does not require the exclusion of evidence in any proceeding under the Canons which is otherwise discoverable and admissible.

(b) In the course of proceedings under this Canon, if a charge is made by the Vestry against the Rector that could give rise to a disciplinary proceeding under Canon IV.1, all proceedings under this Canon with respect to such charge shall be suspended until the charge has been resolved or withdrawn.

Application of this Canon.

Sec. 9. This Canon shall not apply in any Diocese which has made a provision on this subject in its Canons which is consistent with this Canon. This Section 9 shall become effective on January 1, 1990.

CANON 16: Of the Election and Ordination of Bishops

Rules to be followed for an election.

Sec. 1 (a) The election of a person to be a Bishop in a Diocese shall be held in accordance with the rules prescribed by the Convention of the Diocese and pursuant to the provisions of the Constitution and Canons of this Church. With respect to the election of a Bishop Suffragan, the Diocese shall establish a nominating process either by Canon or by the adoption of rules and procedure for the election of the Bishop Suffragan at a regular or special Diocesan Convention with sufficient time preceding the election of the Bishop Suffragan.

Other provisions for election.

(b) The Convention of a Diocese may request that an election be made on its behalf by the House of Bishops of the Province of which the Diocese is a part, subject to confirmation by the Provincial Synod, or it may request that an election be made on its behalf by the House of Bishops of the Episcopal Church.

Joint Nominating Committee.

(c) If either option in Sec. l(b) is chosen, a special Joint Nominating Committee shall be appointed unless the Diocesan Convention has otherwise provided for the nominating process. The Committee shall be composed of three persons from the Diocese, appointed by its Standing Committee, and three members of the electoral body, appointed by the President of that body. The Joint Nominating Committee shall elect its own officers and shall nominate three persons whose names it shall communicate to the Presiding Officer of the electoral body. The Presiding Officer shall communicate the names of the nominees to the electoral body at least three weeks before the election when the names shall be formally placed in nomination. Opportunity for nominations from the floor shall be given.

Certificate and Testimonial.

(d) If either option in Sec. l(b) is chosen, the evidence of the election shall be a certificate signed by the Presiding Officer of the electoral body and by its Secretary, with a testimonial signed by a constitutional majority of the body, in the form required in Canon III.16.3, which shall be sent to the Standing Committee of the Diocese on whose behalf the election was held. The Standing Committee shall thereupon proceed as set forth in Canon III.16.3 or 4.

Notification of election.

(e) The Secretary of the body electing a Bishop Diocesan, Bishop Coadjutor, or Bishop Suffragan, shall inform the Presiding Bishop promptly of the name of the person elected. It shall be the duty of the Bishop-elect to notify the Presiding Bishop of acceptance or declination of the election, at the same time as the Bishop-elect notifies the electing Diocese.

(f) No Diocese shall elect a Bishop within thirty days before a meeting of the General Convention.

Special meeting of Diocesan Convention.

Sec. 2. It shall be lawful, within six months prior to the effective date of the resignation or retirement of a Diocesan Bishop, for the Bishop, with the advice and consent of the Standing Committee, to call a special meeting of the Convention of the Diocese to elect a successor; *Provided*, that if the Convention is to meet in regular session meanwhile, it may hold the election during the regular session. The proceedings incident to preparation for the ordination of the successor shall be as provided in this Canon; but the Presiding Bishop shall not take order for the ordination to be on any date prior to that upon which the resignation is to become effective.

If election is within three months of General Convention.

Sec. 3 (a) When a Diocese desires the ordination of a Bishop-elect, if the date of the election occurs within three months before a meeting of the General Convention, the Standing Committee of the Diocese shall, by its President, or by some person or persons specially appointed, forward to the Secretary of the House of Deputies evidence of the election of the Bishop-elect by the Convention of the Diocese, together with evidence that the Bishop-elect has been duly ordered Deacon and Priest, evidence of acceptance of election, and a testimonial signed by a constitutional majority of the Convention, and a summary of biographical information relating to the Bishop-elect; in the following words:

We, whose names are hereunder written, fully sensible of how important it is that the Sacred Order and Office of a Bishop should not be unworthily conferred, and firmly persuaded that it is our duty

to bear testimony on this solemn occasion without partiality, do, in the presence of Almighty God, testify that we know of no impediment on account of which the Reverend A.B. ought not to be ordained to that Holy Office. We do, moreover, jointly and severally declare that we believe the Reverend A.B. to have been duly and lawfully elected and to be of such sufficiency in learning, of such soundness in the Faith, and of such godly character as to be able to exercise the Office of a Bishop to the honor of God and the edifying of the Church, and to be a wholesome example to the flock of Christ.
(Date) __________ (Signed) _______________

The Secretary of the Convention shall certify upon this testimonial that it has been signed by a constitutional majority of the Convention.

Testimonial and other documents.

(b) The Standing Committee shall also forward to the Secretary of the General Convention, with the testimonial and other documents, certificates from a licensed medical doctor and licensed psychiatrist, appointed by the Ecclesiastical Authority with the approval of the Presiding Bishop, that they have thoroughly examined the Bishop-elect as to that person's medical, psychological and psychiatric condition and have not discovered any reason why the person would not be fit to undertake the work for which the person has been chosen. Forms and procedures agreed to by the Presiding Bishop and the Church Pension Fund shall be used for this purpose.

(c) The Secretary of the House of Deputies shall present the testimonials to the House, and if the House consents to the ordination of the Bishop-elect, notice of its consent, certified by the President and the Secretary of the House, together with the testimonials, shall be sent to the House of Bishops.

(d) If a majority of the Bishops of this Church exercising jurisdiction consent to the ordination, the Presiding Bishop shall, without delay, notify the Standing Committee of the Diocese electing and the Bishop-elect of the consent.

If election is more than 120 days before General Convention.

Sec. 4 (a) If the date of the election of a Bishop occurs more than 120 days before the meeting of the General Convention, the Standing Committee of the Diocese electing shall by its President, or by some person or persons specially appointed, immediately send to the Presiding Bishop and to the Standing Committees of the several Dioceses a certificate of the election by the Secretary of Convention of the Diocese, bearing a statement that evidence of the Bishop-elect's having been duly ordered Deacon and Priest and the certificates as to the Bishop-elect's medical, psychological and psychiatric examination required in Sec. 3(b) of this Canon have been received and that a testimonial in the form set out in Sec. 3(a) of this Canon has been signed by a constitutional majority of the Convention. The Presiding Bishop, without delay, shall notify every Bishop of this Church exercising jurisdiction of the Presiding Bishop's receipt of the certificates mentioned in this Section and request a statement of consent or withholding of consent. Each Standing Committee, in not more than 120 days after the sending by the electing Diocese of the certificate of the election, shall respond by sending the Standing Committee of the Diocese electing either the testimonial of consent in the form set out in paragraph (b) of this

Section or written notice of its refusal to give consent. If a majority of the Standing Committees of all the Dioceses consents to the ordination of the Bishop-elect, the Standing Committee of the Diocese electing shall then forward the evidence of the consent, with the other necessary documents described in Sec. 3(a) and (b) of this Canon, to the Presiding Bishop. If the Presiding Bishop receives sufficient statements to indicate a majority of those Bishops consents to the ordination, the Presiding Bishop shall, without delay, notify the Standing Committee of the Diocese electing and the Bishop-elect of the consent.

Testimonial.

(b) Evidence of the consent of each Standing Committee shall be a testimonial in the following words, signed by a majority of all the members of the Committee:

We, being a majority of all the members of the Standing Committee of ______________, and having been duly convened at ______________, fully sensible how important it is that the Sacred Order and Office of a Bishop should not be unworthily conferred, and firmly persuaded that it is our duty to bear testimony on this solemn occasion without partiality, do, in the presence of Almighty God, testify that we know of no impediment on account of which the Reverend A.B. ought not to be ordained to that Holy Order. In witness whereof, we have hereunto set our hands this _____ day of _________in the year of our Lord _________.

(Signed) _______________

Presiding Bishop to take order for ordination.

Sec. 5. Upon receipt of the consents and assurance of the acceptance of the election by the Bishop-elect, the Presiding Bishop shall take order for the ordination of the Bishop-elect either by the Presiding Bishop or the President of the House of Bishops of the Province of which the Diocese electing is part, and two other Bishops of this Church, or by any three Bishops to whom the Presiding Bishop may communicate the testimonials.

In case of nonconsent.

Sec. 6. In case a majority of all the Standing Committees of the Dioceses do not consent to the ordination of the Bishop-elect within 120 days from the date of the notification of the election by the Standing Committee of the Diocese electing, or in case a majority of all the Bishops exercising jurisdiction do not consent within 120 days from the date of notification to them by the Presiding Bishop of the election, the Presiding Bishop shall declare the election null and void and shall give notice to the Standing Committee of the Diocese electing and to the Bishop-elect. The Convention of the Diocese may then proceed to a new election.

Ordination service.

Sec. 7. In all particulars the service at the ordination of a Bishop shall be under the direction of the Bishop presiding at the ordination.

Sec. 8. No person shall be ordained Bishop unless the person shall at the time, and in the presence of the ordaining Bishops and congregation, subscribe to and make the declaration required in Article VIII of the Constitution.

Objections to election process.

Sec. 9 (a) Within ten days after the election of a Bishop Diocesan, a Bishop Coadjutor, or a Bishop Suffragan by a Diocesan Convention, delegates constituting no less than 10% of the number of delegates casting votes on the final ballot may file with the Secretary of the Convention written objections to the election process, setting forth in detail all alleged irregularities. Within ten days after receipt thereof, the Secretary of the Convention shall forward copies of the same to the Bishop Diocesan, the Chancellor and Standing Committee of the Diocese, and to the Presiding Bishop, who shall request the Court of Review of the Province in which the Diocese is located to investigate the complaint. The Court of Review may invite response by the Bishop Diocesan, the Chancellor, the Standing Committee and any other persons within the electing Diocese. Within thirty days after receipt of the request, the Court of Review shall send a written report of its findings to the Presiding Bishop, a copy of which report the Presiding Bishop, within fifteen days, shall cause to be sent to the Bishop Diocesan, the Chancellor, the Standing Committee and the Secretary of the Convention of the electing Diocese. The Secretary shall send a copy of the report to each of the delegates who filed objection to the election process.

Report on election review.

(b) If the election has taken place within three months before a meeting of the General Convention, the report shall be sent with the evidence of election and testimonials as provided in Section 3(a) of this Canon.

(c) If the election has taken place more than three months before the meeting of the General Convention, the report of the Court of Review shall be sent to the Standing Committees of the several Dioceses, with the Certificate of the Secretary of the electing Convention relating to consent to ordain. Likewise, the Presiding Bishop shall include the report in the communication to the Bishops exercising jurisdiction.

CANON 17: Of Missionary Bishops

Election by Convention of Diocese.

Sec. 1 (a) The election of a person to be a Bishop in a Missionary Diocese shall be held in accordance with the procedures set forth in the Constitution and Canons of the said Diocese, and, except as hereinafter provided, pursuant to the provisions of Canon III.16.

May request Synod of Province to elect.

(b) The Convention of a Missionary Diocese may, in lieu of electing a Bishop, request that such election be made on its behalf by the Synod of the Province, or the House of Bishops of the Province subject to confirmation of the Provincial Council, or the Regional Council of Churches in communion with this Church of which the Diocese is a member, as provided in paragraph (c) of this Section; or it may request that such election be made on its behalf by the House of Bishops as provided in Sec. 2(a) of this Canon.

Certificate.

(c) In the event of an election of a Bishop by the Provincial Synod or House of Bishops of the Province, or by a Regional Council of Churches, as provided in the foregoing paragraph (b), a Certificate of the Election, signed by the presiding officer and the Secretary of the Synod or Provincial House of Bishops, or Regional Council, and a testimonial in the form required in Canon III.16.1(d) signed by a constitutional majority of the Synod, Provincial House of Bishops or Regional Council, shall be transmitted by its presiding officer to the Standing Committee of the Missionary Diocese on whose behalf such election was made. The Standing Committee shall thereupon proceed as set forth in Canon III.16.1, the above Certificate of Election and Testimonial serving in lieu of evidence of election and testimonial therein required.

Sec. 2 (a) The House of Bishops may, upon the request of the Convention of a Missionary Diocese, as provided in Sec. 1(b) of this Canon, elect a person to be a Bishop therein. Such choice shall be subject to confirmation by the House of Deputies during the session of the General Convention, and at other times to confirmation by a majority of the Standing Committees of the several Dioceses. The medical certificate as required in Canon III.16.3(b) shall also be required of Missionary Bishops-elect.

May ask House of Bishops to elect a Bishop.

(b) When the House of Bishops is to elect a Bishop for a Missionary Diocese within a given Province, the President of the Province may convene the Synod of the Province prior to the meeting of the House of Bishops at which a Bishop for such Missionary Diocese is to be elected. The Synod of the Province may thereupon nominate not exceeding three persons to the House of Bishops for that office. It shall be the duty of the President of the Province to transmit such nominations, if any be made, to the Presiding Officer of the House of Bishops, who shall, three weeks before the meeting of the House of Bishops, communicate the same to the Bishops, along with other nominations that have been made, in accordance with the Rules of Order of the House. Each Province containing a Missionary Diocese shall, by Ordinance, provide the manner of convening the Synod and making such nomination.

Synod of Province may nominate.

(c) The evidence of such choice shall be a certificate signed by the Bishop presiding in the House of Bishops and by its Secretary, with a testimonial, or certified copy thereof, signed by a majority of the Bishops of the House, in the form required in Canon III.16.1(d), which shall be sent to the Presiding Officer of the House of Deputies, or the Standing Committees of the several Dioceses, if the General Convention be not in session.

Evidence of election.

(d) When the Presiding Bishop shall have received a certificate signed by the President and Secretary of the House of Deputies (or certificates signed by the Presidents and Secretaries of a majority of the Standing Committees as the case may be), that the election has been approved, and shall have received notice of the acceptance by the Bishop-elect of his election, he shall take order for the consecration of the said Bishop-elect either by himself and two other Bishops of this Church, or by three Bishops of this Church to whom he may communicate the certificates and testimonial.

Approval required.

Sec. 3. In the case of the permanent disability of the Bishop of a Missionary Diocese, where the said Bishop shall not have submitted his resignation of his jurisdiction, the Presiding Bishop shall, upon certification of the said permanent disability by at least three reputable physicians, declare the jurisdiction vacant.

Vacancy in a Missionary Diocese.

Sec. 4. When the Bishop of a Missionary Diocese is unable, by reason of age or other permanent cause of disability, fully to discharge the duties of

Provision for a Bishop Coadjutor.

his office, a Bishop Coadjutor may be elected by the said Diocese, subject to the provisions of Canon III.16.2.

Seat and vote in House of Bishops.

Sec. 5. Any Bishop or Bishops elected and consecrated under this Canon shall be entitled to a seat and vote in the House of Bishops, and shall be eligible to the office of Bishop or Bishop Coadjutor or Bishop Suffragan in any organized Diocese within the United States; *Provided*, that such Bishop shall not be so eligible within five years from the date of his consecration, except to the office of Bishop of a Diocese formed in whole or in part out of such Missionary Diocese.

Election of a Missionary Bishop as a Diocesan, Coadjutor, or Suffragan.

Sec. 6 (a) When a Diocese, entitled to the choice of a Bishop, shall elect as its Bishop Diocesan, or as its Bishop Coadjutor, or as a Bishop Suffragan, a Missionary Bishop of this Church, if such election shall have taken place within 120 days before a meeting of the General Convention, evidence thereof shall be laid before each House of the General Convention, and the concurrence of each House, and its express consent, shall be necessary to the validity of said election, and shall complete the same; so that the Bishop thus elected shall be thereafter the Bishop of the Diocese which has elected such Bishop.

Election during recess.

Consent of Bishops and Standing Committees.

(b) If the said election has taken place more than 120 days before a meeting of the General Convention, the above process may be adopted, or the following instead thereof, viz.: The Standing Committee of the Diocese electing shall give duly certified evidence of the election to every Bishop of this Church having jurisdiction, and to the Standing Committee of every Diocese. On receiving notice of the concurrence of a majority of such Bishops and of the Standing Committees in the election, and their express consent thereto, the Standing Committee of the Diocese electing shall transmit notice thereof to the Ecclesiastical Authority of every Diocese within the United States; which notice shall state what Bishops and what Standing Committees have consented to the election. On receiving this notice the Presiding Bishop shall certify to the Secretary of the House of Bishops the altered status and style of the Bishop so elected.

Notice of election.

The Standing Committee of such Diocese shall transmit to every Congregation thereof, to be publicly read therein, a notice of the election thus completed, and also cause public notice thereof to be given in such other way as they may think proper.

Standing Committee as Ecclesiastical Authority.

Sec. 7. In the event of a vacancy in the episcopate of a Missionary Diocese, on account of death, resignation, or other cause, the Standing Committee shall become the Ecclesiastical Authority thereof until the vacancy is filled.

Area Mission under charge of Presiding Bishop.

In the event of a vacancy in the office of Bishop assigned jurisdiction in an Area Mission, the charge thereof shall devolve upon the Presiding Bishop, with the power of appointing some other Bishop as his substitute in such charge, until the vacancy is filled by the House of Bishops.

CANON 18: Of Bishops and Their Duties

Bishop to keep record of official acts.

Sec. 1. Each Bishop shall keep a record of all official acts, which record shall be the property of the Diocese and shall be transmitted to the Bishop's successor.

Sec. 2. No Bishop shall perform episcopal acts or officiate by preaching, ministering the Sacraments, or holding any public service in a Diocese other than that in which the Bishop is canonically resident, without permission or a license to perform occasional public services from the Ecclesiastical Authority of the Diocese in which the Bishop desires to officiate.

Permission required for Bishop not canonically resident.

Sec. 3 (a) Each Bishop serving in a Diocese shall reside in that Diocese.

Bishop to reside in jurisdiction.

(b) The Bishop Diocesan shall not be absent from the Diocese for a period of more than three consecutive months without the consent of the Convention or the Standing Committee of the Diocese.

(c) A Bishop Diocesan, whenever leaving the Diocese for six consecutive months, shall authorize in writing, under hand and seal, the Bishop Coadjutor, the Bishop Suffragan if the Constitution and Canons of the Diocese so provide, or, should there be none, the Standing Committee of the Diocese, to act as the Ecclesiastical Authority thereof during the absence. The Bishop Coadjutor, or the Bishop Suffragan if the Constitution and Canons of the Diocese so provide, or, should there be none, the Standing Committee may at any time become the Ecclesiastical Authority upon the written request of the Bishop and continue to act as such until the request is revoked by the Bishop Diocesan in writing.

Sec. 4 (a) Each Diocesan Bishop shall visit the Congregations within the Diocese at least once in three years. Interim visits may be delegated to another Bishop of this Church.

Bishop to visit each Congregation every three years.

(b) At every visitation the visiting Bishop shall preside at the Holy Eucharist and at the Initiatory Rites, as required, preach the Word, examine the records of the Congregation required by Canon III.9.5(c), and examine the life and ministry of the Clergy and Congregation according to Canon III.9.5(b)(5).

(c) If a Diocesan Bishop has declined to visit a Parish or Congregation for three years, the Member of the Clergy in charge and Vestry (or the Corporation), or the Bishop, may apply to the Presiding Bishop to appoint five Diocesan Bishops who live nearest to the Diocese in which such Parish or Congregation is situated as a Council of Conciliation, who shall determine all matters of difference between the parties, and each party shall conform to the decision of the Council. *Provided*, that, in case of any subsequent trial of either party for failure to conform to the decision, any right of the Accused under the Constitutions and Canons of this Church or the Diocese holding the trial may be pleaded and established as a sufficient defense, notwithstanding the former decision; and *Provided, further*, that, in any case, the Bishop may at any time apply for such Council of Conciliation.

Sec. 5. The Diocesan Bishop may deliver, from time to time, a Charge to the Clergy of the Diocese and a Pastoral Letter to the people of the Diocese on points of doctrine, discipline, or worship. The Bishop may require the Clergy to read the Pastoral Letter to their Congregations.

Charges and Pastoral Letters.

Sec. 6. At each Annual Meeting of the Diocesan Convention the Diocesan Bishop shall make a report of the State of the Diocese since the last Annual Meeting of the Convention; including the names of the Congregations visited; the number of persons confirmed and received; the names of those

Bishop to deliver a report at every annual Convention.

who have been admitted as Postulants and Candidates for Holy Orders, of those ordained, and of those suspended or deposed from Holy Orders; the changes by death, removal, or otherwise, which have taken place among the Clergy; and other matters the Bishop desires to present to the Convention; which statement shall be inserted in the Journal.

CANON 19: Of Bishops Coadjutor

Occasion for election.

Sec. 1 (a) When the Diocesan Bishop is unable, by reason of permanent medical, psychological or psychiatric condition, or by reason of the extent of Diocesan work, fully to discharge the duties of the office, or in order to provide an orderly transition in the office, a Bishop Coadjutor, who shall have the right of succession, may be elected by and for the Diocese, in accordance with Canon III.16.

Consents.

(b) Before the election of a Bishop Coadjutor based on the extent of Diocesan work, or in order to provide an orderly transition in the office, the consent of the General Convention or, if General Convention is not in session, the consent of a majority of the Bishops exercising jurisdiction and of the several Standing Committees must be obtained.

Duties assigned.

(c) Before an election of a Bishop Coadjutor, the Diocesan Bishop shall read, or cause to be read, to the Convention the Bishop's written consent to the election. The consent shall state the duties to be assigned to the Bishop Coadjutor when ordained. The consent shall form part of the proceedings of the Convention. The duties assigned by the Diocesan Bishop to the Bishop Coadjutor may be enlarged by mutual consent.

(d) In the case of the inability of the Diocesan Bishop to issue the required consent, the Standing Committee of the Diocese may request the Convention to act without the consent. The request shall be accompanied by a certificate by at least two licensed medical doctors, psychologists or psychiatrists as to the inability of the Diocesan Bishop to issue the written consent.

Grounds for election to be communicated.

(e) The grounds for the election of a Bishop Coadjutor, as stated in the record of the Convention, shall be communicated with the other required testimonials to the General Convention or to the Standing Committees and the Presiding Bishop.

(f) When a Diocese desires the ordination of a Bishop Coadjutor, the Standing Committee shall forward to the Presiding Bishop, in addition to the evidence and testimonials required by Canon III.16, a certificate of the Presiding Officer and Secretary of the Convention that every requirement of this Section has been complied with.

Only one Bishop Coadjutor in a Diocese.

Sec. 2. There shall be only one Bishop Coadjutor in any Diocese. *Provided*, if it is certified to the Ecclesiastical Authority of a Diocese by two licensed medical doctors, psychologists or psychiatrists, selected by the Ecclesiastical Authority, that the Bishop Coadjutor in the Diocese is permanently unable, by reason of medical, psychological or psychiatric condition, to carry out the duties of Bishop Coadjutor, the Ecclesiastical

Authority, upon the advice of three Bishops of three neighboring Dioceses, may declare that the right of succession of the Bishop Coadjutor is terminated and a new Bishop Coadjutor may then be elected as provided in Canon III.22.1.

CANON 20: Of Bishops Suffragan

Consents.

Sec. 1 (a) With the consent of the Bishop Diocesan, a Bishop Suffragan shall be elected in accordance with Canon III.16.1.

(b) Before the election of a Bishop Suffragan in a Diocese, the consent of the General Convention or, if General Convention is not in session, the consent of a majority of the Bishops exercising jurisdiction and of the several Standing Committees must be obtained.

To act under Diocesan Bishop.

Sec. 2 (a) A Bishop Suffragan shall act as an assistant to and under the direction of the Bishop Diocesan.

(b) Before the election of a Bishop Suffragan in a Diocese, the Bishop Diocesan shall submit a description of the role and the duties of the Bishop Suffragan to the Convention of the Diocese.

Sec. 3. The tenure of office of a Bishop Suffragan shall not be determined by the tenure of office of the Bishop Diocesan.

Sec. 4. No Bishop Suffragan, while acting as such, shall be Rector or Member of the Clergy in charge of a Parish or Congregation.

CANON 21: Of Assistant Bishops

Diocesan Convention to approve position.

Sec. 1. When a Diocese, in the opinion of its Bishop, requires additional episcopal services, the Bishop may, with the consent of the Standing Committee of the Diocese, ask the Convention of the Diocese to approve the creation of the position of Assistant Bishop and to authorize the Bishop to appoint a Bishop for the position, with the consent of the Standing Committee of the Diocese, and under such conditions as the Bishop may determine.

Eligibility.

Sec. 2. An Assistant Bishop may be appointed from among the following:

(a) Bishops Diocesan, Bishops Coadjutor, or Bishops Suffragan, who under the Constitution and Canons of this Church would be eligible for election in that Diocese; *Provided*, that at the time of accepting any such appointment a Bishop Diocesan, Bishop Coadjutor or Bishop Suffragan shall resign that office;

(b) Bishops of this Church who, having resigned their previous responsibilities, are qualified to perform episcopal acts in this Church; and

(c) Bishops of a Church in communion with this Church, in good standing therein, if they:

(1) have previously resigned their former responsibilities;

(2) have received approval, by a competent authority within the Church of their ordination of their appointment to the position of Assistant Bishop;

(3) have exhibited satisfactory evidence of moral and godly character and having met theological requirements;

(4) have promised in a writing submitted to the Bishop making the appointment to submit in all things to the Doctrine, Discipline and Worship of this Church; and

(5) have submitted to and satisfactorily passed a thorough examination covering their medical, psychological and psychiatric condition by recognized and licensed professionals appointed by the Ecclesiastical Authority of the Diocese with the approval of the Presiding Bishop. The forms for medical, psychological and psychiatric reports prepared by The Church Pension Fund shall be used for these purposes.

(d) Before the appointment of a Bishop who is not otherwise a member of the House of Bishops as an Assistant Bishop under the provisions of Secs. 2(b) or 2(c) of this Canon, the consent of the House of Bishops or, if the appointment is to be made more than three months prior to a meeting of the House of Bishops, the consent of a majority of Bishops exercising jurisdiction must be obtained.

Certified evidence of appointment.

Sec. 3. Before an Assistant Bishop so appointed begins service in this position, the Bishop of the Diocese shall give certified evidence of the appointment to the Secretary of the House of Bishops and shall transmit notice of the appointment to the Presiding Bishop and to the Ecclesiastical Authority of every Diocese.

Sec. 4. No person may serve as an Assistant Bishop beyond the termination of the jurisdiction of the appointing Bishop or after attaining the age of 72 years.

To act under Diocesan Bishop.

Sec. 5. An Assistant Bishop shall serve at the discretion, and under the control and direction of, the Diocesan Bishop.

CANON 22: Of the Incapacity, Resignation, and Retirement of Bishops

Presiding Bishop to declare.

Sec. 1. When it is certified to the Presiding Bishop, by at least two licensed medical doctors, psychologists or psychiatrists, who have examined the case, that a Bishop Diocesan is incapable of authorizing the Bishop Coadjutor, if there is one, or a Bishop Suffragan, if there is one, or the Standing Committee to act as the Ecclesiastical Authority, then, upon the advice of five Bishops of neighboring Dioceses selected by the Presiding Bishop, the Presiding Bishop shall declare the Bishop Coadjutor, or a Bishop Suffragan, if the Constitution and Canons of the Diocese so provide, or the Standing Committee to be the Ecclesiastical Authority for all purposes set forth in these Canons and to retain such canonical authority until the Presiding Bishop, acting upon a like certificate, declares the Bishop Diocesan competent to resume official duties.

Bishop to resign at age seventy-two.

Sec. 2 (a) Each Bishop, upon attaining the age of seventy-two years, shall resign as required by Article II, Sec. 9 of the Constitution. The resignation shall be sent to the Presiding Bishop, who shall immediately communicate it to every Bishop of this Church exercising jurisdiction and shall declare the resignation accepted, effective at a designated date not later than three months from the date the resignation was tendered.

(b) The Presiding Bishop shall communicate to the resigning Bishop the acceptance of the resignation effective as of the date fixed. In the case of a Diocesan Bishop or Bishop Coadjutor, the Presiding Bishop shall certify the resignation to the Standing Committee of the Diocese concerned, and in the case of other Bishops, to the Ecclesiastical Authority of the Diocese concerned. The Presiding Bishop shall also order the Secretary of the House of Bishops to record the resignation, effective as of the date fixed, to be incorporated in the Journal of the House.

Presiding Bishop to certify resignation.

(c) If any Bishop, for any reason, fails to resign upon attaining the age of seventy-two years, as provided in Sec. 2 of this Canon, the Presiding Bishop shall certify that fact to the House of Bishops. The House of Bishops shall then declare the Bishop's position terminated, effective at a date not later than three months from the date of declaration; and shall order the Presiding Bishop's certificate and its own declaration and action to be recorded in its Journal. The Presiding Bishop shall then pronounce the position terminated, effective as of the date fixed, and shall communicate the fact to the Diocesan Bishop and Standing Committee of each Diocese.

If Bishop fails to resign.

Sec. 3 (a) Any Bishop who desires to resign shall send the resignation with the reasons therefor in writing to the Presiding Bishop at least thirty days before the date set for a meeting of the House of Bishops. The Presiding Bishop shall notify without delay every Bishop of this Church, and the Standing Committee of the Diocese of the Bishop desiring to resign, in order that the Standing Committee may be heard on behalf of the Diocese, either in person or by correspondence, upon the subject. The House during its session shall accept or refuse the resignation by a majority of those present.

Resignation procedure.

(b) If a resignation has been tendered more than three months before a meeting of the House of Bishops, the Presiding Bishop shall communicate it, together with any statement from the Standing Committee of the Diocese concerned, to every Bishop of this Church. If a majority of the Bishops consents to the resignation, the Presiding Bishop, without delay, shall notify the resigning Bishop and the Standing Committee of the Diocese concerned of the acceptance of the resignation, effective as of the date fixed. The Presiding Bishop shall also order the Secretary of the House of Bishops to record the resignation, effective as of the date fixed, to be incorporated in the Journal of the House.

(c) At each meeting of the General Convention, the Presiding Bishop shall communicate to the House of Deputies, when in session, a list of the resignations which have been accepted since the preceding meeting of the General Convention.

Sec. 4 (a) A resigned or retired Bishop shall be subject in all matters to the Constitution and Canons of this Church and to the authority of the General Convention.

Resigned or retired Bishops subject to Canons.

(b) A resigned or retired Bishop may perform any episcopal act, at the request of any Diocesan Bishop within that Bishop's Diocese. A resigned or retired Bishop may, by vote of the Convention of any Diocese and with the consent of the Bishop of that Diocese, be given an honorary seat in the

Official acts of resigned or retired Bishops.

Convention, with voice but without vote, or be given an honorary seat in the Cathedral of any Diocese, by and subject to the authority competent to grant such seat. The resigned or retired Bishop shall report all official acts to the Diocesan Bishop and to the Diocese in which the acts are performed. These provisions shall also be applicable to a resigned Bishop of another Church in communion with this Church, subject to the approval of competent authority within the other Church, where such approval may be required.

Resigned Bishop may be enrolled among Diocesan Clergy.

(c) A resigned Bishop may, at the discretion of the Bishop of the Diocese in which the resigned Bishop resides, and upon presentation of Letters Dimissory from the Ecclesiastical Authority of the Diocese in which the resigned Bishop has had canonical residence most recently, be enrolled among the Clergy of the new Diocese, and become subject to its Constitution and Canons including being given a seat and vote in the Diocesan Convention, in accordance with its canonical provisions for qualification of clergy members.

(d) When a resigned Bishop accepts a pastoral charge or other ministerial post within a Diocese, the Diocesan Bishop shall process the Letters Dimissory, and the resigned Bishop shall be enrolled among the Clergy of the Diocese and be given seat and vote in the Diocesan Convention in accordance with the canonical provisions of the Diocese for qualification of clergy members, and subject to the provisions of paragraph (h) of this section.

May accept pastoral charge.

(e) A resigned Bishop may, with the approval of the Bishop of the Diocese in which the resigned Bishop resides, accept a pastoral charge in that Diocese, and, subject to the Diocese's canonical provisions for the filling of vacancies, may accept election as the Rector of a Parish therein.

May accept position created by Diocesan Convention.

(f) A resigned Bishop may, with the approval of the Bishop of the Diocese in which the resigned Bishop resides, accept any position created under the authority of the Diocesan Convention, including that of Assistant Bishop and may, at the same time, occupy a pastoral charge.

Retains rights in House of Bishops.

(g) Enrollment among the Clergy of, or acceptance of any position within, a Diocese shall not deprive a resigned Bishop of the seat and vote in the House of Bishops to which the Bishop may be entitled under Article I, Sec. 2 of the Constitution.

(h) The provisions of this section shall be applicable to a resigned Bishop who continues to reside within the limits of the resigned Bishop's former Diocese, except that the resigned Bishop shall not have the right to vote in the Diocesan Convention, unless the Canons of the Diocese specifically so provide.

CANON 23: Of Dioceses without Bishops

Dioceses under the provisional charge of another Bishop Diocesan.

Sec. 1. A Diocese without a Bishop may, by an act of its Convention, and in consultation with the Presiding Bishop, be placed under the provisional charge and authority of a Bishop of another Diocese or of a resigned Bishop, who shall by that act be authorized to exercise all the duties and offices of the Bishop of the Diocese until a Bishop is elected and ordained for that Diocese or until the act of the Convention is revoked.

Sec. 2. Any Bishop may, on the invitation of the Convention or of the Standing Committee of any Diocese where there is no Bishop, visit and exercise episcopal offices in that Diocese or any part of it. This invitation shall be for a stated period and may be revoked at any time.

Bishop may be invited to visit and officiate.

Sec. 3. A Diocese, while under the provisional charge of a Bishop, shall not invite any other Bishop to visit and exercise episcopal acts or authority without the consent of the Bishop in charge.

CANON 24: Of Religious Orders and Other Christian Communities

Sec. 1 (a) A Religious Order of this Church is a society of Christians (in communion with the See of Canterbury) who voluntarily commit themselves for life, or a term of years: to holding their possessions in common or in trust; to a celibate life in community; and obedience to their Rule and Constitution.

Religious Order defined.

(b) To be officially recognized, a Religious Order must have at least six professed members, and must be approved by the Standing Committee on Religious Communities of the House of Bishops and be registered with the Committee.

Official recognition.

(c) Each Order shall have a Bishop Visitor or Protector, who need not be the Bishop of the Diocese in which the Order is established. If, however, the Bishop Visitor or Protector is not the Bishop of the Diocese in which the Mother House of the Order is situated, the Bishop Visitor or Protector shall not accept election without the consent of the Bishop of that Diocese. The Bishop Visitor or Protector shall be the guardian of the Constitution of the Order, and shall serve as an arbiter in matters which the Order or its members cannot resolve through its normal processes.

Bishop Visitor or Protector.

(d) Any person under vows in a Religious Order, having exhausted the normal processes of the Order, may petition the Bishop Visitor or Protector for dispensation from those vows. In the event the petitioner is not satisfied with the ruling of the Bishop Visitor or Protector on such petition, the person may file a petition with the Presiding Bishop, who shall appoint a Board of three Bishops to review the petition and the decision thereon, and to make recommendation to the Presiding Bishop, who shall have the highest dispensing power for Religious Orders, and whose ruling on the petition shall be final.

Dispensation from vows.

(e) A Religious Order may establish a house in a Diocese only with the permission of the Bishop of the Diocese. This permission once granted shall not be withdrawn by the Bishop or any succeeding Bishop.

Permission to establish a house.

(f) The Constitution of every Religious Order shall make provision for the legal ownership and administration of the temporal possessions of the Order, and in the event of dissolution of the Order, or should it otherwise cease to exist, shall provide for the disposition of its assets according to the laws governing non-profit (religious) organizations in the State wherein the Order is incorporated.

Provision for legal ownership of property.

(g) It is recognized that a Religious Order is not a Parish, Mission, Congregation or Institution of the Diocese within the meaning of Canon I.7.3, and its provisions shall not apply to Religious Orders.

Not regarded as a Parish or Institution.

Christian Community defined.

Sec. 2 (a) A Christian Community of this Church under this Canon is a society of Christians (in communion with the See of Canterbury) who voluntarily commit themselves for life, or a term of years, in obedience to their Rule and Constitution.

Official recognition.

(b) To be officially recognized such a Christian Community must have at least six full members in accordance with their Rule and Constitution, and must be approved by the Standing Committee on Religious Communities of the House of Bishops and be registered with the Committee.

Bishop Visitor or Protector.

(c) Each such Christian Community of this Church shall have a Bishop Visitor or Protector, who need not be the Bishop of the Diocese in which the community is established. If, however, the Bishop Visitor or Protector is not the Bishop of the Diocese in which the Mother House of the Community is situated, the Bishop Visitor or Protector shall not accept election without the consent of the Bishop of that Diocese. The Bishop Visitor or Protector shall be the guardian of the Constitution of the Community, and shall serve as an arbiter in matters which the Community or its members cannot resolve through its normal processes.

Dispensation from commitment.

(d) Any person under full commitment in such a Christian Community, having exhausted the normal processes of the Community, may petition the Bishop Visitor or Protector for dispensation from that full commitment. In the event the petitioner is not satisfied with the ruling of the Bishop Visitor or Protector on such petition, the person may file a petition with the Presiding Bishop of the Church, who shall appoint a Board of three Bishops to review the petition and the decision thereon, and to make recommendation to the Presiding Bishop, who shall have the highest dispensing power for Christian Communities, and whose ruling on the petition shall be final.

Permission to establish a house.

(e) Each such Christian Community may establish a house in a Diocese only with the permission of the Bishop of the Diocese. This permission once granted shall not be withdrawn by the Bishop or any succeeding Bishop.

Provision for legal ownership of property.

(f) The Constitution of each Christian Community shall make provision for the legal ownership and administration of the temporal possessions of the Community, and in the event of dissolution of the Community, or should it otherwise cease to exist, shall provide for the disposition of its assets according to the laws governing non-profit (religious) organizations in the State wherein the Community is incorporated.

Not regarded as a Parish or Institution.

(g) It is recognized that a Christian Community is not a Parish, Mission, Congregation or Institution of the Diocese within the meaning of Canon I.7.3, and its provisions shall not apply to such Christian Communities.

Record to be kept of special vocational vows.

Sec. 3. Any Bishop receiving vows of an individual not a member of a Religious Order or other Christian Community, using the form for "Setting Apart for a Special Vocation" in the *Book of Occasional Services* , or a similar rite, shall record the following information with the Standing Committee on Religious Communities of the House of Bishops: the name of the person making vows; the date of the service; the nature and contents of the vows made, whether temporary or permanent; and any other pastoral considerations as shall be deemed necessary.

CANON 25: Of the General Board of Examining Chaplains

Membership.

Sec. 1. There shall be a General Board of Examining Chaplains, consisting of four Bishops, six Priests with pastoral cures or in specialized ministries, six members of accredited Seminary faculties or of other educational institutions, and six Lay Persons. The members of the Board shall be elected by the House of Bishops and confirmed by the House of Deputies, one-half of the members in each of the foregoing categories being elected and confirmed at each regular meeting of the General Convention for a term of two Convention periods. They shall take office at the adjournment of the meeting of the General Convention at which their elections are confirmed, and shall serve until the adjournment of the second regular meeting thereafter. No member shall serve more than 12 years consecutively. Additionally, the Presiding Bishop, in consultation with the Chair of the Board, may appoint up to four other members for a term. The House of Bishops, at any special meeting that may be held prior to the next meeting of the General Convention, shall fill for the unexpired portion of the term any vacancy that may have arisen in the interim. The Board shall elect its own Chair and Secretary, and shall have the power to constitute committees necessary for the carrying on of its work.

To elect officers.

General Ordination Examination.

Sec. 2 (a) The General Board of Examining Chaplains, with professional assistance, shall prepare at least annually a General Ordination Examination covering the subject matter set forth in Canon III.8.4(e), and shall conduct, administer, and evaluate it in respect to those Candidates for Holy Orders who have been identified to the Board by their several Bishops.

(b) Whenever a Candidate has not demonstrated proficiency in any one or more of the canonical areas covered by the General Ordination Examination, the General Board of Examining Chaplains shall recommend to the Commission on Ministry, and through the Commission to the Board of Examining Chaplains, if one exists, of the Diocese to which the Candidate belongs, how the proficiencies might be attained.

May prepare guidelines.

Sec. 3. The General Board of Examining Chaplains may prepare, in each Convention period, guidelines based upon the subjects contained in Canon Ill.8.4(e), which guidelines shall be available to all persons concerned.

Board to make report on examinations.

Sec. 4. The General Board of Examining Chaplains shall promptly report, in writing, to the Candidate, to the Candidate's Bishop and to the Dean of the Seminary the Candidate is attending, the results of all examinations held by them, together with the examinations themselves, whether satisfactory or unsatisfactory, making separate reports upon each person examined. The Bishop shall transmit these reports to the Standing Committee and to the Commission. Notwithstanding the results of the examinations, in no case shall the Standing Committee recommend a Candidate for Ordination under Canon III.8 until the Standing Committee has received from the Commission on Ministry a certificate to the effect that the Candidate has demonstrated a proficiency in all subjects required by Canon III.8.4(e).

The report of the Board shall be made in the following form:

Form of Report.

To __________ (Candidate), the Right Reverend __________, Bishop of __________ (or in the absence of the Bishop the Standing Committee of) __________: (Place) __________ (Date) _____ To the Dean of (Place) __________ (Date) _____
We, having been assigned as examiners of A.B., hereby testify that we have examined A.B. upon the subject matter prescribed in Canon III.7. Sensible of our responsibility, we give our judgment as follows: (Here specify the proficiency of A.B. in the subject matter appointed, or any deficiency therein, as made apparent by the examination.
(Signed) _______________

Shall report also to Convention.

Sec. 5. The General Board of Examining Chaplains shall make a report concerning its work to each regular meeting of the General Convention, and in years between meetings of the General Convention shall make a report to the House of Bishops.

CANON 26: Of the Board for Church Deployment

Membership.

Sec. 1 (a) There shall be a Board for Church Deployment of the General Convention consisting of twelve members, four of whom shall be Bishops, four of whom shall be Presbyters or Deacons, and four of whom shall be Lay Persons.

Apportionment.

(b) The Bishops shall be appointed by the Presiding Bishop. The Priests or Deacons and Lay Members shall be appointed by the President of the House of Deputies. All appointments to the Board shall be subject to the confirmation of the General Convention.

Terms.

(c) The Members shall serve terms beginning with the adjournment of the meeting of the General Convention at which their appointments are confirmed, and ending with the adjournment of the second regular meeting thereafter. The members shall not serve successive terms.

(d) At each regular meeting of the General Convention one-half of the membership shall be appointed to serve full terms.

Vacancies.

(e) Vacancies shall be filled by appointment by the Presiding Bishop or by the President of the House of Deputies, as appropriate. Such appointments shall be for the remaining unexpired portion of the members' terms, and, if a regular meeting of the General Convention intervenes, appointments for terms extending beyond such meetings shall be subject to confirmation of the General Convention. Members appointed to fill the vacancies shall not thereby be disqualified from appointment to full terms thereafter.

Duties.

Sec. 2. The duties of the Board shall be:

(a) To oversee the Church Deployment Office.

(b) To study the deployment needs and trends in the Episcopal Church and in other Christian bodies.

(c) To issue and distribute such reports and information concerning deployment as it deems helpful to the Church.

(d) To cooperate with the other Boards, Commissions, and Agencies which are concerned with ministry, and particularly with the Executive Council.

(e) To report on its work and the work of the Church Deployment Office at each regular meeting of the General Convention.

(f) To report to the Executive Council at regular intervals as a part of its accountability to the Council for the funding which the Church Deployment Office receives.

(g) To work in cooperation with the Church Center Staff.

(h) To fulfill other responsibilities assigned to it by the General Convention.

TITLE IV
ECCLESIASTICAL DISCIPLINE

CANON 1: Of Offenses for Which Bishops, Priests, or Deacons May Be Presented and Tried, and Of Inhibitions

Sec. 1. A Bishop, Priest, or Deacon of this Church shall be liable to Presentment and Trial for the following offenses, viz.:

Offenses.

(a) Crime.
(b) Immorality.
(c) Holding and teaching publicly or privately, and advisedly, any doctrine contrary to that held by this Church.
(d) Violation of the Rubrics of the Book of Common Prayer.
(e) Violation of the Constitution or Canons of the General Convention.
(f) Violation of the Constitution or Canons of the Diocese in which the person is canonically resident.
(g) Violation of the Constitution or Canons of a Diocese of this Church wherein the person may have been located temporarily.
(h) Any act which involves a violation of Ordination vows.

Presentment for violation of ordination vows.

(1) If a Charge against a Priest or Deacon alleges an act or acts which involve a violation of ordination vows and specifies as the act that the Priest or Deacon has disobeyed or disregarded a Pastoral Direction of the Bishop having authority over such person, the Charge must be made by the Bishop giving the Pastoral Direction or by the Ecclesiastical Authority of that Diocese or by another Bishop if the Bishop who issued the Pastoral Direction has resigned, retired, died or is unable to act and shall set out the Pastoral Direction alleged to have been disregarded or disobeyed and wherein the disregard or failure to obey constitutes a violation of ordination vows. Unless the Charge by the Bishop and the Presentment by the Diocesan Review Committee comply with the foregoing provisions, no finding of a violation based on an act of disregarding a Pastoral Direction of or failing to obey the Bishop having authority over the person charged may be made.

Presentment for disregarding a Pastoral Drection.

(2) In order for the disregard or disobedience of a Pastoral Direction to constitute a violation of ordination vows the Pastoral Direction must have been a solemn warning to the Priest or Deacon; it must have been in writing and set forth clearly the reasons for the Pastoral Direction; it must have been given in the capacity of the pastor, teacher and canonical overseer of the Priest or Deacon; it must have been neither capricious nor arbitrary in nature nor in any way contrary to the Constitution and Canons of the Church, both national and diocesan; and it must have been directed to some matter which concerns the Doctrine, Discipline or Worship of this Church or the manner of life and behavior of the Priest or Deacon concerned. Upon Trial under any such

Presentment, the question of whether the disregard or disobedience of the Pastoral Direction specified constitutes a violation of ordination vows is a matter of ultimate fact upon which testimony may be offered.

(i) Habitual neglect of the exercise of the Ministerial Office, without cause; or habitual neglect of Public Worship, and of the Holy Communion, according to the order and use of this Church.

(j) Conduct Unbecoming a Member of the Clergy.

Temporary Inhibition.

Sec. 2 (a) If a Priest or Deacon is charged with an Offense or Offenses or serious acts are complained of to the Bishop that would constitute the grounds for a Charge of an Offense, and, in the opinion of the Bishop, the Charge or complaint of serious acts is supported by sufficient facts, the Bishop may issue a Temporary Inhibition.

Terms of a Temporary Inhibition.

(b) Any Temporary Inhibition shall: (i) be in writing, (ii) set forth the reasons for its issuance, (iii) be specific in its terms, (iv) define the Offense or Offenses charged or serious acts complained of, (v) describe in reasonable detail the act or acts inhibited, (vi) be promptly served upon the Priest or Deacon to be inhibited, and (vii) become effective upon being served upon the Priest or Deacon to be inhibited.

(c) A Temporary Inhibition may be issued without prior written or oral notice to the Priest or Deacon.

Diocesan Review Committee hearing.

(d) Any Priest or Deacon against whom a Temporary Inhibition has been issued, modified, or extended may request a hearing concerning the Temporary Inhibition before the Diocesan Review Committee, which shall hear the same at the earliest possible time, but not later than fourteen days after the date of receipt of the request. The Diocesan Review Committee by a two-thirds vote may dissolve or modify the Temporary Inhibition. The Bishop and the Church Attorney shall be given notice of such hearing and shall be permitted to attend and be heard or to designate a representative to attend and be heard.

(e) At any time, a Bishop may dissolve or modify the terms of a Temporary Inhibition.

Conditions to end Temporary Inhibition.

(f) A Temporary Inhibition shall continue in force and effect until the earlier of (i) the issuance of an Inhibition as otherwise permitted by this Title, (ii) the withdrawal of the Charge or the allegations, (iii) the refusal of the Diocesan Review Committee to make a Presentment on the Charges alleged, (iv) dissolution of the Temporary Inhibition, (v) imposition of Sentence following a voluntary submission to discipline under Canon IV.2., or (vi) a period of ninety days measured from the date of service of the Temporary Inhibition; *Provided, however*, the ninety-day period may be extended by the Bishop for additional ninety-day periods upon good cause.

(g) In the event that the Temporary Inhibition is dissolved, reduced, or otherwise expires, the Ecclesiastical Authority shall so notify all persons to whom notice of the Temporary Inhibition was given.

Issuing an Inhibition

Sec. 3. If a Presentment has been made by the Diocesan Review Committee against a Priest or Deacon, or if a Priest or Deacon has been convicted in a criminal Court of Record in a cause involving immorality, or if a judgment has been entered against a Priest or Deacon in a civil Court of Record in a cause involving immorality, the Bishop in whose jurisdiction the Priest or Deacon is canonically resident or of the jurisdiction wherein the conviction or judgment has been entered may issue an Inhibition to the Priest or Deacon until after the Judgment of the Ecclesiastical Trial Court becomes final.

Inhibition issued by Bishop of canonical residence.

Sec. 4. No Bishop shall issue an Inhibition or Temporary Inhibition except as expressly permitted by this Title.

Temporary Inhibition if issued by Presiding Bishop.

Sec. 5 (a) If a Bishop is charged with an Offense or Offenses or serious acts are complained of to the Presiding Bishop that would constitute the grounds for a Charge of an Offense and, in the opinion of the Presiding Bishop, the Charge or complaint of serious acts is supported by sufficient facts, the Presiding Bishop may issue a Temporary Inhibition. The consent of a majority of All the Members of the Standing Committee is required for Bishops with jurisdiction.

Terms of Temporary Inhibition of Bishop.

(b) Any Temporary Inhibition shall: (i) be in writing, (ii) set forth the reason for its issuance, (iii) be specific in its terms, (iv) define the Offense or Offenses charged or serious acts complained of, (v) describe in reasonable detail the act or acts inhibited, (vi) be promptly served upon the Bishop to be inhibited, and (vii) become effective upon being served upon the Bishop to be inhibited.

(c) A Temporary Inhibition may be issued without prior written or oral notice to the Bishop.

Review Committee hearing.

(d) Any Bishop against whom a Temporary Inhibition has been issued, modified, or extended may request a hearing concerning the Temporary Inhibition before the Review Committee, which shall hear the same at the earliest possible time, but not later than thirty days after the date of receipt of the request. The Review Committee by a two-thirds vote may dissolve or modify the Temporary Inhibition. The Church Attorney and Presiding Bishop shall be given notice of such hearing and each shall be permitted to attend and be heard or to designate a representative to attend and be heard.

May dissolve or modify terms.

(e) At any time, the Presiding Bishop may dissolve or modify the terms of a Temporary Inhibition. If the Bishop is a Bishop with jurisdiction, the consent of a majority of All the Members of the Standing Committee shall be required for such a dissolution or modification.

Conditions to end Temporary Inhibition.

(f) A Temporary Inhibition shall continue in force and effect until the earlier of (i) the issuance of an Inhibition as otherwise permitted by this Title, (ii) the withdrawal of the Charge or the allegations, (iii) the refusal of the Review Committee to make a Presentment on the Charges alleged, (iv) a dissolution of the Temporary Inhibition, (v) imposition of Sentence following a voluntary submission to discipline under Canon IV.2.9, or (vi) a period of one year measured from the date of service of the Temporary Inhibition.

Sec. 6. If a Presentment has been made by the Review Committee against a Bishop, or if a Bishop has been convicted in a criminal Court of Record

Presiding Bishop may issue inhibition until judgment becomes final.

in a cause involving immorality, or if a judgment has been entered against a Bishop in a civil Court of Record in a case involving Immorality, the Presiding Bishop may issue an Inhibition to the Bishop until after the Judgment of The Court for the Trial of a Bishop becomes final. The consent of a majority of All the Members of the Standing Committee is required for Bishops with jurisdiction.

Sec. 7. The Temporary Inhibition shall be an extraordinary remedy, to be used sparingly and limited to preventing immediate and irreparable harm to individuals or to the good order of the Church.

CANON 2: Of Voluntary Submission to Discipline

(A) Priests and Deacons

Voluntary Submission.

Sec. 1. If an alleged commission of an Offense has been made known to the Ecclesiastical Authority, or if Charges of an Offense have been filed, or if a Presentment has been issued against a Priest or Deacon, the Priest or Deacon may, with the Consent of the Ecclesiastical Authority, voluntarily submit to the discipline of the Church at any time before Judgment by an Ecclesiastical Trial Court, and waive all rights to formal Charges, Presentment, Trial and further opportunity to offer matters in excuse or mitigation, as applicable, and accept a Sentence imposed and pronounced by the Bishop.

Waiver and Voluntary Submission evidenced in writing.

Sec. 2. The Waiver and Voluntary Submission shall be evidenced by a written instrument, which shall contain: (i) the name of the Priest or Deacon, (ii) a reference to the Canon specifying the Offense, (iii) general information sufficient to identify the Offense, and (iv) a statement that the Priest or Deacon is aware of the Sentence to be imposed and the effect thereof, and shall be signed and Acknowledged by the Priest or Deacon, after opportunity to consult with and obtain advice from independent legal counsel of the Priest or Deacon's choosing. If the Priest or Deacon has so consulted with legal counsel, that counsel shall also be identified in the Waiver and Voluntary Submission. Legal counsel shall not be a Chancellor, a Vice Chancellor, the Church Attorney or a Lay Assessor in that Diocese. The Waiver and Voluntary Submission may be withdrawn by the Priest or Deacon within three days of execution by the Priest or Deacon and thereafter shall be effective and irrevocable. The Church Attorney, each Complainant and Victim shall be given an opportunity to be heard on the Sentence by the Bishop who is to impose and pronounce Sentence prior to the execution of the Waiver and Voluntary Submission.

Other conditions.

Sec. 3. If there be no Bishop of the Diocese and if the Ecclesiastical Authority be not a Bishop, the Ecclesiastical Authority shall designate a Bishop of a Diocese of the Province to accept the Waiver and Voluntary Submission to discipline and to impose and pronounce the Sentence.

Sentence.

Sec. 4. Except as otherwise provided in this Canon, the Sentence so imposed and pronounced shall be as if it were imposed and pronounced after Judgment by an Ecclesiastical Trial Court and as if all time provided for all required notices and the right of the Priest or Deacon to offer matters of excuse and mitigation had been given and expired.

Sec. 5. No Priest or Deacon shall have the right to appeal the Sentence imposed and pronounced under this Canon to a Court of Review for the Trial of a Priest or Deacon, and the Sentence shall be final for all purposes.

No right to appeal.

Sec. 6. Where a Sentence is to be imposed and pronounced, as a condition of the acceptance of the Waiver and Voluntary Submission to discipline, the Ecclesiastical Authority may require the resignation of the Priest or Deacon from ecclesiastical and related secular offices, and in the case of a Sentence of Deposition, from a Rectorship held by a Priest, upon such terms and conditions as the Ecclesiastical Authority may deem to be just and proper.

Resignation of offices may be required.

Sec. 7. Prior to Presentment, a Priest or Deacon may voluntarily submit to discipline to the Bishop of the Diocese in which that person is canonically resident or the Bishop of the Diocese wherein the commission of the Offense was alleged to have occurred. Subsequent to Presentment, the Priest or Deacon shall voluntarily submit to discipline in the Diocese wherein the Presentment has issued.

May voluntarily submit to discipline.

Sec. 8. In the event that a Sentence is imposed and pronounced by a Bishop other than the Bishop of the Diocese wherein the Priest or Deacon is canonically resident, the Bishop pronouncing Sentence shall immediately so advise the Ecclesiastical Authority of the Diocese of canonical residence.

Advise Ecclesiastical Authority.

(B) Bishops

Sec. 9. If an alleged commission of an Offense has been made known to the Presiding Bishop, or if Charges of an Offense have been filed, or if a Presentment has been issued against a Bishop, the Bishop may, with the consent of the Presiding Bishop, voluntarily submit to the discipline of the Church at any time before Judgment by an Ecclesiastical Trial Court, and waive all rights to formal Charges, Presentment, Trial and further opportunity to offer matters in excuse or mitigation, as applicable, and accept a Sentence imposed and pronounced by the Presiding Bishop.

May voluntarily submit to discipline.

Sec. 10. The Waiver and Voluntary Submission shall be evidenced by a written instrument, which shall contain: (i) the name of the Bishop, (ii) a reference to the Canon specifying the Offense, (iii) general information sufficient to identify the Offense, and (iv) a statement that the Bishop is aware of the Sentence to be imposed and the effect thereof, and shall be signed and Acknowledged by the Bishop, after opportunity to consult with and obtain advice from independent legal counsel of the Bishop's choosing. If the Bishop has so consulted with legal counsel, that counsel shall also be identified in the Waiver and Voluntary Submission. Legal counsel shall not be the Presiding Bishop's Chancellor. The Waiver and Voluntary Submission may be withdrawn by the Bishop within three days of execution by the Bishop and thereafter shall be effective and irrevocable. The

Written instrument required.

Presiding Bishop to pronounce Sentence.

Church Attorney, each Complainant and Victim shall be given an opportunity to be heard on the Sentence by the Presiding Bishop who is to impose and pronounce Sentence prior to the execution of the Waiver and Voluntary Submission.

Sec. 11. Except as otherwise provided in this Canon, the Sentence so imposed and pronounced shall be as if it were imposed and pronounced after Judgment by an Ecclesiastical Trial Court and as if all time provided for all required notices and the right of the Bishop to offer matters of excuse and mitigation had been given and expired.

No Right to Appeal under this Canon.

Sec. 12. No Bishop shall have the right to appeal the Sentence imposed and pronounced under this Canon to a Court of Review of the Trial of a Bishop, and the Sentence shall be final for all purposes.

Resignation may be required.

Sec. 13. Where a Sentence is to be imposed and pronounced, as a condition of the acceptance of the Waiver and Voluntary Submission to discipline, the Presiding Bishop may require the resignation of the Bishop from ecclesiastical and related secular offices, upon such terms and conditions as the Presiding Bishop may deem to be just and proper.

Sec. 14. In order to become effective, prior to the imposition and pronouncement of the Sentence, the Review Committee must approve the Sentence without conducting further proceedings.

CANON 3: Of Presentments

(A) Of a Priest or Deacon

Diocesan Review Committee.

Sec. 1 In each Diocese there shall be a Diocesan Review Committee. Each Diocese shall provide by Canon for the establishment of the Diocesan Review Committee. The Canon of a Diocese may designate the Standing Committee as the Diocesan Review Committee. If the Standing Committee is not so designated, the Canon of a Diocese establishing the Diocesan Review Committee shall provide that the Diocesan Review Committee shall (i) include lay persons and Priests or Deacons, the majority of the Diocesan Review Committee to be Priests or Deacons (but by no more than one), and (ii) annually elect from its members a President. In the absence of a Canon of the Diocese establishing a Diocesan Review Committee, the Standing Committee shall serve as the Diocesan Review Committee. A Presentment to the Ecclesiastical Trial Court may be issued only by the Diocesan Review Committee as provided in this Canon.

Filing a Charge.

Sec. 2. A Charge against a Priest or Deacon shall be in writing, Verified and addressed to the Diocesan Review Committee of the Diocese wherein the Priest or Deacon is canonically resident, except as otherwise expressly provided in this Title. It shall concisely and clearly inform as to the nature of and facts surrounding each alleged Offense.

Who may Charge.

Sec. 3. A Charge may be made:

(a) by a majority of the lay Members of the Vestry of the Parish of the Respondent; or

(b) by any three Priests canonically resident in the Diocese wherein the Respondent is canonically resident or canonically resident in the

Diocese wherein the Respondent is alleged to have committed the Offense; or

(c) by any seven adult communicants in good standing as defined in Canon I.17 in the Diocese wherein the Respondent is canonically resident or in the Diocese wherein the Respondent is alleged to have committed the Offense; or

(d) in a case where the alleged Offense is the violation of Ordination vows involving the disregard or disobedience of a Pastoral Direction issued by a Bishop, only by that Bishop or the Ecclesiastical Authority of that Diocese, or by another Bishop if the Bishop who issued the Pastoral Direction has resigned, retired, or died or is unable to act; or

(e) in a case where the Offense alleged is a Charge specifying the Offenses of Crime, Immorality or Conduct Unbecoming a Member of the Clergy, by any adult who is (i) the alleged Victim, or (ii) a parent or guardian of an alleged minor Victim or of an alleged Victim who is under a disability, or (iii) the spouse or adult child of an alleged Victim; or

(f) in a case where the Offense alleged is that of holding and teaching publicly or privately any doctrine contrary to that held by this Church, only by a majority of the members of the Standing Committee of the Diocese in which the Priest or Deacon is canonically resident or of the Diocese wherein the Respondent is alleged to have committed the Offense; or

(g) by a majority of the Standing Committee of the Diocese in which the Priest or Deacon is canonically resident or of the Diocese wherein the Respondent is alleged to have committed the Offense whenever the Standing Committee shall have good and sufficient reason to believe that any Priest or Deacon has committed the Offense; or

(h) by the Ecclesiastical Authority of the Diocese in which the Respondent is alleged to have committed the Offense, if different from the Diocese of canonical residence.

Bishop may appoint Advocate for alleged Victim.

Sec. 4. If a complaint or accusation is brought to the Bishop by any adult who is (i) the alleged Victim, or (ii) a parent or guardian of an alleged minor Victim or of an alleged Victim who is under a disability, or (iii) the spouse or adult child of an alleged Victim, of an Offense of Crime, Immorality or Conduct Unbecoming a Member of the Clergy, the Bishop, after consultation with the alleged Victim, the alleged Victim's spouse, or the alleged Victim's parent or guardian or adult child, may appoint an Advocate to assist those persons in understanding and participating in the disciplinary processes of this Church, to obtain assistance to formulate and submit an appropriate Charge and in obtaining assistance in spiritual matters, if the alleged Victim, spouse, parent or guardian or adult child so choose. Any alleged Victim or Complainant shall also be entitled to the counsel of an attorney and/or Advocate of their choice.

Entitled to counsel.

Bishop to inform Diocesan Review Committee.

Sec. 5. Whenever the Bishop has sufficient reason to believe that any Priest or Deacon canonically resident in that Diocese has committed an Offense and the interests and good order and discipline of the Church require investigation by the Diocesan Review Committee, the Bishop shall concisely and clearly inform the Diocesan Review Committee in writing as to the nature of and facts surrounding each alleged Offense but without judgment or comment upon the allegations, and the Diocesan Review Committee shall proceed as if a Charge had been filed.

Priest or Deacon may request inquiry.

Sec. 6. Any Priest or Deacon canonically resident in the Diocese who deems himself or herself to be under imputation, by rumor or otherwise, of any Offense or misconduct for which he or she could be tried in an Ecclesiastical Court, may on his or her own behalf complain to and request of the Bishop that an inquiry with regard to such imputation be instituted. Upon receipt of such request by a Priest or Deacon, it shall be the duty of the Bishop to cause the matter to be investigated and to report the result to the Priest or Deacon.

Sec. 7. Except as expressly provided in this Canon, no Bishop of the Diocese shall prefer a Charge against a Priest or Deacon canonically resident in that Diocese.

Sec. 8. Any Charge against a Priest or Deacon shall be promptly filed with the President of the Diocesan Review Committee.

Sec. 9. Upon the filing of a Charge with the Diocesan Review Committee, the Diocesan Review Committee shall promptly communicate the same to the Bishop and the Respondent.

In cause involving immorality.

Sec. 10. In a case of a Priest or Deacon convicted in a criminal Court of Record in a cause involving immorality, or against whom a judgment has been entered in a civil Court of Record in a cause involving immorality, the Priest or Deacon shall notify the Ecclesiastical Authority of the Diocese in which the Priest or Deacon is canonically resident, in writing, of such conviction or entry of judgment, within thirty days thereof, whether or not any time for appeal has expired. It shall be the duty of the Ecclesiastical Authority to give notice of the conviction or entry of judgment to the Diocesan Review Committee of the Diocese in which the Priest or Deacon is canonically resident in which case, or if the Diocesan Review Committee shall otherwise have knowledge of such conviction or judgment, it shall be the duty of the Diocesan Review Committee to institute an inquiry into the matter. If the conviction or judgment be established, the Diocesan Review Committee shall issue a Presentment against the Priest or Deacon for Trial. The time periods specified in Canon IV.14.4 shall be tolled until the Priest or Deacon provides the required notification to the Ecclesiastical Authority. Nothing in this section shall prevent Charges from being filed against the Priest or Deacon based on the conviction, judgment, or underlying acts pursuant to Sections 3 or 4.

Sec. 11. Within thirty days after the filing of a Charge, other than a Charge alleging a conviction in a criminal Court of Record in a cause involving immorality or alleging the entry of a judgment in a civil Court of Record in a cause involving immorality, the Diocesan Review Committee shall convene to consider the Charge. If after such consideration the Diocesan Review Committee determines that an Offense may have occurred if the facts alleged be true, the Diocesan Review Committee shall prepare a written general statement of the Charge and the facts alleged to support the Charge and transmit the same to the Church Attorney.

Diocesan Review Committee to consider the charge.

Sec. 12. The Church Attorney shall promptly make an investigation of the matter.

Sec. 13. Within sixty days after receipt of the statement from the Diocesan Review Committee, unless delayed for good and sufficient cause stated, the Church Attorney shall render a confidential Report to the Diocesan Review Committee of the findings of that investigation and as to whether or not an Offense may have been committed if the facts disclosed by the investigation be found to be true upon Trial, and with a recommendation as to the matter in the interest of justice and the good order and discipline of this Church and based upon such other matters as shall be pertinent. The report of the Church Attorney shall be confidential for all purposes as between the Church Attorney and the Diocesan Review Committee. *Provided, however*, the Diocesan Review Committee shall share the report of the Church Attorney with the Bishop of the Diocese.

Church Attorney to render confidential report.

Sec. 14 (a) Within thirty days after the receipt of the report of the Church Attorney, the Diocesan Review Committee shall convene to consider the report and whether or not a Presentment shall issue.

Diocesan Review Committee to deliberate.

(b) In its deliberations, the Diocesan Review Committee may consider the Church Attorney's report, responsible writings or sworn statements pertaining to the matter, including experts' statements, whether or not submitted by the Church Attorney. To assist in its deliberations, the Diocesan Review Committee may itself, or through a subcommittee of its members or others appointed by the Diocesan Review Committee, provide an opportunity to be heard to the Respondent, the alleged Victim, the Complainant or other persons and receive additional evidence which it in its sole discretion deems appropriate.

(c) The Diocesan Review Committee may issue a Presentment for an Offense when the information before it, if proved at Trial, provides Reasonable Cause to believe that (i) an Offense was committed, and (ii) the Respondent committed the Offense.

(d) If at any time after a Charge has been made under Canon IV.3.2 a criminal or civil action is brought against the Respondent, the Ecclesiastical Court may, with the consent of the Respondent, suspend proceedings until the conclusion of the criminal or civil action.

Sec. 15 (a) The vote of a majority of All the Members of the Diocesan Review Committee shall be required to issue a Presentment. If the provisions of Canon IV.7.1 apply, the consent of a majority of All the Members of the Diocesan Review Committee of the Diocese in which the Offense is alleged to have occurred must be obtained. No member shall disclose his

Voting provsions to issue Presentment.

or her vote or the vote of any member to any person not a member of the Diocesan Review Committee.

(b) In the event that, due to members who have been excused or vacancies in office, the Diocesan Review Committee does not have sufficient voting members to meet the requirements of Sec. 15(a), the action of the Diocesan Review Committee shall be postponed until such time as there are sufficient members in office to fulfill the voting requirements of this Section.

Contents of Presentment.

Sec. 16. If a Presentment be issued, it shall be in writing, dated, and signed by the President or the Secretary of the Diocesan Review Committee on behalf of the Diocesan Review Committee, whether or not that officer voted in favor of the Presentment. In the event that there be no President or Secretary, or they be absent, a member of the Diocesan Review Committee appointed for that purpose shall sign the Presentment. The Presentment also shall contain (i) a separate accusation addressed to each Offense, if there be more than one, and (ii) a plain and concise factual statement of each separate accusation sufficient to clearly apprise the Respondent of the conduct which is the subject of the Presentment.

Presentment filed and served.

Sec. 17. Promptly after the issuance of a Presentment, the Diocesan Review Committee shall cause the original to be filed with the President of the Ecclesiastical Trial Court with a true copy thereof served upon the Bishop, the Respondent, the Church Attorney and each Complainant, and, unless waived in writing, the alleged Victim, and the Ecclesiastical Authority of the Diocese in which the Respondent is canonically resident, in which the Respondent is licensed, and in which the Respondent resides. The proceeding commences with the filing of the Presentment with the President of the Ecclesiastical Trial Court.

Decision not to issue Presentment.

Sec. 18 . If the Diocesan Review Committee votes not to issue a Presentment, then that decision shall be in writing and shall include an explanation. A copy shall be served upon the Bishop who shall file it with the Secretary of the Convention of the Diocese, the Respondent, the Church Attorney, each Complainant, and, unless waived in writing, the alleged Victim.

Confidentiality.

Sec. 19. Prior to the issuance of a Presentment or a determination not to issue a Presentment, as the case may be, the matter shall be confidential, except (i) as may be determined to be appropriate by the Ecclesiastical Authority or (ii) as necessary to seek or secure diocesan authority for resolution of the matter or any part thereof.

Noncompliance with time limits.

Sec. 20. Non-compliance with time limits set forth in this Canon shall not be grounds for the dismissal of a Presentment unless such non-compliance shall cause material and substantial injustice to be done or seriously prejudice the rights of a Respondent as determined by the Trial Court on motion and hearing.

(B) Of a Bishop Charged with the Offense of Holding and Teaching Publicly or Privately, and Advisedly, Any Doctrine Contrary to that Held by This Church

Sec. 21 (a) For alleged violations of Canon IV.1.1(c) for holding and teaching publicly or privately, and advisedly, any doctrine contrary to that held by this Church, the procedures set out in this section must be followed.

Request for Statement of Disassociation.

(b) No Presentment for violation(s) of Canon IV.1.1(c) shall be filed unless a Statement of Disassociation from the doctrine alleged to be contrary to that held by this Church has been issued by the House of Bishops. A Request for a Statement of Disassociation shall include a statement of the doctrine alleged to be contrary to that held by this Church, the Bishop or Bishops alleged to have held and taught publicly or privately, and advisedly, that doctrine, and a concise statement of the facts upon which the Request for the Statement of Disassociation is based. The written Request for a Statement of Disassociation from the doctrine alleged, signed by any ten Bishops exercising jurisdiction in this Church, must be filed with the Presiding Bishop together with the proposed Statement of Disassociation and a brief in support thereof. The Presiding Bishop shall thereupon serve a copy of the Request for a Statement of Disassociation upon the Bishop charged, together with the proposed Statement of Disassociation and a copy of the supporting brief. The Presiding Bishop shall fix a date for the filing of a response, and brief in support thereof, within three months from the date of service, and may extend the time for responding for not more than two additional months. Upon the filing of a response and supporting brief, if any, or upon the expiration of the time fixed for a response, if none be filed, the Presiding Bishop shall forthwith transmit copies of the Request for a Statement of Disassociation, proposed Statement of Disassociation, response, and briefs to each member of the House of Bishops.

Request for Statement shall be considered at next meeting of House of Bishops.

The Request for a Statement of Disassociation shall be considered no later than the next regularly scheduled House of Bishops' meeting held at least one month after copies of the Request for a Statement of Disassociation, proposed Statement of Disassociation, response, and briefs are transmitted to each member of the House of Bishops. The House of Bishops may amend the proposed Statement of Disassociation. If a Statement of Disassociation is not issued by the conclusion of the meeting, there shall be no further proceedings under Title IV for holding and teaching the doctrine alleged in the Request for a Statement of Disassociation.

Ten Bishops may file a Presentment.

(c) A Bishop may be Presented for an Offense under Canon IV.1.1(c) and any other Offenses arising out of acts alleged to be contrary to the doctrine of the Church which was the subject of the Statement of Disassociation only upon a written Presentment signed by any ten Bishops exercising jurisdiction in this Church. The Presentment shall be filed with the Presiding Bishop, together with a brief in support thereof, and a statement why the issuance of a Statement of Disassociation was not a sufficient response to the acts alleged, within six months of the issuance of a Statement of Disassociation based upon the same doctrine as was alleged in the Request for a Statement of Disassociation. The Presiding Bishop shall thereupon serve a copy of the Presentment upon the Bishop presented, together with a copy of the supporting brief and statement. The Presiding Bishop shall fix a date for the filing of an answer, brief in support thereof, and statement why the issuance of a Statement of Disassociation was a sufficient response to the acts alleged, within three months from the date of service, and may extend the time for answering for not more than two additional months. Upon the filing of an answer, supporting brief, and statement, if any, or upon the expiration of the time fixed for an answer, if none be filed, the Presiding Bishop shall forthwith transmit copies of the Presentment, answer, briefs, and statements to each member of the House of Bishops. The written consent of one-third of the Bishops qualified to vote in the House of Bishops shall be required before the proceeding may continue. In case the Presiding Bishop does not receive the written consent of one-third of all the Bishops eligible to vote within sixty days of the date the notification by the Presiding Bishop was sent to them, the Presiding Bishop shall declare the Presentment dismissed and no further proceedings may be had thereon.

Presiding Bishop shall serve the Presentment.

Consent required.

If the Presiding Bishop receives the necessary written consents within sixty days as specified above, the Presiding Bishop shall forthwith forward the Presentment, answer, briefs, and statements to the Presiding Judge of The Court for the Trial of a Bishop.

(d) Any Offenses other than those specified in this Section 21 will be governed by Canon IV.3, Sections 22-50.

(C) Of a Bishop Charged with Other Offenses

Presiding Bishop shall institute an inquiry.

Sec. 22. In the case of a Bishop convicted in a criminal Court of Record in a cause involving immorality, or against whom a judgment has been entered in a civil Court of Record in a cause involving immorality, it shall be the duty of the Presiding Bishop to institute an inquiry into the matter. If the conviction or judgment be established, the Presiding Bishop shall cause the Chancellor to the Presiding Bishop to prepare a Presentment, which the Presiding Bishop shall sign and issue against the Bishop for Trial. The Bishop shall notify the Presiding Bishop, in writing, of such conviction or entry of judgment, within thirty days thereof, whether or not any time for appeal has expired. The time periods specified in Canon IV.14.4 shall be tolled until the Bishop provides the required notification to the Presiding Bishop. Nothing in this section shall prevent Charges from being filed against the Bishop based on the conviction, judgment, or underlying acts pursuant to Section 23(a).

Who may charge Bishop with Offenses.

Sec. 23 (a) A Bishop may be charged with any one or more of the Offenses other than Offenses specified in Canon IV.3.21(c) by

(1) three Bishops; or
(2) ten or more Priests, Deacons, or adult communicants of this Church in good standing, of whom at least two shall be

Priests. One Priest and not less than six Lay Persons shall be of the Diocese of which the Respondent is canonically resident; or

(3) in a case when the Offense alleged is the Offense of Crime, Immorality or Conduct Unbecoming a Member of the Clergy, as specified in (1) or (2) or by any adult who is (i) the alleged Victim, or (ii) a parent or guardian of an alleged minor Victim or of an alleged Victim who is under a disability, or (iii) the spouse or adult child of an alleged Victim.

(b) Whenever the Presiding Bishop has sufficient reason to believe that any Bishop has committed an Offense and the interests and good order and discipline of the Church require investigation by the Review Committee, the Presiding Bishop shall concisely and clearly inform the Review Committee in writing as to the nature and facts surrounding each alleged Offense but without judgment or comment upon the allegations, and the Review Committee shall proceed as if a Charge had been filed.

A Bishop may demand investigation with consent of any two Bishops.

(c) A Bishop who shall have reason to believe that there are in circulation rumors, reports, or allegations affecting such Bishop's personal or official character, may, acting in conformity with the written advice and consent of any two Bishops of this Church, demand in writing of the Presiding Bishop that investigation of said rumors, reports, and allegations be made. It shall be the duty of the Presiding Bishop to cause the matter to be investigated and report the results to the requesting Bishop.

Charge to be in writing.

Sec. 24. A Charge against a Bishop shall be in writing, verified and addressed to the Presiding Bishop, except as otherwise expressly provided in this Title. It shall concisely and clearly inform as to the nature of and facts surrounding each alleged Offense.

Bishop may appoint Advocate for alleged Victim.

Sec. 25. If a complaint or accusation is brought to the Presiding Bishop by any adult who is (i) the alleged Victim, or (ii) a parent or guardian of an alleged minor Victim or of an alleged Victim who is under a disability, or (iii) the spouse or adult child of an alleged Victim, of an Offense of Crime, Immorality or Conduct Unbecoming a Member of the Clergy, the Presiding Bishop, after consulting with the alleged Victim, the alleged Victim's spouse or adult child, or the alleged Victim's parent or guardian, may appoint an Advocate to assist those persons in understanding and participating in the disciplinary processes of this Church, to obtain assistance to formulate and submit an appropriate Charge and in obtaining assistance in spiritual matters, if the alleged Victim, spouse, adult child, parent or guardian so choose.

Entitled to counsel.

Any alleged Victim or Complainant shall also be entitled to the counsel of an attorney and/or Advocate of their choice.

Sec. 26. Any Charge against a Bishop shall be filed with the Presiding Bishop who shall promptly communicate the same to the Respondent. The Presiding Bishop shall forward the Charge to the Review Committee at such time as the Presiding Bishop shall determine or when requested in writing by the Complainant or Respondent after 90 days of receipt of the charge by the Presiding Bishop.

Review Committee.

Sec. 27. There shall be a Review Committee consisting of five Bishops of this Church, two Priests, and two confirmed adult lay communicants of this Church in good standing. Five Bishops shall be appointed by the Presiding Bishop at each regular meeting of General Convention, to serve until the adjournment of the succeeding regular meeting of General Convention. Two Priests and two adult lay communicants shall be appointed by the President of the House of Deputies at each regular meeting of General Convention to serve until the adjournment of the succeeding regular meeting of General Convention. All Committee members shall serve until their successors are appointed and qualify; *Provided, however*, there shall be no change in composition of a Review Committee as to a proceeding pending before it, while that proceeding is unresolved.

Sec. 28. The Review Committee shall, from time to time, elect from its own membership a President and a Secretary.

Review Committee vacancy.

Sec. 29. The death, disability rendering the person unable to act, resignation or declination to serve as a member of the Review Committee shall constitute a vacancy on the Committee. The recusal or disqualification of a member of the Review Committee from consideration of a particular Charge or matter shall constitute a temporary vacancy on the Committee.

Sec. 30. Notice of resignations, declinations to serve or recusal shall be given by the members of the Committee in writing to the President.

Sec. 31. If any Priest appointed to the Review Committee is elected a Bishop, or if any lay person appointed to the Review Committee is ordained, that person shall immediately cease to be a member of the Committee. If either event occurs following the filing of a Charge or referral of a matter for investigation or other action, the person may continue to serve until the completion of the investigation or of the consideration of that Charge or matter.

Filling a vacancy.

Sec. 32. A vacancy occurring in the Review Committee shall be filled as follows:

(a) In the case of a temporary vacancy due to the recusal or disqualification of any Committee member, the Presiding Bishop in the case of Bishops and the President of the House of Deputies in the case of Priests or lay persons shall appoint a person to fill the temporary vacancy, the replacement being of the same order as the order in which the vacancy exists.

(b) In the case of a vacancy in the Review Committee, the Presiding Bishop in the case of Bishops and the President of the House of Deputies in the case of Priests or lay persons shall have power to fill such vacancy until the next General Convention, the replacement being of the same order as the order in which the vacancy exists. The persons so chosen shall serve during the remainder of the term.

Sec. 33. The Church Attorney for the proceedings before the Review Committee shall be the Church Attorney appointed by the Court for the

Trial of a Bishop pursuant to Canon IV.5.9 to serve at the discretion of the Review Committee.

Sec. 34. The Review Committee may appoint a Clerk and, if necessary, Assistant Clerks, who shall be Members of the Clergy or adult lay communicants of this Church in good standing, to serve during the pleasure of the Committee.

Clerks.

Sec. 35. The Review Committee shall appoint at least one but not more than three Lay Assessors. Lay Assessors shall have no vote.

Lay Assessors.

Sec. 36. The members of the Review Committee may be challenged by the Respondent or the Church Attorney.

Sec. 37. The Review Committee may adopt and publish rules of procedure not inconsistent with the Constitution and Canons of this Church, with the power to alter or rescind the same from time to time.

May adopt rules of procedure.

Sec. 38. Prior to the issuance of a Presentment or a determination not to issue a Presentment, as the case may be, the matter shall be confidential, except as may be determined to be pastorally appropriate by the Presiding Bishop.

Confidentiality.

Sec. 39. Not less than five of the Review Committee members of whom at least two shall be Bishops shall constitute a quorum, but any lesser number may adjourn the Review Committee from time to time.

Quorum.

Sec. 40. Within sixty days after receiving a Charge, the Review Committee shall convene to consider the Charge. If after such consideration the Review Committee determines that an Offense may have occurred if the facts alleged be true, the Review Committee shall prepare a written general statement of the Charge and the facts alleged to support the Charge and transmit the same to the Church Attorney.

Consideration and preparation of a Charge.

Sec. 41. The Church Attorney shall promptly make an investigation of the matter.

Sec. 42. Within one hundred twenty days after receipt of the statement from the Review Committee, unless delayed for good and sufficient cause stated, the Church Attorney shall render a confidential report to the Review Committee of the findings of that investigation and as to whether or not an Offense may have been committed if the facts disclosed by the investigation be found to be true upon Trial, and with a recommendation as to the matter in the interest of justice and the good order and discipline of this Church and based upon such other matters as shall be pertinent. The report of the Church Attorney shall be confidential for all purposes as between the Church Attorney and the Review Committee. *Provided, however*, the Review Committee shall share the Report of the Church Attorney with the Presiding Bishop.

Confidential Report.

Sec. 43 (a) Within forty-five days after the receipt of the report of the Church Attorney, the Review Committee shall convene to consider the report and whether or not a Presentment shall issue.

(b) In its deliberations, the Review Committee may consider the Church Attorney's report, responsible writings or sworn statements pertaining to the matter, including experts' statements, whether or not submitted by the Church Attorney. To assist in its deliberations, the Review Committee may provide an opportunity to be heard to the Respondent, the alleged Victim, the Complainant or other persons and receive additional evidence which it in its sole discretion deems appropriate.

May issue presentment.

(c) The Review Committee may issue a Presentment for an Offense when the information before it, if proved at Trial, provides Reasonable Cause to believe that (i) an Offense was committed, and (ii) the Respondent committed the Offense.

Majority required.

Sec. 44 (a) A majority of All the Members of the Review Committee shall be required to issue a Presentment. No member shall disclose his or her vote or the vote of any member to any person not a member of the Review Committee.

(b) In the event that, due to vacancies or temporary vacancies in office, the Review Committee does not have sufficient voting members to meet the requirements of this Section, the action of the Review Committee shall be postponed until such time as there are sufficient members in office to fulfill the voting requirements of this Section.

Church Attorney to prepare Presentment.

(c) When the Review Committee votes to issue a Presentment it shall cause the Church Attorney to prepare the Presentment.

Decision shall be in writing.

Sec. 45. If a Presentment be issued, it shall be in writing, dated, and signed by the President or the Secretary of the Review Committee on behalf of the Review Committee, whether or not that officer voted in favor of the Presentment. In the event that there be no President or Secretary, or if they be absent, a member of the Review Committee appointed for that purpose by the Review Committee shall sign the Presentment. The Presentment also shall contain (i) a separate accusation addressed to each Offense, if there be more than one, and (ii) a plain and concise factual statement of each separate accusation sufficient to clearly apprise the Respondent of the conduct which is the subject of the Presentment.

Explanation required if Presentment not issued.

Sec. 46. If the Review Committee votes not to issue a Presentment, then that decision shall be in writing and shall include an explanation. A copy shall be served upon the Respondent, the Church Attorney, each Complainant, the alleged Victim, unless waived in writing, and the Presiding Bishop who shall file it with the Secretary of the House of Bishops.

Presentment filed and served.

Sec. 47. Promptly after the issuance of a Presentment, the Review Committee shall cause the original to be filed with the Presiding Judge of the Court for the Trial of a Bishop with a true copy thereof served upon the Presiding Bishop, the Respondent, each Complainant, and, unless waived in writing, the alleged Victim. The proceeding commences with the filing of the Presentment with the Presiding Judge of the Court for the Trial of a Bishop.

Sec. 48. [reserved]

Sec. 49. If the Presiding Bishop is a Complainant, except in a case of a Bishop convicted in a criminal Court of Record in a cause involving immorality or against whom a judgment has been entered in a civil Court of Record in a cause involving immorality, or if the Presiding Bishop is the Respondent, is disabled, or otherwise unable to act, the duties of the Presiding Bishop under this Canon shall be performed by the presiding officer of the House of Bishops. If the presiding officer is similarly unable to act, such duties shall be performed by the Secretary of the House of Bishops.

If Presiding Bishop is Complainant or Respondent.

Sec. 50. Non-compliance with the time limits or any procedural requirements set forth in this Canon shall not be grounds for the dismissal of a Presentment unless the non-compliance shall cause material and substantial injustice to be done or seriously prejudice the rights of a Respondent as determined by the Trial Court on motion and hearing.

Noncompliance.

Sec 51. The reasonable and necessary expenses of the Review Committee, including but not limited to, the fees, costs, disbursements and expenses of the Members, Clerks, Church Attorney, Lay Assessors and Reports shall be charged upon the General Convention and shall be paid by the Treasurer of General Convention upon the order of the President of the Review Committee. The Review Committee shall have the authority to contract for and bind the General Convention to payment of these expenses.

Expenses.

CANON 4: Of Diocesan Courts, and Courts of Review for the Trial of a Priest or Deacon, Their Membership and Procedure

(A) Diocesan Courts for the Trial of a Priest or Deacon

Sec. 1. In each Diocese there shall be an Ecclesiastical Court for the Trial of any Priest or Deacon subject to its jurisdiction, and it shall be the duty of each Diocese to provide by Canon for the establishment of the Court and the mode of conducting Trials of the same; *Provided, however*, that the provisions of this Canon shall be included therein.

Ecclesiastical Court established.

Sec. 2. The Canon of a Diocese establishing an Ecclesiastical Trial Court shall make provision for a Church Attorney and shall provide that the Court shall: (i) be elected by the Convention of the Diocese, (ii) include lay persons and Priests or Deacons, the majority of the Court to be Priests or Deacons (but by no more than one), and (iii) annually elect from its members a Presiding Judge within two months following the Diocesan Convention.

Organization of Court.

Sec. 3. The provisions of Canon IV.14 shall apply to each Diocesan Ecclesiastical Trial Court.

Sec. 4. The death, disability rendering a person unable to act, resignation or declination to serve as a member of an Ecclesiastical Trial Court shall constitute a vacancy on the Court.

Court vacancy.

Sec. 5. Notice of resignations or declinations to serve shall be given by members of the Court in writing to the Presiding Judge of the Court.

Disqualification of Court member.

Sec. 6. If any Priest elected to an Ecclesiastical Trial Court is elected a Bishop, or if any lay person elected to an Ecclesiastical Trial Court is ordained prior to the commencement of a Trial, that person shall immediately cease to be a member of the Ecclesiastical Trial Court. If either event occurs following the commencement of a Trial, the person shall continue to serve until the completion of the Trial and the rendering of a Judgment thereon.

Filling vacancies.

Sec. 7. Vacancies, other than for cause under Section 8 of this Canon, occurring in any Ecclesiastical Trial Court shall be filled as provided by Diocesan Canon.

System of challenge.

Sec. 8. The canons of each Diocese may provide a system of challenge as to the members of the Ecclesiastical Trial Court and the filling of vacancies arising therefrom. If the canons of a Diocese make no provisions for Challenge, the members of the Ecclesiastical Trial Court may be challenged by either the Respondent or the Church Attorney for cause stated to the Court. The Court shall determine the relevancy and validity of challenges for cause. Vacancies caused by challenges determined by the Court shall be filled by majority vote of the Court from persons otherwise qualified for election under the diocesan canons. Vacancies filled by the Court shall be from the same order as the person challenged was when first elected to the Court.

Rules to govern procedure.

Sec. 9. An Ecclesiastical Trial Court shall be governed by the Rules of Procedure set forth in Appendix A to this Title and such other procedural rules or determinations as the Ecclesiastical Trial Court deems appropriate and not inconsistent with this Title.

Sec. 10. The Ecclesiastical Trial Court shall be governed by the Federal Rules of Evidence in the conduct of the Trial.

Clerks.

Sec. 11. Each Ecclesiastical Trial Court shall appoint a Clerk and, if necessary, Assistant Clerks who shall be Priests or Deacons or adult lay communicants in good standing of this Church and who shall serve at the pleasure of the Court.

Reporter.

Sec. 12. Each Ecclesiastical Trial Court shall appoint a Reporter who shall provide for the recording of the proceedings and who shall serve at the pleasure of the Court.

Lay Assessors.

Sec. 13. Each Ecclesiastical Trial Court shall appoint at least one but no more than three Lay Assessors. Lay Assessors shall have no vote. It shall be their duty to give the Ecclesiastical Trial Court an opinion on any question of law, procedure or evidence.

Record of Proceedings.

Sec. 14 (a) The Ecclesiastical Trial Court shall keep a complete and accurate record of its proceedings. When all proceedings on a Presentment have been concluded, including any and all appeals, the Presiding Judge shall certify the record. If the Presiding Judge did not participate in the proceeding for any reason, by majority vote, the Court shall designate another member to certify the record.

(b) The Court shall promptly deliver the original certified record of the proceedings to The Archives of the Episcopal Church.

Delivery to Archives.

Sec. 15. The Ecclesiastical Trial Court shall permit the Respondent to be heard in person and by counsel of the Respondent's own selection. In every Trial the Court may regulate the number of counsel who may address the Court or examine witnesses.

Respondent to be heard.

Sec. 16 (a) Upon receiving a Presentment, the Presiding Judge shall, within 30 days, send to each member of the Court a copy of the Presentment.

(b) The Presiding Judge of the Court shall, within not more than three calendar months from the Presiding Judge's receipt of the Presentment, summon the Respondent to answer the Presentment in accordance with the Rules of Procedure.

Court to issue summons within three months.

(c) The Respondent's answer or other response to the Presentment in accordance with the Rules of Procedure shall be duly recorded and the Trial shall proceed; *Provided*, that for sufficient cause the Court may adjourn from time to time; and *Provided, also*, that the Respondent shall, at all times during the Trial, have liberty to be present, and may be accompanied by counsel and one other person of his or her own choosing, and in due time and order to produce testimony and to make a defense.

Respondent's answer to be recorded.

(d) If the Respondent fails or refuses to answer or otherwise enter an appearance, except for reasonable cause to be allowed by the Court, the Church Attorney may, no sooner than thirty days after the answer is due, move for Summary Judgment of Offense in accordance with the Rules of Procedure. If the motion is granted, the Bishop shall be notified, and the Respondent shall be given notice that Sentence of Admonition, Suspension or Deposition will be adjudged by the Court and pronounced by the Bishop at the expiration of thirty days after the date of the Notice of Sentence, or at such convenient time thereafter as the Bishop shall determine. Sentence of Admonition, Suspension or of Deposition from the Ordained Ministry may, thereafter, be adjudged by the Court and pronounced by the Bishop.

Nonappearance of Respondent.

Sec. 17. In all Ecclesiastical Trials, the Church Attorney shall appear on behalf of the Diocese, which shall then be considered the party on one side and the Respondent the party on the other. Each Complainant and alleged Victim shall be entitled to be present throughout and observe the Trial and each may be accompanied by counsel and another person of his or her own choosing.

Church Attorney shall appear.

Sec. 18. Before a vote is taken on the findings and in the presence of the Respondent and counsel, counsel for the parties may submit requested proposed instructions. The Presiding Judge of the Ecclesiastical Trial Court, after consultation with the Lay Assessors, shall declare which of the proposed instructions shall be issued and shall instruct the members of the Court as to the elements of the Offense and charge them (i) that the Respondent must be presumed not to have committed the Offense alleged until established by clear and convincing evidence, and unless such standard of proof be met the Presentment must be dismissed, and (ii) that the burden of proof to establish the Respondent's commission of the Offense is upon the Church Attorney in the name of the Diocese.

Proposed instructions.

Sec. 19. A separate vote shall be taken first upon the findings as to the commission of an Offense by the Respondent.

Two-thirds vote needed for Judgment.

Sec. 20. For a Judgment that the Respondent has committed an Offense, the affirmative vote of two-thirds of the Members of the Ecclesiastical Trial Court then serving for that Trial shall be necessary. Failing such two-thirds vote, the Presentment shall be dismissed.

Sec. 21. The Presiding Judge shall cause the Respondent, the Church Attorney, each Complainant, and, unless waived in writing, the Victim to be advised of and provided with a copy of the findings of the Court.

Voting on the Sentence.

Sec. 22. No vote shall be taken on the Sentence to be imposed until at least 30 days after the Respondent, Church Attorney, each Complainant and, unless waived in writing, the Victim have been informed of the Judgment and each has had a reasonable opportunity to offer matters in excuse or mitigation or to otherwise comment on the Sentence.

Sec. 23. All matters in excuse or mitigation or comments on the Sentence shall be served on the Respondent, Church Attorney, Complainants and, unless waived in writing, the Victim. The Court shall provide a reasonable time for responses to the Court which shall also be served as provided above. The Court may schedule hearings on the submissions.

Two-thirds vote needed to impose Sentence.

Sec. 24. The concurrence of two-thirds of the Members of the Ecclesiastical Trial Court then serving for that Trial shall be necessary to adjudge and impose a Sentence upon a Respondent found to have committed an Offense.

Sec. 25. The Court shall then vote upon a Sentence to be adjudged and imposed upon the Respondent and the decision so signed shall be recorded as the Judgment of the Court.

Sec. 26. The decision of the Court as to all the Charges shall be reduced to writing, and signed by those who assent to it.

Communication of Judgment.

Sec. 27. The Judgment and any Sentence adjudged on a Judgment shall be communicated promptly to the Bishop of the Diocese wherein the Trial was held, the Ecclesiastical Authority, if there be no Bishop, the Standing Committee, the Ecclesiastical Authority of the Diocese in which the Respondent is canonically resident, the Respondent, each Complainant, and, unless waived in writing, the Victim.

(B) Appeals to Courts of Review for the Trial of a Priest or Deacon

Respondent may appeal.

Sec. 28. The Ecclesiastical Authority of the jurisdiction within which a Trial was held shall cause written notice to be served on the Respondent, the Church Attorney, each Complainant, and, unless waived in writing, the Victim of (i) the Judgment, (ii) the Sentence adjudged, and (iii) the Sentence to be pronounced by the Bishop. Within thirty days after the service of that notice the Respondent may appeal to the Court of Review by serving a written notice of appeal on the Ecclesiastical Authority of that jurisdiction and a copy on the Presiding Judge of the Ecclesiastical Trial Court and the Presiding Judge of the Court of Review. The notice shall be signed by the Respondent or the Respondent's counsel and shall briefly set forth the decision from which the appeal is taken and the grounds of the appeal, and a copy of the decision of the Trial Court shall be attached.

Sec. 29. After Judgment by an Ecclesiastical Trial Court, the Bishop shall not pronounce Sentence on the Respondent before the expiration of thirty days after the Respondent shall have been served as set forth in Section 28 with the notice of the decision of the Court and the Sentence adjudged, nor, in case an appeal is taken, shall Sentence be pronounced pending the hearing and final determination thereof.

Pronouncement of Sentence.

Sec. 30. In each of the Provinces there shall be a Court of Review of the Trial of a Priest or Deacon, which shall be composed of a Bishop of the Province, three Priests canonically resident in Dioceses within the Province, and three Lay Persons who are adult communicants of this Church in good standing, having domicile in the Province; at least two of the Lay Persons shall be learned in the law.

Court of Review.

Sec. 31. During the period between General Conventions, each Provincial Synod shall elect the Judges of the Court of Review in the Province. The Synod shall prescribe the time and the manner in which such Judges shall be elected. The persons so elected, except in case of death, resignation, or declination to serve, shall continue to be members of the Court for such terms as the Synod may set and until their successors shall be elected. The Bishop elected by the Synod shall be the Presiding Judge of the Court.

Mode of electing Judges.

Sec. 32 (a) No person shall sit as a member of any Court of Review who is excused pursuant to Canon IV.14.13; nor shall any Bishop, Priest, or Lay Member who for any reason upon objection made by either appellant or appellee is deemed by the other members of the Court to be disqualified.

Conditions for disqualification.

(b) The death, disability rendering the person unable to act, resignation, or declination to serve as a member of a Court of Review shall constitute a vacancy in the Court of Review.

(c) Notices of resignations or declinations to serve shall be given as follows:

Resignations.

(1) By the Presiding Judge of the Court of Review of the Trial of a Priest or Deacon; by written notice sent to the President of the Provincial Synod.

(2) By a Priest or Lay Member of the Court, by written notice sent to the Presiding Judge of the Court.

(d) If any Priest appointed to the Court of Review is elected a Bishop, or if any Lay Member appointed to the Court of Review is ordained to the ministry prior to the hearing of the appeal, the person shall immediately cease to be a member of the Court of Review. If either event occurs following the hearing of the appeal, the person shall continue to serve until the completion of the appeal and the rendering of a decision by the Court of Review.

Change of Order.

Filling vacancies.

Sec. 33. Vacancies occurring in the Court of Review shall be filled as follows:

(a) In the case of a vacancy in the office of the Bishop elected as a member of the Court of Review, the President of the Provincial Synod shall give written notice thereof to the Bishop with jurisdiction senior by consecration in the Province. Thereupon the Bishop so notified shall become a member of the Court until a new election is made. If the Bishop so appointed is unable or unwilling to serve as a member of the Court, notification shall be given by the Bishop to the President of the Provincial Synod of this fact, who shall thereupon appoint the Bishop with jurisdiction next senior by consecration in that Province who is willing and able to serve.

(b) In case any vacancy shall exist in the membership of the Court of Review's Priests or Deacons or Lay Members, the remaining Judges of the Court shall appoint another person similarly domiciled or canonically resident in the Province from the same order to fill such vacancy.

Jurisdiction of Court.

Sec. 34. The several Courts of Review are vested with jurisdiction to hear and determine appeals from decisions of Ecclesiastical Trial Courts in Dioceses within that Province in Ecclesiastical Trials of Priests or Deacons.

Right of appeal.

Sec. 35. The Respondent may take an appeal to the Court of Review of the Province within which an Ecclesiastical Trial was held from a Judgment. The right of appeal is solely that of the Respondent, except as provided in Section 36 of this Canon.

Appeal.

Sec. 36 (a) Upon the written request of at least two Bishops of other jurisdictions within the Province, the Ecclesiastical Authority of the Diocese within which a Trial was held shall appeal from a decision of the Ecclesiastical Trial Court that the Respondent had not committed an Offense involving a question of Doctrine, Faith, or Worship; *Provided, however*, that such appeal shall be on the question of the Church's Doctrine, Faith, or Worship only, and that the decision of the Court of Review shall not be held to reverse the finding of the non-commission of an Offense by the Respondent on other Charges. An appeal by the Standing Committee can be taken only when there is a vacancy in the office of Bishop or in case the Bishop is unable to act.

(b) An appeal under this Section may be taken by the service by the appellant of a written notice of appeal upon the Respondent, and also upon the Presiding Judge of the Ecclesiastical Trial Court and the Presiding Judge of the Court of Review, within thirty days after the decision from which the appeal is taken.

Appeal if Diocese is non-provincial.

Sec. 37. If the Ecclesiastical Trial was held in a Diocese not specified in Canon I.9.1, the appeal shall lie to the Court of Review of the Province which is geographically closest to that Diocese or is otherwise most appropriate as determined by the Presiding Bishop.

Sec. 38. An appeal shall be heard upon the Record on Appeal of the Ecclesiastical Trial Court. Except for the purpose of correcting the Record on Appeal, if defective, no new evidence shall be taken by the Court of Review.

Sec. 39. The Presiding Judge of the Court of Review of the Province having jurisdiction, within ninety days but not less than sixty days after having received the Record on Appeal, shall appoint a time and place within such Province for the hearing of the appeal. At least thirty days prior to the day appointed, the Presiding Judge shall give written notice of such time and place to the other members of the Court, and also to the Respondent, and to the Bishop and Diocesan Review Committee of the Diocese in which the Ecclesiastical Trial was held.

Appointment of time and place to hear appeal.

Sec. 40. It shall be the duty of the Ecclesiastical Trial Court to prepare a copy of the Record on Appeal of the Ecclesiastical Trial as transcribed, to be printed or otherwise reproduced as shall be permitted by the Presiding Judge of the Court of Review. Within thirty days after receiving the copy of the Record on Appeal, the appellant shall serve two copies of the Record on Appeal, the notice of appeal and the appellant's brief, if any, upon the opposite party, and shall deliver seven copies of each to the Presiding Judge of the Court for the use of the Judges.

Record on Appeal.

The appellee shall serve the appellee's brief, if any, on the appellant with seven copies to the Presiding Judge of the Court of Review not later than thirty days following the service upon the appellee of the record, notice of appeal and appellant's brief. Any reply brief shall be served likewise within ten days following service of the prior brief upon the party.

Sec. 41. The Diocesan Review Committee of the Diocese which issued the Presentment shall be deemed to be the opposite party for the purpose of this appeal.

Sec. 42. At the time and place appointed, the Court shall organize, and proceed to hear the appeal; *Provided, however*, that at least six Judges, of whom the Presiding Judge of the Court shall be one, shall participate in the hearing. But the members present, if less than that number, may adjourn the Court from time to time, until the requisite number of Judges are present.

Court to organize with at least six Judges.

Sec. 43. The Court of Review shall appoint a Clerk and, if necessary, Assistant Clerks, who shall be Priests canonically resident in a Diocese of that Province or adult lay communicants in good standing of this Church residing in the Province, to serve at the pleasure of the Court.

Clerks.

Sec. 44. The Court of Review shall appoint at least one but no more than three Lay Assessors. Lay Assessors shall have no vote.

Lay Assessors.

Sec. 45. The Court of Review shall appoint a Reporter who shall provide for the recording of the proceedings and who shall serve at the pleasure of the Court

Reporter.

Sec. 46. The Court of Review shall be guided by the Rules of Appellate Procedure in Appendix B to this Title and may adopt rules of procedure not inconsistent with the Constitution and Canons of the Church, with the

Rules of procedure.

power to alter or rescind the same from time to time, provided the same shall not cause material and substantial injustice to be done or seriously prejudice the rights of the parties.

Respondent to be heard.

Sec. 47. The Court of Review shall permit the Respondent to be heard in person or by counsel of the Respondent's own selection but may regulate the number of counsel who may address the Court and shall permit the Church Attorney to be heard.

Record to be kept.

Sec. 48 (a) The Court of Review shall keep a complete and accurate record of its proceedings. When all proceedings on an appeal have been concluded, the Presiding Judge shall certify the record. If the Presiding Judge did not participate in the proceeding for any reason, by majority vote the Court shall designate another member to certify the record.

(b) The Court shall promptly deliver the original certified record of the proceedings to The Archives of the Episcopal Church.

Sec. 49. No determination or Judgment of any Ecclesiastical Trial Court shall be disturbed for technical errors not going to the merits of the case.

Power of Court to dispose of case.

Sec. 50. The Court may reverse or affirm in whole or in part the determination or Judgment of the Ecclesiastical Trial Court, or, if in its opinion justice shall so require, may grant a new Trial. If after having been duly notified, the appellant fails to appear, and no sufficient excuse be shown, the Court, in its discretion, may dismiss the appeal for want of prosecution, or may proceed to hear and determine the appeal in the appellant's absence.

Concurrence necessary to pronounce a judgment.

Sec. 51. The concurrence of five members of a Court of Review shall be necessary to pronounce a judgment. The judgment or decision of the Court shall be in writing, signed by the members of the Court concurring therein, and shall distinctly specify the grounds of the decision and shall be attached to the record. If the concurrence of five of the members cannot be obtained, that fact shall be stated in the record, and the determination or Judgment of the Trial Court shall stand as affirmed except as to any reversal in part in which there has been concurrence. Immediately after the determination of the appeal, the Presiding Judge of the Court shall give notice thereof in writing to the appellant and appellee and to the Bishop and the Diocesan Review Committee of the Diocese in which the Trial was had.

Sentence.

Sec. 52. The Court of Review shall not pronounce Sentence on the affirmation of a Judgment. When the appeal is so finally determined, if the decision of the Ecclesiastical Trial Court be affirmed in whole or in part, upon receipt of the record and the Judgment or decision of the Court of Review by the Ecclesiastical Authority of the jurisdiction of the Trial Court, the Respondent shall be sentenced in accordance with Canon IV.12.

Expenses.

Sec. 53. The necessary charges and expenses of the Court of Review, including the necessary expenses of the members of the Court, Lay Assessors, Reporters and Clerks and the reasonable and necessary out-of-pocket disbursements and expenses, except the cost of printing any records or briefs, shall be a charge upon the Province and shall be paid by the Treasurer of the Synod of that Province upon the order of the President of the Synod. Any legal fees and other disbursements of the Church Attorney shall be the responsibility of the Diocese in which the Trial was held, unless the Trial was held as a service or convenience to a Diocese from which the Presentment issued, in which case the responsibility therefor shall be that of the Diocese from which the Presentment was issued.

CANON 5: Of the Court for the Trial of a Bishop

Sec. 1. The Court for the Trial of a Bishop is vested with jurisdiction to try a Bishop who is duly Presented for one or more Offenses.

Jurisdiction.

Sec. 2. The Court for the Trial of a Bishop shall consist of nine Bishops of this Church. Three Bishops shall be elected by the House of Bishops at each regular meeting of General Convention, to serve until the adjournment of the third succeeding regular meeting of General Convention. All judges shall serve until their successors are elected and qualify; *Provided, however*, there shall be no change in composition of a Court as to a proceeding pending before it, while that proceeding is unresolved except as specified in Canon IV.5.3.

Mode of electing Judges.

Sec. 3 (a) No Judge shall sit as a member of a Court for the Trial of a Bishop who is a Complainant, or is related to the Respondent or Complainant by affinity or consanguinity, or who is excused pursuant to Canon IV.14.13; nor shall any Judge sit who, upon objection made by either party for any reason, is deemed by the other members of the Court to be disqualified.

Conditions for disqualification.

(b) The death, permanent disability rendering the person unable to act, resignation or declination to serve as a member of the Court for the Trial of a Bishop shall constitute a vacancy in the Court. The recusal or disqualification of a member of the Court from consideration of a particular Presentment shall constitute a temporary vacancy in the Court.

(c) Notices of resignations or declinations to serve shall be given by any Bishop chosen to serve as a member of the Court for the Trial of a Bishop by written notice sent to the Presiding Bishop.

(d) Notices of recusal shall be given by a Judge to the Presiding Judge.

Sec. 4. The Court for the Trial of a Bishop shall from time to time elect from its own membership a Presiding Judge, who shall hold office until the expiration of the term for which chosen. If in any proceeding before the Court the Presiding Judge is disqualified or is for any cause unable to act, the Court shall elect from its members a Presiding Judge *pro tempore*.

Presiding Judge.

Sec. 5. When the Court is not in session, if there is a vacancy in the office of the Presiding Judge, the Bishop who is senior by consecration shall perform the duties of the office of Presiding Judge.

Filling vacancies.

Sec. 6. Vacancies occurring in the Court for the Trial of a Bishop shall be filled as follows:

(a) In the case of a temporary vacancy due to the recusal or disqualification of any Judge, the remaining Judges may appoint a Judge to take the place of the one so disqualified in that particular case. If the recused or disqualified Judge participated in any proceedings other than consideration of whether any Judge should be disqualified, the remaining Judges shall decide whether or not the Judge will be replaced for the remainder of that case.

(b) In the case of a vacancy in the Court, the remaining Judges shall have power to fill such vacancy until the next General Convention, when the House of Bishops shall choose a person to fill such vacancy. The person so chosen shall serve during the remainder of the term.

Quorum.

Sec. 7. Not less than five of the Judges shall constitute a quorum, but any less number may adjourn the Court from time to time.

Presiding Judge to send Presentment.

Sec. 8 (a) Upon receiving a Presentment, the Presiding Judge shall, within 30 days, send to each member of the Court a copy of the Presentment. If the Presentment is issued pursuant to Canon IV.3.21(c) the Presiding Judge shall also send a copy of the supporting briefs, answer, and statements.

(b) The Presiding Judge of the Court shall, within not more than three calendar months from the Presiding Judge's receipt of the Presentment, summon the Respondent to answer the Presentment in accordance with the Rules of Procedure.

Location of Court proceedings.

(c) Court proceedings at which the Respondent and Church Attorney are to appear shall be held within the Diocese of the accused Bishop, or within the Diocese where the accused Bishop lives or serves, at the discretion of the Court. The Court may, for good cause, appoint another place for any such proceedings or conduct such proceedings by telephone conference provided that all participants can hear and be heard by all other participants in the telephone conference.

Church Attorney.

Sec. 9. Within three months following each regular meeting of General Convention, the Court for the Trial of a Bishop shall appoint a Church Attorney to serve until the next regular meeting of General Convention and until a successor is duly appointed and qualified, and from time to time for good cause and upon the request of the Church Attorney, appoint one or more assistant Church Attorneys to act for and in the place of the Church Attorney.

Clerks.

Sec. 10. The Court shall appoint a Clerk and, if necessary, Assistant Clerks, who shall be Members of the Clergy or adult lay communicants in good standing of this Church, to serve at the pleasure of the Court.

Reporter.

Sec. 11. The Court shall appoint a Reporter who shall provide for the recording of the proceedings and serve at the pleasure of the Court.

Lay Assessors.

Sec. 12. The Court shall appoint at least one but no more than three Lay Assessors. Lay Assessors shall have no vote.

Bishops may select Church Attorney.

Sec. 13. If the Presentment is issued pursuant to Canon IV.3.21(c), the ten Bishops of this Church exercising jurisdiction who signed the Presentment may select a Church Attorney, subject to confirmation of their selection by the Court, which confirmation shall not be unreasonably withheld.

Sec. 14. In all cases, the Church Attorney, or the assistants to the Church Attorney shall appear in behalf of the Church. The Church shall then be considered the party on one side, and the Respondent the party on the other.

Sec. 15. The Court shall be governed by the Rules of Procedure set forth in Appendix A to this Title, and such other procedural rules or determinations as the Court deems appropriate and not inconsistent with this Title.

Rules of procedure.

Sec. 16. The Court shall be governed by the Federal Rules of Evidence.

Sec. 17. The Court shall permit the Respondent to be heard in person or by counsel of the Respondent's own selection, but the Court may regulate the number of counsel who may address the Court or examine witnesses.

Respondent to be heard.

Sec. 18 (a) The Respondent's answer or other response to the Presentment in accordance with the Rules of Procedure shall be duly recorded and the Trial shall proceed; *Provided*, that for sufficient cause the Court may adjourn from time to time; and *Provided*, *also*, that the Respondent shall, at all times during the Trial, have liberty to be present, and may be accompanied by counsel and one other person of his or her own choosing, and in due time and order to produce testimony and to make a defense.

Response to be recorded.

(b) If the Respondent fails or refuses to answer or otherwise enter an appearance, except for reasonable cause to be allowed by the Court, the Church Attorney may, no sooner than thirty days after the answer is due, move for Summary Judgment of Offense. If the motion is granted, the Respondent shall be given notice that Sentence will be adjudged and pronounced by the Court at the expiration of thirty days after the date of the Notice of Sentence, or at such convenient time thereafter as the Court shall determine. Sentence may thereafter be adjudged and pronounced by the Court.

Nonappearance.

Sec. 19. The Complainant and the alleged Victim shall each have the right to be present throughout and observe the Trial and to be accompanied by counsel and one other person of his or her choosing.

Sec. 20. The Respondent being present, the Trial shall proceed in accordance with this Canon. The Respondent shall in all cases have the right to be a defense witness, subject to cross-examination in the same manner as any other witness. No testimony shall be received at the Trial except from witnesses who have signed a declaration in the following words or the Oath provided by the Federal Rules of Evidence, to be read aloud before the witness testifies and to be filed with the records of the Court.

"I, A.B., a witness on the Trial of a Presentment against the Right Reverend __________, a Bishop of the Episcopal Church, now pending, do most solemnly call God to witness that the evidence I am about to give shall be the truth, the whole truth, and nothing but the truth, so help me God."

Declaration of witnesses.

Sec. 21. Before a vote is taken on the findings and in the presence of the Respondent and counsel, counsel for the parties may submit requested proposed instructions. The Presiding Judge of the Court, after consultation with the Lay Assessors, shall instruct the members of the Court as to the

Presiding Judge to instruct Court.

elements of the Offense and charge them (i) that the Respondent must be presumed not to have committed the Offense alleged until established by clear and convincing proof, and unless the standard of proof be met the Presentment must be dismissed, and (ii) that the burden of proof to establish the Respondent's commission of the Offense is upon the Church.

Voting on findings and sentence.

Sec. 22. Separate and distinct votes shall be taken first upon the findings as to the commission of an Offense by the Respondent, and, if the Respondent be found to have committed an Offense, then upon the Sentence to be imposed.

Two-thirds vote needed for Judgment.

Sec. 23. For a Judgment that the Respondent has committed an Offense, the affirmative vote of two-thirds of the members of the Court shall be necessary. Failing such two-thirds vote, the Presentment shall be dismissed.

Sec. 24. The decision of the Court as to all the Charges shall be reduced to writing, and signed by those who assent to it.

Parties to be informed of Judgment.

Sec. 25. No vote shall be taken on the Sentence to be imposed until at least thirty days after the Respondent, Church Attorney, each Complainant, and, unless waived in writing, the Victim have been informed of the Judgment and each has had a reasonable opportunity to offer matters in excuse or mitigation or to otherwise comment on the Sentence.

Sec. 26. All matters in excuse or mitigation or comments on the sentence shall be served on the Respondent, Church Attorney, Complainants and, unless waived in writing, the Victim. The Court shall provide a reasonable time for responses to the Court which shall also be served as provided above. The Court may schedule hearings on the submissions.

Sec. 27. The Court shall then vote upon a Sentence to be adjudged and imposed upon the Respondent and the decision so signed shall be recorded as the Judgment of the Court.

Communication of Judgment and Sentence.

Sec. 28 (a) The Judgment and Sentence adjudged shall be communicated promptly to the Respondent, each Complainant, and, unless waived in writing, the Victim, the Presiding Bishop and the Standing Committee of the Diocese in which the Respondent is canonically resident.

Motion to modify Sentence.

(b) Any Respondent who shall be found to have committed an Offense may file a motion for a modification of Sentence. Any such motion shall be filed within 30 days from the date of the filing of the decision, and the motion shall set forth all the reasons therefor, and no other shall be relied on at the hearing of the motion without the consent of the Court. The Presiding Judge of the Court shall set a place and time for hearing the motion and shall reconvene the Court to hear and determine the same.

Court may modify Sentence.

(c) The Court may in the interest of justice modify the Sentence. Upon determination of the motion to modify, the Clerk of the Court shall enter Judgment. If no motion for modification of Sentence shall be filed within the time limited for filing such motions, the Clerk of the Court shall on the next business day enter, as final, the Judgment rendered by the Court. An appeal from a final Judgment of a Court for the Trial of a Bishop to the Court of Review of the Trial of a Bishop, as provided in Canon IV.6, may be taken within thirty days from the entry of the Judgment.

(d) The final Judgment shall be in writing signed by a majority of the Court and direct what Sentence is to be incorporated in the final Judgment to be entered by the Clerk.

Sentence to be pronounced.

(e) After the entry of final Judgment, the Presiding Judge of the Court shall appoint a time and place not less than sixty days thereafter for pronouncing the Sentence adjudged. At the time and place appointed, if the Respondent shall not have an appeal pending in the Court of Review of the Trial of a Bishop, or the action of the Court of Review has not made it unnecessary for the Trial Court to proceed to pronounce Sentence, the Presiding Judge of the Court, or a member thereof designated in writing by a majority of the members thereof to do so, shall in the presence of the Respondent, if the Respondent shall see fit to attend, pronounce the Sentence which has been adjudged by the Court, and direct the same to be entered by the Clerk; and *Provided, further*, that Sentence shall not be imposed upon a Bishop found to have committed an Offense of holding and teaching doctrine contrary to that held by this Church unless and until the said finding shall have been approved by a vote of two-thirds of the Bishops present at a meeting of the House of Bishops.

Record of proceedings.

Sec. 29 (a) The Court for the Trial of a Bishop shall keep a complete and accurate record of its proceedings. When all proceedings on a Presentment have been concluded, including any and all appeals, the Presiding Judge shall certify the record. If the Presiding Judge did not participate in the proceeding for any reason, by majority vote the Court shall designate another member to certify the record.

(b) The Court shall promptly deliver the original certified record of the proceedings to The Archives of the Episcopal Church.

Expenses.

Sec. 30. The reasonable and necessary expenses of the Court including but not limited to the fees, costs, disbursements and expenses of the Judges, Church Attorneys, Clerks, Reporters and Lay Assessors, shall be a charge upon the General Convention and shall be paid by the Treasurer of General Convention upon the order of the Presiding Judge of the Court. The Court shall have the authority to contract for and bind the General Convention to payment of these expenses.

CANON 6: Of Appeals to the Court of Review of the Trial of a Bishop

Right to appeal.

Sec. 1. A Bishop found to have committed an Offense shall have the right to appeal from the Judgment of the Trial Court to the Court of Review of the Trial of a Bishop.

Sec. 2. The Court of Review of the Trial of a Bishop is vested with jurisdiction to hear and determine appeals from the determination of the Court for the Trial of a Bishop.

Court of Review.

Sec. 3. There shall be a Court of Review of the Trial of a Bishop, consisting of nine Bishops. Three Bishops shall be elected by the House of Bishops at each regular meeting of General Convention, to serve until the adjournment of the third succeeding regular meeting of General Convention. All Judges shall serve until their successors are elected and qualify; *Provided, however*, there shall be no change in composition of a Court following the hearing and while a proceeding is pending, unresolved, before the Court.

Conditions for disqualification.

Sec. 4 (a) No Bishop shall sit as a member of this Court who is a Complainant, is related to the Respondent or Complainant by affinity or consanguinity, or who is excused pursuant to Canon IV.14.13; nor shall any Bishop sit who, upon objection made by either party for any reason, is deemed by the other members of the Court to be disqualified.

Court vacancy.

(b) The death, permanent disability rendering the person unable to act, resignation, or declination to serve as a member of this Court shall constitute a vacancy in the Court. The recusal or disqualification of a member of the Court from consideration of a particular appeal shall constitute a temporary vacancy on the Court.

(c) Notices of resignations or declinations to serve shall be given by any Bishop chosen to serve as a member of the Court by written notice sent to the Presiding Bishop.

(d) Notices of recusal shall be given by a Judge to the Presiding Judge.

Presiding Judge.

Sec. 5. The Court shall from time to time elect from its own membership a Presiding Judge, who shall hold office until the expiration of the term for which chosen. If in any proceeding before the Court the Presiding Judge is disqualified or is for any cause unable to act, the Court shall elect from its members a Presiding Judge *pro tempore*.

Sec. 6. When the Court is not in session, if there is a vacancy in the office of the Presiding Judge, the Bishop who is senior by consecration shall perform the duties of the office of Presiding Judge.

Filling vacancies.

Sec. 7. Vacancies occurring in this Court shall be filled as follows:

(a) In the case of a temporary vacancy due to the recusal or disqualification of any Judge, the remaining Judges may appoint a Judge to take the place of the one so disqualified in that particular case. If the recused or disqualified Judge participated in any proceedings other than consideration of whether any Judge should be disqualified, the remaining Judges shall decide whether or not the Judge will be replaced for the remainder of the case.

(b) In the case of a vacancy in the Court, the remaining Judges shall have power to fill the vacancy until the next General Convention, when the House of Bishops shall choose a Bishop to fill the vacancy. The Bishop so chosen shall serve during the remainder of the term.

Quorum.

Sec. 8. Not less than five Judges shall constitute a quorum.

Sec. 9. The concurrence of six Judges shall be necessary to pronounce a Judgment, but any lesser number may adjourn the Court from time to time.

Sec. 10. The Court shall appoint a Clerk and, if necessary, Assistant Clerks who shall be Members of the Clergy or adult lay communicants in good standing of this Church, to serve during the pleasure of the Court.

Clerks.

Sec. 11 . The Court shall appoint a Reporter who shall provide for the recording of the proceedings and serve during the pleasure of the Court.

Reporter.

Sec. 12. The Court shall appoint at least one but no more than three Lay Assessors. Lay Assessors shall have no vote.

Lay Assessors.

Sec. 13. The Court shall be guided by the Rules of Appellate Procedure and may adopt rules of procedure not inconsistent with the Constitution and Canons of the Church, with the power to alter or rescind the same from time to time, provided the same shall not cause material and substantial injustice to be done or seriously prejudice the rights of the parties.

Rules of procedure.

Sec. 14. The Court shall permit the Respondent to be heard in person and by counsel of the Respondent's own selection, but the Court may regulate the number of counsel who may address the Court.

Respondents to be heard.

Sec. 15 (a) Unless within thirty days from the date of entry of Judgment in the Trial Court the appellant has given notice of the appeal in writing to the Trial Court, to the party against whom the appeal is taken, and to the Presiding Judge of the Court of Review of the Trial of a Bishop, assigning in the notice the reasons of appeal, the appellant shall be held to have waived the right of appeal although in its discretion the Court of Review of the Trial of a Bishop may entertain and hear an appeal not taken within the prescribed period.

Right of appeal.

(b) The Presiding Judge of the Court of Review upon receiving the notice of appeal shall appoint a time within 60 days thereafter, unless for good cause extended, for hearing the appeal and fix the place of the hearing. At least 30 days prior to the day appointed, the Presiding Judge shall give written notice of the time and place to the other members of the Court and also the appellant and appellee.

Appoint time for hearing.

Sec. 16. Upon notice of appeal being given, the Clerk of the Trial Court shall send to the Clerk of the Court of Review of the Trial of a Bishop a transcript of the record, including all the evidence, certified by the Presiding Judge and Clerk of the Trial Court, and the Clerk shall lay the same before the Court of Review at its next session.

Transcript of the record.

Sec. 17. An appeal shall be heard upon the Record on Appeal of the Court for the Trial of a Bishop. Except for the purpose of correcting the Record on Appeal, if defective, no new evidence shall be taken by the Court of Review.

Sec. 18. The Court of Review of the Trial of a Bishop may affirm or reverse any Judgment brought before it on appeal, and may enter final Judgment in the case or may remand the same to the Trial Court for a new Trial or for such further proceedings as the interests of justice may require.

Court may affirm or reverse Judgment.

Sec. 19 (a) If the Court of Review of the Trial of a Bishop enters final Judgment in the case, and if by that Judgment the Respondent is found to have committed any of the Charges upon which tried, the Court of Review

Sentences.

of the Trial of a Bishop may review the Sentence adjudged by the Trial Court and may adjudge a lesser Sentence than that adjudged by the Trial Court. Before final Sentence is adjudged by the Court of Review the Respondent shall have the opportunity to make a statement to the Court in excuse or mitigation. The Church Attorney, each Complainant, and, unless waived in writing, the Victim shall have the opportunity to make a statement to the Court regarding the Sentence to be adjudged and imposed.

(b) The final Sentence adjudged shall be pronounced pursuant to Canon IV.5.28 and the notices thereof required by Canon IV.12 shall be given.

Stay of proceedings in Trial Court.

Sec. 20. In case of appeal, all proceedings in the Trial Court and the pronouncement of Sentence shall be stayed until the appeal is dismissed by the Court of Review of the Trial of a Bishop, or the case be remanded by the Court to the Trial Court for further proceedings, or until final Judgment has been adjudged by the Court of Review.

May discontinue an appeal.

Sec. 21. The appellant may discontinue the appeal at any time before a hearing thereof has begun before the Court of Review of the Trial of a Bishop. After the hearing has begun, the appellant may discontinue the appeal only with the consent of the Court. If the appeal is discontinued, the Trial Court shall proceed as if no appeal had been taken.

Record of proceedings.

Sec. 22 (a) The Court of Review of a Trial of a Bishop shall keep a complete and accurate record of its proceedings. When all proceedings on an appeal have been concluded, the Presiding Judge shall certify the record. If the Presiding Judge did not participate in the proceeding for any reason, by majority vote the Court shall designate another member to certify the record.

(b) The Court shall promptly deliver the original certified record of the proceedings to The Archives of the Episcopal Church.

Expenses.

Sec. 23. The reasonable and necessary expenses of the Court of Review of the Trial of a Bishop, including but not limited to the fees, costs, disbursements and expenses of the Judges, Church Attorneys, Clerks, Reporters and Lay Assessors, shall be charged upon the General Convention and shall be paid by the Treasurer of General Convention upon the order of the Presiding Judge of the Court. The Court shall have the authority to contract for and bind the General Convention to payment of these expenses.

CANON 7: Of a Priest or Deacon in Any Diocese Chargeable with Offense in Another

Ecclesiastical Authority to give notice of liability.

Sec. 1. If a Priest or Deacon canonically resident in a Diocese shall have acted in any other Diocese in such a way as to be liable to Presentment, the Ecclesiastical Authority thereof shall give notice of the same to the Ecclesiastical Authority where the Priest or Deacon is canonically resident, exhibiting, with the information given, reasonable ground for presuming its truth. If the Ecclesiastical Authority, after due notice given, shall omit, for the space of three months, to proceed against the offending Priest or Deacon, or shall request the Ecclesiastical Authority of the Diocese in which the Offense or Offenses are alleged to have been committed to proceed against that Priest or Deacon, it shall be within the power of the Ecclesiastical Authority of the Diocese within which the Offense or Offenses are alleged to have been committed to institute proceedings pursuant to this Title.

Inhibition of Clergy from another Diocese.

Sec. 2. If a Priest or Deacon shall come temporarily into any Diocese, under the imputation of having elsewhere committed any Offense or if any Priest or Deacon, while temporarily in any Diocese, shall so offend, the Bishop of that Diocese, upon probable cause, may Admonish or Inhibit the Priest or Deacon from officiating in that Diocese. And if, after Inhibition, the Priest or Deacon so officiate, the Bishop shall give notice to all the Clergy and Congregations in that Diocese that the officiating of the Priest or Deacon is inhibited; and like notice shall be given to the Ecclesiastical Authority of the Diocese in which the Priest or Deacon is canonically resident, and to the Recorder. The Inhibition shall continue in force until the soonest of (i) the Bishop dissolves the Inhibition, (ii) the Standing Committee assuming jurisdiction thereof votes not to issue a Presentment, or (iii) if presented, the Presentment is dismissed.

Sec. 3. The provisions of Section 2 shall apply to Clergy ordained in foreign lands by Bishops in communion with this Church; but in such case notice of the Inhibition shall be given to the Bishop from whose jurisdiction the Priest or Deacon shall appear to have come, and also to all the Bishops exercising jurisdiction in this Church, and to the Recorder.

CANON 8: Of Renunciation of the Ministry by Members of the Clergy Amenable for Presentment for an Offense

Priest or Deacon.

Sec. 1. Subject to the provisions of Section 3 of this Canon, if any Priest or Deacon (i) Amenable for but not under Presentment for an Offense of Crime, of Immorality or of Conduct Unbecoming a Member of the Clergy, or (ii) Amenable for or under a Presentment for any other Offense, shall declare in writing to the Ecclesiastical Authority of the Diocese in which that person is canonically resident a renunciation of the Ministry of this Church and a desire to be removed therefrom, the Ecclesiastical Authority if it be a Bishop, or if the Ecclesiastical Authority not be a Bishop a Bishop acting for the Ecclesiastical Authority, may accept the renunciation and pronounce Sentence of Deposition with the consent of a majority of All the Members of the Standing Committee of the Diocese. Upon receiving the consent of the Standing Committee, the Bishop or the Bishop acting for the Ecclesiastical Authority may proceed to impose a Sentence of Deposition in accordance with Canon IV.12.4.

Bishop.

Sec. 2. If any Bishop Amenable for but not under Presentment for an Offense of Crime, Immorality or Conduct Unbecoming a Member of the Clergy or Amenable for or under a Presentment for any other Offense shall declare in writing to the Presiding Bishop, or if there then be none to the presiding officer of the House of Bishops, a renunciation of the Ministry of this Church and a desire to be removed therefrom, the Presiding Bishop or the presiding officer may accept the renunciation and pronounce Sentence of Deposition with the consent of a majority of All the Members of the

Review Committee. Upon receiving the consent of the Review Committee, the Presiding Bishop or the presiding officer of the House of Bishops may proceed to impose a Sentence of Deposition in accordance with Canon IV.12.

Renunciation while under Presentment.

Sec. 3. If a Member of the Clergy making a declaration of renunciation of the Ministry be under a Presentment for an Offense involving Crime, Immorality or Conduct Unbecoming a Member of the Clergy, or shall have been placed on Trial for the same, the declaration shall not be considered or acted upon until after the Presentment has been dismissed or the Trial has been concluded and Sentence, if any, adjudged. Thereafter, unless the renunciation be revoked by the Member of the Clergy, the Bishop, or Presiding Bishop as the case may be, may accept the renunciation and impose and pronounce a Sentence of Deposition.

Sec. 4. No declaration of renunciation of the ministry of this Church under this Canon shall become effective until it has been accepted and Sentence has been pronounced.

CANON 9: Of Abandonment of the Communion of This Church by a Bishop

Sec. 1. If a Bishop abandons the communion of this Church (i) by an open renunciation of the Doctrine, Discipline, or Worship of this Church, or (ii) by formal admission into any religious body not in communion with the same, or (iii) by exercising episcopal acts in and for a religious body other than this Church or another Church in communion with this Church, so as to extend to such body Holy Orders as this Church holds them, or to administer on behalf of such religious body Confirmation without the express consent and commission of the proper authority in this Church; it shall be the duty of the Review Committee, by a majority vote of All the Members, to certify the fact to the Presiding Bishop and with the certificate to send a statement of the acts or declarations which show such abandonment, which certificate and statement shall be recorded by the Presiding Bishop. The Presiding Bishop, with the consent of the three senior Bishops having jurisdiction in this Church, shall then inhibit the said Bishop until such time as the House of Bishops shall investigate the matter and act thereon. During the period of Inhibition, the Bishop shall not perform any episcopal, ministerial or canonical acts, except as relate to the administration of the temporal affairs of the Diocese of which the Bishop holds jurisdiction or in which the Bishop is then serving.

Inhibition of Bishop.

Written statement from the Bishop to be considered.

Sec. 2. The Presiding Bishop, or the presiding officer, shall forthwith give notice to the Bishop of the certification and Inhibition. Unless the inhibited Bishop, within two months, makes declaration by a Verified written statement to the Presiding Bishop, that the facts alleged in the certificate are false or utilizes the provisions of Canon IV.8 or Canon III.13, as applicable, the Bishop will be liable to Deposition. If the Presiding Bishop is reasonably satisfied that the statement constitutes (i) a good faith retraction of the declarations or acts relied upon in the certification to the Presiding Bishop or (ii) a good faith denial that the Bishop made the declarations or committed the acts relied upon in the certificate, the

Presiding Bishop, with the advice and consent of a majority of the three senior Bishops consenting to Inhibition, terminate the Inhibition. Otherwise, it shall be the duty of the Presiding Bishop to present the matter to the House of Bishops at the next regular or special meeting of the House. If the House, by a majority of the whole number of Bishops entitled to vote, shall give its consent, the Presiding Bishop shall depose the Bishop from the Ministry, and pronounce and record in the presence of two or more Bishops that the Bishop has been so deposed.

Deposition.

CANON 10: Of Abandonment of the Communion of This Church by a Priest or Deacon

Role of the Standing Committee.

Sec. 1. If it is reported to the Standing Committee of the Diocese in which a Priest or Deacon is canonically resident that the Priest or Deacon, without using the provisions of Canon IV.8 or III.13, has abandoned the Communion of this Church, then the Standing Committee shall ascertain and consider the facts, and if it shall determine by a vote of three-fourths of All the Members that the Priest or Deacon has abandoned the Communion of this Church by an open renunciation of the Doctrine, Discipline, or Worship of this Church, or by a formal admission into any religious body not in communion with this Church, or in any other way, it shall be the duty of the Standing Committee of the Diocese to transmit in writing to the Bishop of such Diocese, or if there be no such Bishop, to the Bishop of an adjacent Diocese, its determination, together with a statement setting out in reasonable detail the acts or declarations relied upon in making its determination. If the Bishop affirms the determination, the Bishop shall then inhibit the Priest or Deacon from officiating in the Diocese for six months and shall send to the Priest or Deacon a copy of the determination and statement, together with a notice that the Priest or Deacon has the rights specified in Section 2 and at the end of the six-months period the Bishop will consider deposing the Priest or Deacon in accordance with the provisions of Section 2.

Inhibition.

Expiration of period of Inhibition.

Sec. 2. Prior to the expiration of the six-month period of Inhibition, the Bishop may permit the Priest or Deacon to utilize the provisions of Canon IV.8 or Canon III.13, as applicable. If within such six-month period the Priest or Deacon shall transmit to the Bishop a statement in writing signed by the Priest or Deacon which the Bishop is reasonably satisfied constitutes a good faith retraction of such declarations or acts relied upon in the determination or a good faith denial that the Priest or Deacon committed the acts or made the declarations relied upon in the determination, the Bishop shall withdraw the notice and the Inhibition shall expire. If, however, within the six-month period, the Bishop does not pronounce acceptance of the renunciation of the Priest or Deacon in accordance with Canon IV.8 or Canon III.13, as applicable, or the Priest or Deacon does not make retraction or denial as provided above, then it shall be the duty of the Bishop either (i) to depose the Priest or Deacon as provided in Canon IV.12, or (ii) if the Bishop is satisfied that no previous irregularity or misconduct is involved, with the advice and consent of the Standing

Committee to pronounce and record in the presence of two or more Priests that the Priest or Deacon is released from the obligations of Priest or Deacon and (for causes which do not affect the person's moral character) is deprived of the right to exercise the gifts and spiritual authority conferred in Ordination.

CANON 11: Of a Priest or Deacon Engaging in Secular Employment without Consent, Being Absent from the Diocese, or Abandoning the Work of the Ministry

Diocesan Review Committee to institute inquiry.

Sec. 1. If a Priest or Deacon has engaged in any secular calling or business without the consent of the Bishop of the Diocese in which the Priest or Deacon is canonically resident as provided in Canon III.9.3(e), it shall be the duty of the Diocesan Review Committee of the Diocese, upon the case being brought to its attention by the written statement of the Bishop, to institute an inquiry into the matter. If in the judgment of the Diocesan Review Committee there is sufficient reason for further proceedings, it shall be the duty of the Diocesan Review Committee to Present the offending Priest or Deacon for Trial for violation of Ordination vows and these Canons.

Priest or Deacon to be presented for trial.

Sec. 2. If a Priest or Deacon has substantially and materially abandoned the work of the ministry of this Church and the exercise of the office to which ordained without having given reasons satisfactory to the Bishop of the Diocese wherein the Priest or Deacon is canonically resident, or without renouncing the ministry as provided in Canon III.13 or without seeking to be released from the obligations of the office pursuant to Canon III.9.3(e), it shall be the duty of the Diocesan Review Committee of the Diocese, upon the case being brought to its attention by the written statement of the Bishop, to institute an inquiry into the matter. If in the judgment of the Diocesan Review Committee there is sufficient reason for further proceedings, it shall be the duty of the Diocesan Review Committee to Present the offending Priest or Deacon for Trial for violation of Ordination vows and these Canons.

Absent from Diocese for more than two years.

Sec. 3 (a) Whenever a Priest or Deacon of this Church shall have been absent from the Diocese for a period of more than two years and has failed to make the annual report required by Canon I.6.1, the Bishop shall bring the case to the attention of the Diocesan Review Committee by written statement, whereupon the Diocesan Review Committee may institute an inquiry into the matter. If in the judgment of the Diocesan Review Committee there is sufficient reason for further proceedings, the Diocesan Review Committee shall Present the offending Priest or Deacon for Trial for violation of Ordination vows and these Canons.

Special List of Clergy.

(b) On application either by the Bishop or Priest or Deacon, or at the discretion of the Presiding Bishop, with the approval of the Bishop of that jurisdiction, a Priest or Deacon now on the Special List of Clergy maintained by the Secretary of the House of Bishops may be placed again on a Diocesan Clergy Roll.

(c) A Priest or Deacon whose name remains upon the List of the Secretary of the House of Bishops shall not be considered as canonically resident in a Diocese.

(d) Any Priest or Deacon whose name is on the List, as aforesaid, and who has not made an annual report on the Priest or Deacon's exercise of office to the Presiding Bishop for a period of five years, may be considered to have abandoned the Ordained Ministry of this Church. The Presiding Bishop may, in the exercise of discretion, upon notice in accordance with Canon IV.14, in the presence of two Presbyters, pronounce Sentence of Deposition upon the Priest or Deacon, and authorize the Secretary of the House of Bishops to strike the name from the List and to give notice of the fact to the Priest or Deacon as provided in Canon IV.12.

Failure to make annual report.

(e) A Priest or Deacon whose name remains upon the List of the Secretary of the House of Bishops shall be Amenable for an Offense in either the Diocese wherein the Offense has occurred or the Diocese in which the Priest or Deacon was canonically resident immediately prior to being added to the List.

CANON 12: Of Sentences

Sec. 1 (a) The three Sentences which may be adjudged by a Trial Court and imposed are Admonition, Suspension, or Deposition.

Admonition.

(b) A Sentence of Admonition may be imposed (i) after the filing of a Waiver and Voluntary Submission under Canon IV.2, or (ii) after final Judgment by a Trial Court.

Suspension.

(c) (1) Sentence of Suspension may be imposed (i) after the acceptance of a Waiver and Voluntary Submission under Canon IV.2, or (ii) after final Judgment by a Trial Court.

(2) Whenever the Sentence of Suspension shall be adjudged and imposed on a Member of the Clergy, the Sentence shall specify on what terms and on what conditions and at what time the Suspension shall cease.

(3) The Suspension of a Priest from the exercise of the ordained ministry shall terminate the Pastoral Relationship unless (i) the Vestry by two-thirds vote requests of the Ecclesiastical Authority within thirty days that the relationship continue, and (ii) the Ecclesiastical Authority approves such request. If the Pastoral Relationship has not been terminated, religious services and sacramental ministrations shall be provided for that Parish as though a vacancy exists in the Office of the Rector. This Section shall not prohibit the application of Canon III.15.

Deposition.

(d) (1) A Sentence of Deposition may be imposed (i) after the acceptance of a Waiver and Voluntary Submission under Canon IV.2, (ii) after final Judgment by a Trial Court, (iii) when there has been a renunciation under Canon IV.8, (iv) upon the abandonment of the communion of the Church as set forth in Canons IV.9 and IV.10, or (v) by the Presiding Bishop pursuant to Canon IV.11.3(d).

(2) Upon the pronouncement of a Sentence of Deposition, all ecclesiastical offices held by the Member of the Clergy deposed, including a Rectorship and all ecclesiastical and

related secular offices, shall thereupon be automatically terminated and vacated.

(3) A Member of the Clergy deposed from any order of ordained ministry is deposed entirely from the ordained ministry.

Sec. 2. A Sentence after final Judgment by a Trial Court shall be adjudged by the Trial Court.

Conditions for adjudging and pronouncing Sentence.

Sec. 3. The Bishop shall both adjudge and pronounce Sentence upon a Priest or Deacon (i) after the acceptance of a Waiver and Voluntary Submission under Canon IV.2, (ii) when there has been a renunciation under Canon IV.8, or, (iii) upon the abandonment of the communion of the Church as set forth in Canon IV.10.

Who shall impose Sentence.

Sec. 4 (a) If a Priest or Deacon is liable to Sentence upon Judgment by a Trial Court or upon affirmance of the Judgment by a Court of Review, Sentence shall be imposed by the Bishop of the Diocese in which the original Trial of the Respondent was had, or in case that Bishop is disqualified or there be no Bishop of that jurisdiction, by another Bishop at the request of the Standing Committee of that Diocese.

(b) If a Priest or Deacon is liable to Sentence upon voluntary submission to discipline under Canon IV.2, Sentence shall be imposed by the Bishop to whom the submission was made.

(c) If a Priest or Deacon is liable to Sentence upon renunciation of the ministry of this Church under Canon IV.8, Sentence shall be imposed by the Bishop of the Diocese in which the Respondent is canonically resident, or in case there be no Bishop of that jurisdiction, by another Bishop at the request of the Standing Committee of the Diocese.

(d) If a Priest or Deacon is liable to Sentence upon abandonment of the communion of this Church under Canon IV.10, Sentence shall be imposed by the Bishop of the Diocese in which the Respondent is canonically resident, or in case there be no Bishop of that jurisdiction, by another Bishop at the request of the Standing Committee of the Diocese.

Opportunity for response.

Sec. 5. No Sentence shall be pronounced by a Bishop upon a Priest or Deacon after final Judgment by a Trial Court until an opportunity has been given to the Respondent, the Church Attorney, the Complainant and, unless waived in writing, the Victim to show cause why Sentence should not be pronounced and to offer any matter for the consideration of the Bishop.

Sec. 6. It shall be lawful for the Bishop to pronounce a lesser Sentence upon a Priest or Deacon than that adjudged by the Trial Court, if the Bishop so choose.

Time and place.

Sec. 7. The Bishop who is to pronounce Sentence upon a Priest or Deacon after final Judgment by a Trial Court shall appoint a time and place for pronouncing the Sentence and shall cause notice thereof in writing to be served upon the Respondent, the Church Attorney, each Complainant, and, unless waived in writing, the Victim in the manner provided in Canon IV.14.20.

In the presence of Priests.

Sec. 8. Sentence of Deposition imposed on a Priest or Deacon shall be pronounced in the presence of two or more Priests.

Sec. 9. When the Sentence is pronounced, the Bishop who pronounces it shall give notice thereof without delay in writing to every Member of the Clergy, each Vestry and the Secretary of the Convention and the Standing Committee of the Diocese in which the person so sentenced was canonically resident and in which the Sentence is pronounced, which shall be added to the official records of each Diocese; to the Presiding Bishop, to all other bishops of this Church, and where there is no Bishop, to the Ecclesiastical Authority of each Diocese of this Church; to the Recorder; to the Church Deployment Office; and to the Secretary of the House of Bishops, who shall deposit and preserve such notice among the archives of the House. The notice shall specify under what Canon the Priest or Deacon has been suspended or deposed.

Notice to be given.

Sec. 10. When a Bishop is liable to Sentence under a Judgment of a Trial Court or under a Judgment of a Court of Review of the Trial of a Bishop on an appeal to the Court of Review, the Sentence to be imposed shall be one of the Sentences specified in Canon IV.12.1, the Presiding Bishop to pronounce it, and the procedure to be followed in imposing Sentence shall be as provided in the several Canons governing the procedure of those Courts.

Pronouncing Sentence on a Bishop.

Sec. 11. In the case of the Suspension or Deposition of a Bishop, it shall be the duty of the Presiding Bishop to give notice of the Sentence to the Ecclesiastical Authority of every Diocese of this Church, to the Recorder, to the Church Deployment Office, and to the Secretary of the House of Bishops, and to all Archbishops and Metropolitans, and to all Presiding Bishops of Churches in communion with this Church.

Notice to be given.

Sec. 12. The Court for the Trial of a Bishop shall have the discretion to order that a Bishop: (i) convicted in a criminal Court of Record of a Crime involving immorality, (ii) against whom a judgment has been entered in a civil Court of Record in a cause involving immorality, or (iii) found to have committed an Offense upon a Presentment for a Crime, for Immorality, for holding and teaching publicly or privately, and advisedly, any doctrine contrary to that held by this Church, or for Conduct Unbecoming a Member of the Clergy shall not, on the conviction, the rendering of the judgment or the finding of commission of an Offense, and while the conviction, the judgment or the finding continues unreversed, perform any episcopal, or ministerial or canonical acts, except those that relate to the administration of the temporal affairs of the Diocese in which the Bishop holds jurisdiction or in which the Bishop is then serving.

Discretion of Court to Suspend acts of Bishop.

Administration of temporal affairs.

Sec. 13. The Suspension of a Bishop from the exercise of the episcopal office and ordained ministry shall not terminate any episcopal office held by that Bishop but may by its terms suspend episcopal, ministerial or canonical acts, except as relate to the administration of the temporal affairs of the Diocese of which the Bishop holds jurisdiction or in which the Bishop is then serving. The application of this Canon shall not affect the right to terminate the term of an assistant Bishop.

Suspension of a Bishop.

CANON 13: Of the Remission or Modification of Sentences

In case of a Bishop.

Sec. 1. The House of Bishops may remit and terminate any judicial Sentence which may have been imposed upon a Bishop, or modify the same so far as to designate a precise period of time, or other specific contingency, on the occurrence of which the Sentence shall utterly cease, and be of no further force or effect; *Provided*, that no such Remission or modification shall be made except at a meeting of the House of Bishops, during the session of some General Convention, or at a special meeting of the House of Bishops, which shall be convened by the Presiding Bishop on the application of any five Bishops, after three months' notice in writing of the time, place, and object of the meeting being given to each Bishop; *Provided, also*, that the Remission or modification be assented to by not less than a majority of the Bishops; And *provided*, that nothing herein shall be construed to repeal or alter the provisions of Canon IV.12.

Proviso.

In case of a Priest or Deacon.

Sec. 2 (a) A Bishop who deems the reasons sufficient may, with the advice and consent of two-thirds of All the Members of the Standing Committee, remit and terminate a Sentence of Suspension pronounced in that Bishop's jurisdiction upon a Priest or Deacon.

Conditions for granting remission.

(b) A Bishop who deems the reasons sufficient may also remit and terminate any Sentence of Deposition pronounced in the Bishop's jurisdiction upon a Priest or Deacon, but shall exercise this power only upon the following conditions:

(1) That the Remission shall be done with the advice and consent of two-thirds of All the Members of the Standing Committee;

(2) That the proposed Remission, with the reasons therefor, shall be submitted to the judgment of five of the Bishops of this Church whose Dioceses are nearest to the Bishop's own, and the Bishop shall receive in writing from at least four of the Bishops, their approval of the Remission, and their consent thereto.

(3) That before such Remission, the Bishop shall require the person so Deposed, who desires to be restored to the ordained ministry, to subscribe to the declaration required in Article VIII of the Constitution.

Applicant to be in lay communion.

Sec. 3. In case the person was deposed for abandoning the communion of this Church, or was deposed by reason of renunciation of or release from the exercise of the Office of Priest or Deacon, or for other causes, the person also having abandoned its communion, the Bishop before granting the Remission, shall be satisfied that the person has lived in lay communion with this Church for not less than one year next preceding application for the Remission.

Residence of applicant.

Sec. 4. In case the person applying for Remission shall be residing other than in the Diocese in which deposed, the Bishop to whom application has been made, before granting the Remission, shall be furnished with written evidence of the approval of the application with the reasons therefor from the Bishop of the Diocese in which the person is then residing.

Sec. 5. A Bishop who shall grant Remission for any Sentence of Removal or Deposition shall, without delay, give due notice thereof under the Bishop's own hand sending the notice in a sealed envelope to every Member of the Clergy, each Vestry, the Secretary of the Convention and the Standing Committee of the Diocese, which shall be added to the official records of the Diocese; to the Presiding Bishop, to all other Bishops of this Church, and where there is no Bishop, to the Ecclesiastical Authority of each Diocese of this Church; to the Recorder; to the Church Deployment Office; and to the Secretary of the House of Bishops and Secretary of the House of Deputies, who shall deposit and preserve the notice among the archives of those Houses giving, with the full name of the person restored, the date of the Removal or Deposition, and the Order of the Ministry to which that person is restored.

Bishop to give notice.

CANON 14: Of General Provisions Applicable to This Title

Sec. 1. Ecclesiastical Nature. Disciplinary proceedings under this Title are neither civil nor criminal, but ecclesiastical in nature and represent determinations by this Church of who shall serve as Members of the Clergy of this Church and further represent the polity and order of this hierarchical Church. Clergy who have voluntarily sought and accepted ordination in this Church have given their express consent and subjected themselves to the discipline of this Church and may not claim in proceedings under this Title constitutional guarantees afforded to citizens in other contexts.

Proceedings to be ecclesiastical.

Sec. 2. Resort to secular courts. No Member of the Clergy of this Church may resort to the secular courts for the purpose of interpreting the Constitution and Canons, or for the purpose of resolving any dispute arising thereunder, or for the purpose of delaying, hindering or reviewing or affecting in any way any proceeding under this Title.

Sec. 3. Review of proceedings by secular courts. No secular court shall have authority to review, annul, reverse, restrain or otherwise delay any proceeding under this Title.

Sec. 4. Limitations of Actions.

(a) (1) No Presentment shall be made for any Offense that constitutes Crime, Immorality, or Conduct Unbecoming a Member of the Clergy, unless the Offense was committed within, or continued up to, ten years immediately preceding the time of receipt of a Charge by the Diocesan Review Committee or the Presiding Bishop except:

Time limitations.

(i) in the case of a conviction of the Respondent in a criminal Court of Record or a judgment in a civil Court of Record in a cause involving immorality, a Presentment may be made at any time within three years after the conviction or judgment becomes final;

(ii) in a case where the alleged Victim was a minor at the time of the Offense, a Charge may be made at any time prior to the alleged Victim's attaining the age of twenty-five years; or

(iii) if an alleged Victim entitled to bring a Charge is otherwise under a disability at the time the Offense occurs, or

(iv) if the Offense is not discovered or its effects realized during the ten years immediately following the date of the Offense, the time within which the Charge shall be received by the Diocesan Review Committee shall be extended to two years after the disability ceases or the alleged Victim discovers or realizes the effects of the occurrence of the Offense; *Provided, however*, in the case of clauses (iii) or (iv) above, the time within which the Charge shall be received by the Diocesan Review Committee shall not be extended beyond fifteen years from the date the Offense was committed or continued.

(2) The time limits of this Section shall not apply to Offenses the specifications of which include physical violence, sexual abuse or sexual exploitation, if the acts occurred when the alleged Victim was a Minor.

(3) For Offenses, the specifications of which include physical violence, sexual abuse or sexual exploitation, which were barred by the 1991 Canon on Limitations (Canon IV.1.4). Charges may be made to a Standing Committee or the Presiding Bishop, in the case of a Bishop, no later than July 1, 1998.

(4) Except as provided in clauses (2) and (3) of this Section, these Limitations of Actions shall not be effective retroactively but shall be effective only from the effective dates of this Canon forward.

Time Limit.

(b) No Presentment shall issue for any Offense specified in Canon IV.1.1(c), (d), (e), (f), (g), (h) and (i) unless the Offense was committed within, or continued up to, two years immediately preceding the time the Charge is filed with the Diocesan Review Committee.

(c) Periods in which the Respondent is in the custody of secular authorities shall be excluded in computing the period of limitation prescribed in this Canon, if that custody would prevent the Respondent from participating in an Ecclesiastical Trial.

Request for Statement of Disassociation.

(d) The filing of a Request for a Statement of Disassociation under Canon IV.3.21 shall be the equivalent of filing a Charge for purposes of this Section for alleged violations of Canon IV.1.1(c) for holding and teaching publicly or privately, and advisedly, any doctrine contrary to that held by this Church and all other Offenses for which Presentment may be made pursuant to Canon IV.3.21(c).

Materiality.

Sec. 5. Materiality. In order for the Offenses specified in Canon IV.1.1. (d), (e), (f) and (g) to be considered for Presentment, the Offense complained of must be intentional, material and meaningful as determined by the Diocesan Review Committee or Review Committee.

Sec. 6. Time.

(a) Computation. In computing any period of time the day of the act or event from which the designated period of time begins to run shall not be included. The last day of the period shall be included, unless it is a Saturday, a Sunday or a legal holiday in that jurisdiction, in which event the period runs until the end of the next day which is not a Saturday, a Sunday or a legal holiday in that jurisdiction.

Computation of time.

(b) Additional Time after Service by Mail. Whenever a party has the right or is required to do an act within a prescribed period after the service of a notice or other paper, if service is served by mail, five days shall be added to the prescribed period.

Sec. 7. Quorum. In all cases in this Title where a Canon directs a duty to be performed or a power to be exercised, by a Diocesan Review Committee, by the Review Committee, by a Trial Court or by any other body consisting of several members, a majority of the members, the whole having been duly cited to meet, shall be a quorum; and a majority of the members present when a quorum exists shall be competent to act, unless otherwise expressly required by Canon.

Quorum.

Sec. 8 (a) Each Diocese shall appoint one or more Consultants and shall make a Consultant available to any Member of the Clergy canonically resident or residing in that Diocese charged with or suspected of an Offense. The Consultant shall be available to consult with and advise the Member of the Clergy and his or her legal advisors at reasonable times prior to the issuance of a Presentment. The Consultant shall explain the rights of the Member of the Clergy and the alternatives available under this Title.

Consultants.

(b) A Member of the Clergy shall be notified of the availability and identity of the Consultant at the earliest of (i) the communication to the Member of the Clergy of a Charge, (ii) any interrogation or request for a statement described in Canon IV.14.11(a), (iii) the service of a Temporary Inhibition, (iv) submission to the Ecclesiastical Authority or the Presiding Bishop of a Renunciation under Canon IV.8, or (v) prior to the Execution of a Waiver and Voluntary Submission to Discipline.

(c) Any communications between the Consultant and the Member of the Clergy, or his or her legal advisors shall be Privileged Communications.

(d) No Consultant shall be required to respond to any questions regarding the Member of the Clergy for whom the Consultant has acted as Consultant.

(e) All of the costs and expenses of providing a Consultant shall be the obligation of the Diocese exercising disciplinary jurisdiction over the Member of the Clergy.

Expenses.

Sec. 9. Influencing proceedings. No person subject to the authority of this Church may attempt to coerce or by any other means improperly influence, directly or indirectly, the actions of a Diocesan Review Committee, the Review Committee, an Ecclesiastical Trial Court, any other Court provided for in these Canons, or any member thereof or any person involved in such

Influencing proceedings.

proceedings in reaching the issuance of any Presentment or the findings, Judgment or Sentence of any Trial Court or any review thereof. The foregoing provisions shall not apply with respect to (i) statements and instructions given by the Church Attorney, the Respondent, or counsel for a Respondent to the Diocesan Review Committee prior to Presentment or to the Ecclesiastical Trial Court, or by Lay Assessors of any Court, (ii) sworn testimony or instruments submitted by witnesses or experts during the course of any disciplinary proceedings, or (iii) statements given by Complainants, alleged Victims or their Advocates as provided for in this Title.

Right to representation.

Sec. 10. In all proceedings under this Title, whenever a Respondent or Member of the Clergy suspected of an Offense is required or permitted to appear, the Respondent or Member of the Clergy shall have the right to be represented by counsel of her or his choice.

Involuntary Statements.

Sec. 11. Involuntary Statements.

(a) No person proceeding under the authority of this Title may interrogate, or request a statement from, a Respondent or a person suspected of an Offense without first informing that person of the nature of the accusation and advising that person that no statement need be made regarding the Offense of which the Respondent is accused or suspected and that any statement so made may be used in evidence against that person in any Ecclesiastical Trial.

(b) No Respondent or person suspected of an Offense may be compelled to make any statement or admission or to testify against himself or herself in any proceedings under this Title.

(c) No statement obtained from any person in violation of this Canon, or through the use of coercion, undue influence or improper inducement may be received in evidence against that person in a Trial under this Title.

(d) No Advocate shall be required to respond to any question regarding any Complainant or alleged Victim.

(e) No Consultant shall be required to respond to any question regarding any Respondent or any Member of the Clergy for whom the Consultant has acted as a Consultant.

Effect of Prior Proceedings.

Sec. 12. Effect of Prior Proceedings. A Member of the Clergy shall be liable for Presentment and Trial for an Offense set out in Canon IV.1.1. unless the specific accusation or Charge has previously been included in a Presentment against that Member of the Clergy or has been expressly set forth in the Member of the Clergy's Waiver and Voluntary Submission to Discipline upon which a Sentence has been imposed and pronounced or in the report of a Conciliator under Canon IV.16.4.

Conditions for disqualification.

Sec. 13. Disqualification of Bishop, Judge, or Member of a Review Committee.

(a) Any Bishop exercising authority as provided in this Title shall disqualify himself or herself in any proceeding in which the Bishop's impartiality may reasonably be questioned. The Bishop shall also disqualify himself or herself when the Bishop, the Bishop's spouse, or a person within the third degree of relationship to either of them, or the spouse of such person, (1) is the Respondent, alleged Victim, or Complainant, or (2) is likely to be a witness in the proceeding.

(b) Any member of any Diocesan Review Committee, Review Committee, or any Ecclesiastical Court provided for in this Title, shall disqualify himself or herself in any proceeding in which the member's impartiality may reasonably be questioned. The member shall also disqualify himself or herself when the member, the member's spouse, any person within the third degree of relationship to either of them, or the spouse of such person, (1) is the Respondent, alleged Victim, or Complainant, (2) is likely to be a witness in the proceeding, (3) has a personal bias or prejudice concerning the Respondent, alleged Victim, or Complainant, (4) has personal knowledge of disputed evidentiary facts concerning the proceeding, (5) has a personal financial interest in the outcome of the proceeding or in the Respondent, alleged Victim, Complainant, or any other interest that could be substantially affected by the outcome, or (6) is a member of the same congregation or otherwise has a close personal or professional relationship with the Respondent, any alleged Victim, Complainant, or any witness in the matter.

(c) No Bishop, Ecclesiastical Court, Diocesan Review Committee, or Review Committee shall accept from the parties to the proceeding any waiver of any ground for disqualification enumerated in this Section unless preceded by full disclosure of the basis for the disqualification, on the record, to all parties.

Sec. 14. Presumption of Non-Commission of an Offense. There is a presumption that the Respondent did not commit the Offense alleged until the presumption is overcome by Clear and Convincing evidence.

Sec. 15. Standard of Proof. The standard of proof required to establish an Offense by the Respondent by an Ecclesiastical Trial Court shall be that of Clear and Convincing evidence.

Proof.

Sec. 16. Burden of Proof. The burden of proof to establish an Offense by a Respondent is upon the Church in the Case of Bishops and the Diocesan Review Committee in the Case of Priests or Deacons.

Sec. 17. Duty to Appear, Respond and Give Testimony. Except as otherwise provided in this Title, it shall be the duty of all Members of this Church to appear and testify or respond when duly served with a Notice or Citation by a Diocesan Review Committee, Review Committee, or Ecclesiastical Trial Court in any matter arising under this Title.

Duty to appear.

Sec. 18. Roles of Chancellors, Vice Chancellors, etc. Neither the Chancellor nor a Vice Chancellor of the Diocese shall serve as Church Attorney or Lay Assessor in that Diocese. Neither the Chancellor nor a Vice Chancellor of any Province shall serve as Church Attorney or Lay Assessor in any Diocese including in such Province. The Presiding Bishop's Chancellor shall not serve as Church Attorney or Lay Assessor in any proceeding against a Bishop of this Church. The Church Attorney shall not

Roles of Chancellors.

be from the same law firm as the Chancellor or Vice Chancellor or as the Chancellor to the Presiding Bishop or as a Lay Assessor.

Jurisdiction.

Sec. 19. Jurisdiction. Bishops, Priests, and Deacons are Amenable for Offenses committed by them; a Bishop to a Court of Bishops, and a Priest or Deacon to the Ecclesiastical Authority of the jurisdiction in which the Priest or Deacon is canonically resident at the time the Charge is made or in which the Offense occurred, except as provided in Canon IV.11.3(e).

Notices and Citations.

Sec. 20. Service of Notices and Citations.

(a) A Notice or Citation permitted by any law of this Church to any Member to appear, at a certain time and place for the investigation of a Charge before a Diocesan Review Committee or Review Committee, for deposition in an Ecclesiastical Trial Court, or for a Trial of an Offense, shall be deemed to be duly served if a copy thereof be delivered to the person to be served, be left at the person's usual place of abode within the United States as to Members of the Clergy Canonically resident in the United States and non-Clergy Members resident in the United States, or as to Members of the Clergy Canonically resident or non-Clergy Members resident in countries or territories other than the United States at the place of abode within the country or territory of Canonical residence or residence, as the case may be, with a person of suitable age and discretion, or be mailed by certified mail return receipt requested to the person's usual place of abode within the United States or by similar mail service if mailed in a country other than the United States, at least sixty days before the day of appearance named therein, and in case the Member of the Clergy or non-Clergy Member has departed from the United States or other country or territory of Canonical residence or residence, as the case may be, and has not been duly served, if a copy of the Citation be published once a week for four successive weeks in such newspaper printed in the jurisdiction in which the Member of the Clergy or non-Clergy Member is cited to appear as the Diocesan Review Committee, Review Committee or Ecclesiastical Court shall designate, the last publication to be three months before the day of appearance. Acceptance of service will render unnecessary any further process of Citation.

(b) A notice or Citation, other than those above mentioned, required by any law of this Church, when no other mode of service is provided, may be served personally, or by certified mail return receipt requested, addressed to the person to be served, at the person's last known place of residence, or by leaving a copy at the person's last usual place of abode within the United States as to Members of the Clergy who are Canonically resident and non-Clergy Members who are resident in the United States, or at the person's last known usual place of abode in a country or territory other than the United States where the Member of the Clergy is Canonically resident or the non-Clergy Member resides, with a person of suitable age and discretion.

(c) A notice or Citation to appear may be issued by Diocesan Review Committee, Review Committee or Ecclesiastical Court.

Sec. 21. Bishops. A reference in this Title to a Bishop intending to mean the Bishop holding jurisdiction pursuant to Article II of the Constitution of this Church shall include a Bishop Coadjutor, if specific jurisdiction for matters contemplated by this Title has been assigned to the Bishop Coadjutor pursuant to Canon III.19.1(c).

Alternate Ecclesiastical Trial Court.

Sec. 22. Alternate Ecclesiastical Trial Court. In the event that a Diocese cannot convene an Ecclesiastical Trial Court due to vacancies, declinations to act, absences, resignations, challenges or otherwise or due to the determination by the Diocesan Review Committee for good cause shown that change in venue is needed, the Ecclesiastical Authority shall arrange for the Trial to be held by an Ecclesiastical Trial Court of another Diocese of that Province reasonably convenient for the parties. The reasonable expenses of the alternate Ecclesiastical Trial Court shall be the responsibility of the Diocese from which the Presentment has issued. If the person against whom the Charge or Complaint is made is a Member of the Diocesan Review Committee or if the Diocesan Review Committee is not able to consider a Charge or a Complaint, the Ecclesiastical Authority shall arrange to have the Charge or Complaint reviewed by the Diocesan Review Committee of another Diocese of that Province reasonably convenient to both parties.

Expenses.

Sec. 23. Expenses of Parties and Costs of Proceedings. Except as expressly provided in this Title, or applicable Diocesan canon, all costs, expenses and fees of the several parties shall be the obligation of the party incurring them. The record of proceedings of a Diocesan Ecclesiastical Trial Court shall be the expense of the Diocese. The record of proceedings of a Court of Review of a Trial of a Priest or Deacon shall be the expense of the Province. The record of proceedings of a Review Committee, the Court for the Trial of a Bishop and the Court of Review of a Trial of a Bishop shall be the expense of the General Convention. Nothing in this Title precludes the voluntary payment of a Respondent's costs, expenses and fees by any other party or person, including a Diocese.

Absence of Presiding Bishop.

Sec. 24. Absence, etc. of Presiding Bishop. If the Presiding Bishop should be absent, under a disability rendering the Presiding Bishop unable to act, or otherwise disqualified, except as expressly otherwise provided in this Title duties assigned to the Presiding Bishop under this Title shall be performed by that Bishop who would be the next qualified Presiding Officer of the House of Bishops.

Suspension.

Sec. 25. Effect of the Suspension of a Bishop. If the Bishop of a Diocese shall be subject to a Sentence of Suspension, the body or person who would be the Ecclesiastical Authority of that Diocese if there were no Bishop shall have authority to request episcopal assistance and Episcopal Acts from another Bishop of this Church.

Privileged Communications.

Sec. 26. Privileged Communications. No Privileged Communication shall be required to be disclosed. Further, the secrecy of a confession is morally absolute for the confessor, and must under no circumstances be broken.

Noncompliance.

Sec. 27. Non-compliance with any procedural requirements set forth in this Title shall not be grounds for the dismissal of any proceeding unless the non-compliance shall cause material and substantial injustice to be done or seriously prejudice the rights of a Respondent as determined by the Court on motion and hearing.

Sec. 28. Former Sentence of Removal. Solely for the purposes of the application of these Canons to persons who have received the pronouncement of the former Sentence of removal, the former Sentence of removal shall be deemed to have been a Sentence of Deposition.

Records to be kept and delivered to Archives.

Sec. 29. Record of Certain Title IV Proceedings and Actions.

(a) Each Ecclesiastical Court shall keep a complete and accurate record of its proceedings. When all proceedings on a Presentment or other matter have been concluded, including any and all appeals, the Presiding Judge shall certify the record. If the Presiding Judge did not participate in the proceeding for any reason, the Court, by majority vote, shall designate another member to certify the record.

(b) A Court may make provision for the preservation and storage of a copy of the record of each proceeding in the Diocese in which the Presentment or other proceeding originated.

(c) A Court shall promptly deliver the original certified record of its proceedings to The Archives of the Episcopal Church.

(d) A Bishop, including the Presiding Bishop, who pronounces a Sentence shall deliver a copy of the notice of the Sentence to The Archives of the Episcopal Church.

(e) In the case of a Waiver and Voluntary Submission to discipline of a Deacon, Priest or Bishop, the Ecclesiastical Authority with jurisdiction shall promptly deliver a copy of the required written instrument to The Archives of the Episcopal Church.

(f) Bishops, including the Presiding Bishop, shall promptly deliver a record of any action of remission or modification of a Sentence to The Archives of the Episcopal Church.

CANON 15: Of Terminology Used in This Title

Except as otherwise expressly provided or unless the context otherwise requires, as used in this Title the following terms and phrases shall have the following meanings:

Acknowledged shall mean the execution of an instrument in form sufficient to record a deed in the jurisdiction wherein the instrument has been executed.

Admonish shall mean to caution, advise or counsel against wrong practices or to warn against the danger of an Offense.

Admonition shall mean a censure or reprimand which is a public and formal reproof of the conduct of a Member of the Clergy.

Advocate shall mean a person, lay or clergy, designated to support and assist a Complainant or an alleged Victim in any proceeding contemplated by this Title. The Advocate need not reside in or be a member of the Diocese proceeding under this Title or of the Diocese of the person or body designating the person as Advocate.

All the Members shall mean the total number of members of the body provided for by Constitution or Canon without regard to absences, excused members, abstentions or vacancies.

Amenable shall mean subject, accountable, and responsible to the discipline of this Church.

Amenable for Presentment for an Offense shall mean that a reasonable suspicion exists that the individual has been or may be accused of the commission of an Offense.

Canonically resident shall mean the canonical residence of a Member of the Clergy of this Church established by ordination or letters dimissory.

Chancellor shall mean a person appointed or elected to that office in a Diocese, under its Canons or otherwise by the Ecclesiastical Authority, and shall include Vice Chancellors or similar legal officers of the Diocese. Chancellor shall also include the Presiding Bishop's Chancellor.

Charge shall mean a formal and Verified accusation against a Member of the Clergy that the Member of the Clergy has committed an Offense.

Church Attorney shall mean (i) as to proceedings concerning Priests and Deacons, a duly licensed attorney, appointed to investigate matters of ecclesiastical discipline on behalf of the Diocesan Review Committee, to represent the Church in the prosecution of Presentments against Priests and Deacons and to represent the Church in an appeal to the Court of Review of a Trial of a Priest or Deacon; (ii) as to proceedings concerning Bishops, a duly licensed attorney, appointed to investigate matters of ecclesiastical discipline on behalf of the Review Committee, to represent the Church in the prosecution of Presentments against Bishops and to represent the Church in an appeal to the Court of Review of a Trial of a Bishop pursuant to Canon IV.5.9, and appointed by the Presenters pursuant to Canon IV.5.13. The Church attorney's client shall be the Diocesan Review Committee or the Review Committee, as the case may be. The Church Attorney need not reside in or be a member of the Diocese proceeding under this Title.

Citation shall mean a written direction from a Diocesan Review Committee, Review Committee or Ecclesiastical Court to a member of this Church or person subject to the jurisdiction of this Church to appear and respond to a Diocesan Review Committee or Review Committee or give testimony before an Ecclesiastical Court.

Clear and Convincing shall mean proof sufficient to convince ordinarily prudent people that there is a high probability that what is claimed actually happened. More than a preponderance of the evidence is required but not proof beyond a reasonable doubt.

Clerk of the Court shall mean that person appointed by an Ecclesiastical Court to keep the account of proceedings of the Court. The Clerk of the Court need not reside in or be a member of the Diocese or Province of the Ecclesiastical Court appointing the Clerk of the Court.

Complainant shall mean the person or body by whom a Charge is made.

Conciliator shall mean an adult person, lay or clergy, appointed to seek the conciliation under Canon IV.16. The Conciliator need not reside in or be a member of the Diocese proceeding under Canon IV.16.

Conduct Unbecoming a Member of the Clergy shall mean any disorder or neglect that prejudices the reputation, good order and discipline of the Church, or any conduct of a nature to bring material discredit upon the Church or the Holy Orders conferred by the Church.

Consultant shall mean a priest, pastoral counselor, chaplain, an attorney-at-law or other person familiar with the procedures, alternatives, requirements and consequences of this Title and who is made available to a Member of the Clergy pursuant to Canon IV.14.8. The Consultant need not reside in or be a member of the Diocese proceeding under Canon IV.14.8.

Convention shall mean the governing body or assembly of a Diocese by whatever name it is styled in that Diocese.

Court of Record shall mean a secular civil or criminal court of the national government, a state, territory or other jurisdiction wherein the Diocese is located which keeps a separate record of a trial or issues its Judgment in writing sufficient on its face to state an Offense under this Title and as to be able to be certified or duly authenticated by the judge, justice, clerk or other appropriate officer of that court.

Crime shall mean a positive or negative act in violation of a penal law which embraces acts immoral or wrong in and of themselves. As used in this Title, Crime does not embrace acts or conduct prohibited by statute to which no moral turpitude attaches and constituting Crimes only because they are so prohibited.

Deposition shall mean a Sentence by which a Member of the Clergy is deprived of the right to exercise the gifts and spiritual authority of God's word and sacraments conferred at ordination.

Discipline The Discipline of the Church shall be found in the Constitution, the Canons, and the Rubrics and the Ordinal of the Book of Common Prayer.

Doctrine As used in this Title, the term Doctrine shall mean the basic and essential teachings of the church. The Doctrine of the Church is to be found in the Canon of Holy Scripture as understood in the Apostles' and Nicene Creeds and in the sacramental rites, the Ordinal and Catechism of the Book of Common Prayer.

Ecclesiastical Authority shall mean the Bishop of the Diocese or, if there be none, the Standing Committee or such other ecclesiastical authority established by the Constitution and Canons of the Diocese.

Ecclesiastical Court shall mean a court established under this Title.

Ecclesiastical Trial Court shall mean a Diocesan Court for the Trial of a Priest or Deacon established pursuant to Canon IV.4(A) and The Court for the Trial of a Bishop pursuant to Canon IV.5.1.

Federal Rules of Evidence shall mean the Federal Rules of Evidence for United States District Courts and Magistrates, Title 28 United States Code, as amended from time to time.

Godly Admonition: see **Pastoral Direction**.

Inhibition shall mean a written command from a Bishop that a Priest or Deacon shall cease from exercising the gifts of ordination in the ordained ministry as specified in the Inhibition. When an Inhibition is issued to a Bishop it may also command the Bishop to cease all episcopal, ministerial or canonical acts.

Judgment shall mean the determination by an Ecclesiastical Trial Court that a Respondent has or has not committed the Offense for which presented.

Lay Assessor shall mean a duly licensed attorney to advise in matters of law, procedure and evidence affecting a Court or Review Committee in its proceedings. The Lay Assessor need not reside in or be a member of the Diocese or Province of the Court the Lay Assessor advises.

Limitations of Actions shall mean the time within which a Charge must be filed with a Diocesan Review Committee in a matter concerning a Priest or Deacon or filed with the Presiding Bishop in a matter concerning a Bishop as provided for in Canon IV.14.4.

Member of the Clergy shall mean Bishops, Priests and Deacons of this Church unless the context shall exclude a Bishop.

Minor shall mean a person under the age of twenty-one years of age.

Offense shall mean any conduct or acts proscribed in Canon IV.1.1.

Pastoral Direction shall mean a written solemn warning from a Bishop to a Priest or Deacon setting forth clearly the reasons for the Pastoral Direction given in the capacity of pastor, teacher and canonical overseer, which is neither capricious or arbitrary in nature nor in any way contrary to the Constitution and Canons of the Church, national or diocesan, and directed to some matter which concerns the Doctrine, Discipline or worship of this Church or manner of life and behavior of the Priest or Deacon addressed, and shall be deemed to include without limitation admonition and Godly admonition.

Presentment shall mean the writing under Canon IV.3.21(c) or of a Diocesan Review Committee or Review Committee to an Ecclesiastical Trial Court that there are reasonable grounds to believe (i) an Offense has been committed which is triable, and (ii) the person named therein has committed it.

Presiding Bishop shall mean the Presiding Bishop of this Church or, if there be none or the then Presiding Bishop be absent or disabled, the presiding officer of the House of Bishops.

Privileged Communications shall mean (i) disclosures in confidence made by a person to a Member of the Clergy with the purpose of seeking religious counsel, advice, solace, absolution or ministration wherein the Member of the Clergy is acting in the capacity of spiritual advisor to the person, and where the person making the disclosures has a reasonable expectation that the communication will be kept in confidence, (ii) communications privileged under the law of the state or applicable federal law, (iii) such other privileged communications as are defined under the Federal Rules of Evidence, (iv) communications between an Advocate and a Complainant, alleged Victim, or Victim, (v) communications between a Consultant and a Respondent, and (vi) communications during the

Conciliation process between and among a Conciliator and the participants in a Conciliation; but not necessarily so in federal and state civil or criminal proceedings.

Reasonable Cause shall mean grounds sufficiently strong to warrant reasonable persons to believe that the Charge is true.

Record on Appeal shall mean such part of the Presentment, original papers and exhibits filed in the Trial Court, the transcript of proceedings, the Decision of the Trial Court and the Sentence adjudged and to be imposed, as may be designated by the parties pursuant to Rule 10 of the Federal Rules of Appellate Procedure.

Remission shall mean the forgiveness and termination of a Sentence imposed.

Reporter shall mean that person charged with the responsibility of taking the recording of the proceedings. The Reporter need not reside in or be a member of the Diocese or Province in which proceedings are held under this Title.

Respondent shall mean a Member of the Clergy charged with an Offense.

Restored or Restoration shall mean the act of a Bishop or the Presiding Bishop remitting and terminating a Sentence imposed and returning a Member of the Clergy to good standing in the order to which the Member of the Clergy was ordained.

Rules of Appellate Procedure shall mean the procedural rules for conducting an Appeal of an Ecclesiastical Trial Court Judgment as set forth in Appendix B.

Rules of Procedure shall mean the procedural rules for conducting an Ecclesiastical Trial as set forth in Appendix A, except as modified by express provision of this Title.

Sentence shall mean the sentence adjudged by an Ecclesiastical Court after a finding of a commission of an Offense or the lesser Sentence to be pronounced by a Bishop or the Presiding Bishop, as the case may be. The Sentence, whether Admonition, Suspension or Deposition, shall specify the Canon or Canons under which the action is being taken.

Standard of Proof shall mean that nature of proof required for a Judgment by an Ecclesiastical Court.

Summary Judgment of Offense shall mean the determination by an Ecclesiastical Trial Court that the Respondent has committed the Offense or Offenses described in the Presentment.

Suspension shall mean a Sentence by which the Member of the Clergy is directed to refrain temporarily from the exercise of the gifts of ministry conferred by ordination.

Temporary Inhibition shall mean that Inhibition authorized by Canon IV.1.

Trial shall mean an evidentiary proceeding before an Ecclesiastical Court pursuant to this Title.

Verification shall mean a signature before a notary public or similar person authorized to take acknowledgments of signatures on a document that states that the signer has personal knowledge or has investigated the matters set forth in the document and that they are true to the best of the signer's knowledge and belief.

Verified shall mean that an instrument contains a Verification.

Victim shall mean a person who has been, or is, or is alleged to be the object of acts of the Respondent.

Waiver and Voluntary Submission shall mean a written instrument containing the information required by this Title and Acknowledged by the person executing the same in accordance with Canon IV.2.2.

CANON 16: Of Conciliation of Disciplinary Matters

Conditions for conciliation.

Sec. 1. If the Ecclesiastical Authority or the Standing Committee, as the case may be, shall receive a complaint or Charge against a Priest or Deacon, or if the Presiding Bishop shall receive a complaint or Charge against a Bishop, which complaint or Charge on its face, if true, would constitute an Offense and the Ecclesiastical Authority or Standing Committee or Presiding Bishop, as the case may be, considers the complaint or Charge not to be a serious Offense against the Church and its good order and Discipline, but an interpersonal conflict not involving immorality or serious personal misconduct, or one that may be a technical commission of another Offense, the Ecclesiastical Authority or Standing Committee or Presiding Bishop may offer the persons involved the opportunity for conciliation in lieu of canonical proceedings seeking a Presentment.

Appointment of Conciliator.

Sec. 2. If all persons involved in the matter agree that conciliation is desirable and are willing for the matter to be conciliated, the Ecclesiastical Authority or the Standing Committee or the Presiding Bishop receiving the complaint or Charge shall appoint a Conciliator, who shall labor with those involved in the conflict that they may be reconciled.

Time periods.

Sec. 3. If the Conciliator is unable to achieve conciliation within a period of thirty (30) days, which may be extended by consent of all the participants to the conciliation for additional periods not to exceed a total of ninety (90) days from the date of the appointment of the Conciliator, the Conciliator shall refer the matter back to the appointing authority without recommendation for further proceedings under this Title.

Conciliator to report results.

Sec. 4. If conciliation is achieved, the Conciliator shall report back to the appointing authority with the results of the conciliation. The Conciliator's report shall be in writing, concisely state the allegations of the original complaint or Charge, state the terms, if any, and the results of the conciliation, which shall be agreed to, signed and Acknowledged by and between the participants in the conciliation.

RULES OF PROCEDURE OF THE ECCLESIASTICAL TRIAL COURTS AND THE COURT FOR THE TRIAL OF A BISHOP

Rule 1

These Rules of Procedure to the extent they are not inconsistent with provisions of Title IV, shall govern proceedings held in the Ecclesiastical Trial Courts. Such Courts may adopt further rules of procedure not inconsistent with the Constitution and Canons of this Church, with the power to alter or rescind the same from time to time, provided the same shall not cause material and substantial injustice to be done or seriously prejudice the rights of the parties.

Rule 2: Summons

(a) Form. The summons shall be signed by the Presiding Judge of the Court, identify the Court and the parties, be directed to the Respondent and state the name and address of the Church Attorney. It shall state the time within which the Respondent must file an Answer to the Presentment with the Court, and notify the Respondent that failure to do so will result in a Judgment that an Offense was committed by the Respondent and place the Respondent at risk for a Sentence to be pronounced at a later date. The Court may allow the Summons to be amended.

(b) Service. The service of the Summons and a copy of the Presentment shall be made in accordance with Canon IV.14.20. The Respondent may waive personal service in writing.

(c) Proof of Service. The person effecting service shall make proof of service by affidavit or sworn statement to the Court. If service is waived, the written waiver of service shall be filed with the Court.

Rule 3: Service and Filing of Pleadings and Other Papers.

Except as otherwise provided in these Rules, every pleading, paper, motion and notice required to be served on a party shall be served upon the attorney for the party unless otherwise ordered by the Court. Service upon the attorney or upon a party shall be made by delivering a copy to the attorney or party or by mailing it to the attorney or party at the attorney's or party's last known address. Service by mail is complete upon mailing. The filing of papers with the Court shall be made by filing them with the clerk of the Court unless otherwise directed by the Court.

Rule 4: General Rules of Pleading

(a) Presentment. The content of the Presentment shall conform to the applicable provisions of Canon 3 of this Title. It shall contain a short plain statement of the allegation of each Offense with reference to applicable provisions of Canon I of this Title, and a plain and concise statement of the facts upon which each allegation is made.

(b) Answer. The Answer shall state in short and plain terms the Respondent's defenses to each allegation of the Presentment, and shall admit or deny the factual allegations of the Presentment. If the Respondent is without knowledge or information sufficient to form a belief as to the truth of an allegation, the Respondent shall so state and this has the effect of a denial. Denials may also be made in part or with qualification.

(c) Style. Pleadings are to be direct and concise. No technical forms of pleadings or motions are required.

(d) Construction. All pleadings shall be so construed as to do substantial justice.

(e) Forms of Pleadings. Every pleading shall identify the name of the Court, name of the Respondent, and file number, if any. All allegations of fact or defense shall be made in separately numbered paragraphs. Exhibits may be attached and identified by reference within the pleading.

(f) Signature. All pleadings shall be signed by the attorney for the party on whose behalf it has been prepared, or the party if not represented by an attorney. Each paper shall state the signer's address and telephone number.

Rule 5: Defenses and Objections.

(a) When Presented. Unless a different time period is prescribed, a Respondent shall serve an Answer to the Presentment upon the Church Attorney and the Court within 30 days after being served a Summons and Presentment.

(b) How Presented. The following defenses may be asserted by motion: (1) Insufficiency of service or process, (2) lack of jurisdiction (3) failure to state the factual basis of an Offense; and (4) expiration of the applicable period of limitations as stated in Canon IV.14.4. The Respondent may also move for a more definite statement before filing an Answer if the Presentment is so vague or ambiguous that Respondent cannot reasonably be required to frame a responsive pleading.

Rule 6: Amended and Supplemental Pleadings.

The Court may, in the interest of justice, permit the filing of amended and supplemental pleadings.

Rule 7: Voluntary Disclosures, Discovery.

(a) Voluntary Disclosures. The Parties shall provide to each other and the Court not later than sixty days prior to trial a list of all the witnesses expected to testify at trial, including the name and address of each witness; and copies of all documents and exhibits intended for use at trial.

(b) The Parties may conduct discovery through written or oral depositions or written interrogatories. The Ecclesiastical Trial Court may limit the number, length and scope of depositions or interrogatories. The Respondent shall not be required to make any statement or admission against himself or herself in any discovery procedure.

Rule 8: Taking of Testimony.

In all trials, the testimony of witnesses shall be taken orally in open Court, unless otherwise provided by the Federal Rules of Evidence or other rules adopted by the Court. Such testimony shall be given under oath or solemn affirmation.

Rule 9: Summary Judgment of Offense.

(a) How Made. If the Respondent fails or refuses to Answer the Presentment or otherwise respond by motion, except for reasonable cause to be allowed by the Court, the Church Attorney may, no sooner than thirty days after the Answer is due, move with or without supporting affidavits for Summary Judgment of Offense. The Church Attorney shall file the motion with any supporting affidavits with the Court, serve a copy of the same on the Respondent, and provide copies to each Complainant and, unless waived in writing, the alleged Victim. The motion shall be served upon the Respondent at least twenty days before the time fixed by the Court for a hearing on the Motion.

(b) Opposing Affidavits. Respondent prior to the day of hearing may serve opposing affidavits upon the Court and Church Attorney, and shall provide copies of such affidavits to each Complainant and, unless waived in writing, the alleged Victim.

(c) Proceedings Thereon. The court shall convene a hearing to consider the Motion and may, in the Court's discretion, receive oral testimony. If the Presentment, together with affidavits, if any, and any oral testimony or other admissible evidence presented to the Court show that there is no genuine issue as to any fact material to a determination that the Respondent committed an Offense, the Court shall render Judgment on the matter of the Offense or Offenses described in the Presentment.

(d) Form of Affidavits. Supporting and opposing affidavits shall be made on personal knowledge, shall set forth such facts as would be admissible in evidence, and shall show affirmatively that the affiant is competent to testify as to the matters stated in the affidavit. Copies of papers referred to in an affidavit shall be attached to and served with the affidavit.

(e) Defense Required. When a motion is made and supported as provided in this rule, the opposing party may not rest upon mere allegations or denials of the adverse party's pleading but must, by affidavits or otherwise provided in this rule, set forth specific facts to show that there is a genuine issue for Trial.

FEDERAL RULES OF CIVIL APPELLATE PROCEDURE

(as modified and adopted for use in the administration of Title IV, The Canons of the Protestant Episcopal Church in the United States)

Rule 1. Scope of Rules. These rules govern procedure in appeals to Courts of Review as provided in Canon IV.4.46 and Canon IV.6.13. Courts of Review shall, in addition to these rules, be guided by the Federal Rules of Appellate Procedure.

Rule 2. Suspension of Rules. [FRAP 2 as written.]

Rule 10. The Record of Appeal.

(d) Agreed Statement as the Record on Appeal. In lieu of the Record on Appeal as defined in subdivision (a) of this rule, the parties may prepare and sign a statement of the case showing how the issues presented by the appeal arose and were decided by the Trial Court and setting forth only so many of the facts averred and proved or sought to be proved as are essential to a decision of the issues presented. If the statement conforms to the truth, it, together with such additions as the Court may consider necessary fully to present the issues raised by the appeal, shall be approved by the Trial Court and shall be transmitted to the Court of Review as the Record on Appeal.

(e) Correction or Modification of the Record on Appeal. Any dispute as to whether the Record on Appeal truly discloses what occurred in the Trial Court shall be addressed to and resolved by the Trial Court.

Rule 25. Filing and Service.

(a) Filing. A paper required or permitted to be filed in the Court of Review must be filed with the Clerk of the Court of Review. Filing may be accomplished by mail addressed to the Clerk. Filing is not timely unless the Clerk receives the papers within the time fixed for filing, except that briefs and appendices are treated as filed when mailed. A Court of Review may permit filing by facsimile or other electronic means.

(b) Service of All Papers Required. [FRAP 25(b) as written.]

(c) Manner of Service. [FRAP 25(c) as written.]

(d) Proof of Service. [FRAP 25(c) as written, substituting "Rule 25(a)" for "Rule 25(a)(2)(B)"]

Rule 26. Computation and Extension of Time . [FRAP 26 as written, substituting "Court of Review" for "Court of Appeals" and deleting the second sentence of subdivision (b)]

Rule 28. Briefs.

(a) Appellant's Brief. The brief of the appellant must contain, under appropriate headings and in the order here indicated:

(1) A table of contents with page references, and a table of cases, canons or authorities with page references.

(2) A statement of the issues presented for review.

(3) A statement of the case, including a description of the course of proceedings and a statement of the facts relevant to the

issues presented for review, with appropriate references to the record.

(4) A brief summary of the argument.

(5) An argument. The argument must contain the contentions of the appellant on the issues presented and the reasons therefor, with citations to the authorities and parts of the record relied on.

(6) A short conclusion stating the precise relief sought.

(b) Appellee's Brief. The brief of appellee must conform to the requirements of paragraphs (a)(1), (4), (5), and (6)

(c) Reply Brief. Appellant may file a brief in reply to the brief of appellee, and if the appellee has cross-appealed, the appellee may file a brief in reply to the response of the appellant to the issues presented in the cross-appeal. All reply briefs shall contain a table of contents and a table of authorities cited with page references.

(g) Length of Briefs. Except by permission of the Court of Review, principal briefs shall not exceed fifty (50) pages and reply briefs must not exceed twenty-five (25) pages exclusive of pages containing the table of contents, table of authorities, proof of service and any addendum.

Rule 29. **Brief of an Amicus Curiae**. A brief of an amicus curiae may be filed only by leave of the Court of Review granted on motion or at the request of the Court. A motion of an amicus curiae to participate in the oral argument will be granted only for extraordinary reasons.

Rule 30. **Appendix to the Briefs**. The appellant must prepare and file an appendix to the briefs containing (1) any relevant portions of the pleadings or presentment; (2) the decision or opinion in question; and (3) any other parts of the record to which the parties wish to direct the particular attention of the Court of Review. The appendix must be filed with the brief, unless an extension is granted by the Court of Review.

Rule 32. **Forms of Briefs, the Appendix and Other Papers**. Briefs, appendices and other papers filed with the Court of Review may be produced by standard typographic printing or by any duplicating or copying process which produces a clear black image on white paper. All printed matter must appear in at least 11 point type on unglazed, white paper, and shall be bound in volumes having pages not exceeding 8 1/2 by 11 inches, typed matter must be double spaced, with numbered pages. The front cover shall contain (1) the name of the court; (2) caption of the case; (3) nature of the proceedings in the court; (4) title of the document; and (5) the names and addresses of counsel representing the party on whose behalf the document is filed.

Rule 34. **Oral Argument**.

(a) In General. Oral argument, if requested, shall be allowed in all appeals.

(b) Notice of Argument. The Presiding Judge of the Court of Review shall provide at least thirty (30) day's written notice of the time and place of oral argument to all parties to the appeal.

(c) Order and Content of Argument. The hearing of oral argument shall proceed with the argument of appellant, argument of appellee, and rebuttal by appellant. Additional opportunities to present argument may be afforded by the Court so long as the appellant receives the final opportunity to speak. During the oral argument, the Court may address questions to any participant in the oral argument, but shall not receive any evidence not contained in the Record of Appeal.

TITLE V
GENERAL PROVISIONS

CANON 1: Of Enactment, Amendment, and Repeal

Sec. 1. No new Canon shall be enacted, or existing Canon be amended or repealed, except by concurrent Resolution of the two Houses of the General Convention. Such Resolution may be introduced first in either House, and shall be referred in each House to the Committee on Canons thereof, for consideration, report, and recommendation, before adoption by the House; *Provided*, that in either House the foregoing requirement of reference may be dispensed with by a three-fourths vote of the members present.

Procedure required.

Sec. 2. Whenever a Canon is amended, enacted, or repealed in different respects by two or more independent enactments at the same General Convention, including the enactment of an entire Title, the separate enactments shall be considered as one enactment containing all of the amendments or enactments, whether or not repealed, to the extent that the change made in separate amendments or enactments, are not in conflict with each other. The two members of the Committee on Canons from each House of General Convention appointed pursuant to Canon V.1.5(a) shall make the determination whether or not there is a conflict and certify the text of the single enactment to the Secretary.

Separate enactments effecting the same Canon, how treated.

Sec. 3. Whenever a Canon which repealed another Canon, or part thereof, shall itself be repealed, such previous Canon or part thereof shall not thereby be revived or reenacted, without express words to that effect.

Sec. 4. If a Canon or Section of a Canon or Clause of a Section of a Canon is to be amended or added, the enactment shall be in substantially one of the following forms: "Canon . . . (Canon, Section or Clause designated as provided in Canon V.2.3) . . . is hereby amended to read as follows: (here insert the new reading)"; or "Canon . . . (Canon or Section designated as provided in Canon V.2.3) . . . is hereby amended by adding a Section (or Clause) reading as follows: (here insert the text of the new Section or Clause)." If amendments are to be made at one meeting of the General Convention to more than one-half of the Canons in a single Title of the Canons, the enactment may be in the following form: "Title . . . of the Canons is hereby amended to read as follows: (here insert the new reading of all Canons in the Title whether or not the individual Canon is amended)." In the event of insertion of a new Canon, or a new Section or Clause in a Canon, or of the repeal of an existing Canon, or of a Section or Clause, the numbering of the Canons, or of a division of a Canon, which follow shall be changed accordingly without the necessity of enacting an amendment or amendments to that effect.

Form of amendment.

Sec. 5 (a) The Committee on Canons of each House of the General Convention shall, at the close of each regular meeting of the General Convention, appoint two of its members to certify the changes, if any, made in the Canons, including a correction of the references made in any Canon

Certification of changes.

to another, and to report the same, with the proper arrangement thereof, to the Secretary, who shall publish them in the Journal.

(b) The Committee on Constitution of each House of the General Convention shall, at the close of each regular meeting of the General Convention, appoint a similar committee of two of its members to certify in like manner the changes, if any, made in the Constitution, or proposed to be made therein under the provisions of Article XII of the Constitution, and to report the same to the Secretary, who shall publish them in the Journal. The committee shall also have and exercise the power of renumbering of, and correction of references to, Articles, Sections and Clauses of the Constitution required by the adoption of amendments to the Constitution at a meeting of the General Convention in the same manner as provided with respect to the Canons in the foregoing Sections 4 and 5(a) of this Canon.

When Canons take effect.

Sec. 6. All Canons enacted during the General Convention of 1943, and thereafter, and all amendments and repeals of Canons then or thereafter made, unless otherwise expressly ordered, shall take effect on the first day of January following the adjournment of the General Convention at which they were enacted or made.

CANON 2: Of Terminology Used in These Canons

Use of the term Diocese.

Sec. 1. Whenever the term "Diocese" is used without qualification in these Canons, it shall be understood to refer both to "Dioceses" and to "Missionary Dioceses," as these terms are used in the Constitution, and also, whenever applicable, to the "Convocation of the American Churches in Europe."

Use of the term Canon.

Sec. 2. Whenever in these Canons a reference is made to a Canon or a Section of a Canon or a Clause of a Section of a Canon, the word "Canon" shall be set out, followed in order by the numerical or alphabetical designation of the Title, the Canon, the Section and the Clause, in each case separated by a period.

CANON 3: Of a Quorum

Sec. 1. Except where the Constitution or Canons of the General Convention provide to the contrary, a quorum of any body of the General Convention consisting of several members, the whole having been duly cited to meet, shall be a majority of said members; and a majority of the quorum so convened shall be competent to act.

CANON 4: Of Vacancies on Canonical Bodies

Causes for removal.

Sec. 1 (a) Except where the Constitution or Canons of the General Convention provide to the contrary, the term of a member in any body of the General Convention consisting of several members shall become vacant as follows:

(1) upon absence from two regularly scheduled meetings of the body between successive regular meetings of the General Convention unless excused by the body;

(2) upon Inhibition, Admonition, Suspension, or Deposition of a Member of the Clergy then serving on the body;
(3) upon the renunciation of the ministry of this Church by a Member of the Clergy;
(4) upon the certification to the Presiding Bishop by the Advisory Committee as to the abandonment of the communion of this Church by a Bishop pursuant to Canon IV.9;
(5) upon the certification by the Standing Committee as to the abandonment of the communion of this Church by a Priest or Deacon pursuant to Canon IV.10; or
(6) for cause deemed sufficient by a two-thirds vote of all the members of the body.

Vacancies due to change in status.

(b) The term of any member specified to be filled by a Priest or Deacon shall become vacant upon that member's ordination to the episcopacy.

(c) The term of any Member of the Clergy specified to be filled by virtue of a provincial or diocesan canonical residence shall become vacant upon the change of canonical residence to another diocese or to a diocese in a different province, as the case may be.

(d) The term of any Lay Person specified to be filled by virtue of a provincial or diocesan residence shall become vacant upon the change of residence to another diocese or to a diocese in a different province, as the case may be.

Section 2 (a) The position of a lay member becomes vacant upon loss of status as a communicant in good standing.

(b) The position of any member specified to be filled by a lay person shall become vacant upon that member's ordination.

RULES OF ORDER
HOUSE OF BISHOPS

SERVICES AND DEVOTIONS

I As an indication of our humble dependence upon the Word and Spirit of God, and following the example of primitive Councils, a copy of the Holy Scriptures shall always be reverently placed in view at all meetings of this House.

Placement of Holy Scriptures.

II On each day of the Session of the House, the meeting shall be opened with prayer and the reading of the Holy Scriptures.

Opening devotions.

III At the hour of noon on each day of the Session, there shall be a devotional service, including prayers for the Church in its mission, as provided for in the Book of Common Prayer.

Noonday prayers.

IV The last session of the House shall be closed with the Benediction pronounced by the Bishop presiding.

Close of daily session.

V At every session of the House of Bishops there shall be a daily celebration of the Holy Eucharist at such time and place as the Presiding Bishop or Vice-Chair of the House shall appoint.

Holy Eucharist.

VI Preceding the balloting for the election of a Presiding Bishop, of a Missionary Bishop, or on the proposed transfer of a Missionary Bishop from one Diocese to another, there shall be a celebration of the Holy Eucharist, with a special prayer for the guidance of the Holy Spirit.

VII The opening service of the General Convention and selection of the Preacher shall be in charge of the Presiding Bishop, the Vice-Chair of the House of Bishops, and the Bishop of the Diocese wherein the Convention is to be held. The sermon shall be delivered by the Presiding Bishop, unless the Presiding Bishop shall elect to appoint some other Bishop as Preacher.

Opening Service of General Convention.

FIRST DAY OF SESSION

I The House of Bishops shall meet for business at such time and place as shall have been duly notified by the Presiding Bishop, or the Vice-Chair of the House, to the members of this House, and shall be called to order by the Presiding Bishop or the Vice-Chair, or, in their absence, by the Senior Bishop present.

Call to order.

II The House shall then proceed to elect a Secretary if the office is vacant; and the person elected shall serve until the end of that meeting of the Convention. At the end of each meeting of the Convention, the House shall proceed to elect a Secretary who shall continue in office until the conclusion of the triennial meeting of the Convention following that election. With the approval of the Presiding Officer, the Secretary may then, or later, appoint Assistant Secretaries.

Secretary and Assistant Secretaries.

Roll.

III The roll of members shall be called by the Secretary. On the second and third days the Secretary shall make a note of the late arrivals who shall inform the Secretary of their presence.

Minutes.

The minutes of the last meeting shall then be read by the Secretary and acted on by the House. Such reading may be dispensed with by a majority vote of the House.

Presentation of new Bishops.

IV Bishops appearing in the House for the first time after their Consecration shall then, or at such other time at that meeting appointed by the Presiding Bishop, be presented to the President in a manner prescribed by the Presiding Bishop.

Memorials.

V At a time deemed suitable, the Presiding Bishop shall then announce, without word or comment, the fact and the date of the death of any members who have died since the last preceding meeting; after which the House shall be led in prayer.

Vice-Chair.

VI The House shall then proceed to elect a Vice-Chair, if the office is then vacant, after hearing the report of the nominating committee of the House and after receiving any other nominations from the floor; and the person elected shall serve until the conclusion of that meeting. At the conclusion of each meeting of the Convention, the House, using the same procedure, shall proceed to elect a Vice-Chair who shall continue in office until the conclusion of the triennial meeting of the Convention following that election. The Vice-Chair, in the absence of the Presiding Bishop, or at the request of the Presiding Bishop, shall be the Presiding Officer of the House. In the absence of the Vice-Chair, the Presiding Bishop may ask another member of the House to preside.

DAILY ORDERS

Regular order of business.

I The regular order of business of the House shall be as follows:

(1) Devotions.
(2) Roll call or late registrations.
(3) Minutes of the previous meeting.
(4) Presentation of new members.
(5) Communications from the Presiding Bishop.
(6) Report of the Committee on Dispatch of Business.
(7) Petitions and Memorials.
(8) Messages from the House of Deputies not yet disposed of.
(9) Motions of Reference.
(10) Reports of Legislative Committees in the order in which the Committees are named in General Rule I.
(11) Reports of Commissions.
(12) Reports of Special Committees.
(13) Miscellaneous business.

Special order of business.

II At any Special Meeting of the House, the Secretary shall present the Official Call for such meeting and incorporate such Call in the Minutes. The order of business at any Special Session shall be as follows:

(1) Call to order.
(2) Devotions.
(3) Roll call.
(4) Presentation of new members.
(5) Communications from the Presiding Bishop.
(6) The special Business of the Meeting.
(7) Reports of Special Committees.
(8) Reading of the Minutes.
(9) Adjournment.

III On the second day of the Session, after Devotions, the Presiding Bishop shall lay before the House a statement of official acts during the recess of the General Convention.

Official acts of Presiding Bishop.

IV On the days when the House of Bishops is expected to meet with the House of Deputies and others in Joint Session, the first order of business shall be the consideration of such matters as the Committee on Dispatch of Business shall report as urgently demanding attention. Then shall follow consideration of Messages from the House of Deputies not disposed of, Reports from Standing Committees, and other business for which time shall remain. If the Joint Session shall adjourn before the customary hour for adjournment of the House of Bishops, the House shall resume its sitting. Any part of this rule may be suspended by a majority vote.

Order of business on days when Joint Session is to be held.

V The Secretary shall keep a Calendar of Business, on which shall be placed, in the order in which they are presented, Reports of Committees, Resolutions which lie over, and other matters undisposed of, indicating the subject of each item.

Calendar of Business.

VI The Secretary shall also keep a Consent Calendar, which shall be published daily and distributed to the members before the convening of the House on each legislative day, and designate it as a separate calendar. Matters shall be listed on the Consent Calendar in separate groupings according to the date that they have been placed thereon. All matters to which amendments have been proposed by a Committee shall be so designated. No debate is in order regarding any matter appearing on the Consent Calendar. However, the President shall allow a reasonable time for questions from the floor and answers to those questions. No amendment other than an amendment contained in a Committee report is in order regarding any matter on the Consent Calendar. Any amendments contained in Committee reports on such matters shall be deemed adopted unless the matter is objected to and removed from the Consent Calendar. Immediately prior to a vote on the first matter on the Consent Calendar the President shall call to the attention of the members the fact that the next vote will be on the first matter pending on the Consent Calendar. Matters appearing on the Consent Calendar shall be taken up immediately following the noon recess of the next legislative day following their placement on the Consent Calendar, or otherwise by unanimous consent or by adoption of a special order of business. A matter may be placed on the Consent Calendar by report of a legislative Committee, if the Committee vote to report the

Consent Calendar.

matter with a recommendation for adoption, with or without amendments, or for discharge, or for rejection was by three-quarters (3/4) of the members present and if the Committee recommends placement of the matter on the Consent Calendar. Prior to a vote on final passage of any matter appearing on the Consent Calendar, it shall be removed from the Consent Calendar if (1) any three Bishops, or (2) the sponsor of the matter, or (3) the Committee on Dispatch of Business files with the Secretary written objections to the presence of the matter on the Consent Calendar. Any matter so removed may not be placed thereafter on the Consent Calendar but shall be restored to the Daily Calendar. Any matter removed from the Consent Calendar, to which amendments have been proposed by a Committee, shall stand on the Daily Calendar in its original, unamended form, and amendments shall be treated as if the matter had never been on the Consent Calendar.

Order of Day.

VII The Order of the Day shall be taken up at the hour appointed, unless postponed by a two-thirds vote of those present and voting.

Visiting Bishops.

VIII Bishops invited to honorary seats may be introduced by the Presiding Officer whenever no other business occupies the House.

GENERAL RULES FOR MEETINGS OF THIS HOUSE

Legislative Committees.

I Committees shall be appointed by the Presiding Officer of the House unless otherwise ordered. The Presiding Bishop shall name the members of all the Committees of this House annually, and shall designate the Chair of each Committee. The Chair shall appoint a Vice-Chair and a Secretary; and if the Chair should leave the Convention or the House of Bishops early, the Secretary of the House shall be notified. The Presiding Bishop may refer to Committees of this House, for their consideration, matters which arise and which should receive consideration at the next meeting of the House. The Standing Committees, to be announced not later than the third day of the session, may be as follows:

(1) Dispatch of Business.
(2) Certification of Minutes.
(3) Rules of Order, of which the Presiding Bishop shall be a member, *ex officio*.
(4) Constitution.
(5) Canons.
(6) Structure,
(7) Consecration of Bishops
(8) World Mission.
(9) National and International Concerns
(10) Social and Urban Affairs
(11) Church in Small Communities
(12) Evangelism
(13) Prayer Book, Liturgy and Church Music.
(14) Ministry.
(15) Education

(16) Church Pension Fund.
(17) Stewardship and Development.
(18) Ecumenical Relations.
(19) Communications.
(20) Miscellaneous Resolutions.
(21) Privilege and Courtesy.
(22) Committees and Commissions.
(A) Pastoral Letter.
(B) Resignation of Bishops.
(C) Religious Communities.
(D) On Nominations and Elections.

In addition, the Presiding Bishop shall appoint a Legislative Committee on Admission of New Dioceses if such legislation will be presented to the Convention.

II No Memorial, Petition, or Address shall come before this House unless presented by the Presiding Officer of the House, or some other Bishop present.

Distribution of printed matter.

III Nothing other than Reports and other documents printed for the use and by the order of the House, except the private correspondence of its members, shall be distributed in the House without having first been entrusted to the Secretary, and submitted to the approval of the Presiding Officer.

Resolutions and motions.

IV All Resolutions shall be reduced to writing, and no motion shall be considered as before the House until seconded. In all cases where a Resolution seeks to amend a Canon or an entire Title of Canons, the form of Resolution submitted shall set out the enactment in the form prescribed by Canon V.1, shall include with a dash overstrike on each letter any words which are deleted by the amendment and shall underline any words which are added by the amendment; *Provided*, that if the amendment of an entire Title is to be covered by one enactment under Canon V.1.4, the deleted text and the underlining of the next text need not be included but the proponent shall make adequate written explanation of the changes.

Limitations.

All resolutions of Bishops shall be proposed by one Bishop and be endorsed by not less than two additional Bishops, all three being from different dioceses. Individual Bishops shall be limited to proposing not more than three resolutions.

Rules of debate.

V Members in discussion shall address the Chair, and shall confine themselves to the Question in debate. No member shall speak more than twice in the same debate without leave of the House. At the conclusion of any speech, the Presiding Officer alone, or any member of the House, may call for a vote, without debate, on a proposal for a recess of conference to define and clarify the issues of the debate and the way in which the House is working. If the proposal of a member is supported by at least four other members, it is to be put to a vote. If passed by a two-thirds vote of those present and voting, members of the House will form small groups for a ten-minute conference, at the end of which debate will resume with any speakers who had already been recognized at the time of the motion for conference.

VI Officers of the House of Bishops, when addressing the House in debate, shall in all cases do so from the floor of the House.

Division.

VII When a division is called for, every voting member present shall be counted. When, in such procedure, the vote of the Presiding Officer produces a tie, the motion shall be considered as lost.

On any question before the House the ayes and nays may be required by any six voting members, and shall in such cases be entered on the Journal.

Ballot.

VIII When it is proposed to give consent to the consecration or confirmation of a Bishop-elect, or of a Bishop Coadjutor-elect, or of a Bishop-elect Suffragan, it shall be competent for any six voting members of the House to call for a vote by ballot.

IX The Secretary shall prepare a ballot for each election listing alphabetically the names of all persons nominated. On each ballot, each voting member shall vote for the number of nominees to be or remaining to be elected, and any ballot with votes less than or in excess thereof shall be void. The nominees receiving the largest number of votes shall be deemed elected, provided that votes equal to or in excess of a majority of the ballots cast on any ballot shall be required for election.

Precedence of motions.

X When a Question is under consideration, the following motions shall have precedence in the order listed: to lay upon the table, to postpone to a time certain, to commit or to refer, to substitute another motion dealing with the same Question, to amend, or to postpone indefinitely; *Provided*, that, in consideration of a message from the House of Deputies, the provisions of Rules XXI and XXII shall apply, and a motion made thereunder for a Committee of Conference shall have precedence; and *Provided, further*, that a proposal for a Recess of Conference shall always be in order, under the conditions set forth in Rule V.

Committee of the Whole.

XI On motion duly put and carried, the House may resolve itself into a Committee of the Whole, at which no records shall be made of its action. On separate motion duly put and carried, those present at such sessions may be limited to members of the House.

Executive Session.

XII On motion duly put and carried, the House may go into Executive Session, at which only members of the House shall be present. The Chair of the Committee on Dispatch of Business shall act as clerk and make a record of all motions adopted.

Reports of Committees.

XIII (a) Reports of Committees shall be in writing, and shall be received in due course. Reports recommending or requiring any action or expression of opinion by the House shall be accompanied by specific Resolutions.

(b) At the conclusion of each meeting of a Committee, its Chair shall prepare, or cause to be prepared, in triplicate, on forms provided for the purpose, a separate report with regard to each matter upon which the Committee took final action during the meeting. Each such report shall be in the following alternative form:

Committee recommendations.

(1) Recommends adoption, with or without amendments, in which case the question shall be on the adoption of the Resolution, or the Resolution as amended.

(2) Recommends rejection, with or without reasons, in which case the question shall be on the adoption of the Resolution, notwithstanding the recommendation of the Committee for rejection.

(3) Recommends that it be discharged from further consideration of the Resolution because

- (i) the matter is not within the scope of the Committee's function, in which case it may recommend referral to an appropriate Committee;
- (ii) the matter has already been dealt with by action of the House at this meeting of the General Convention; or
- (iii) the matter is covered by a Resolution of a prior General Convention; or
- (iv) for other reasons.

(4) Recommends referral to a Standing Committee to study the theological, ethical and pastoral questions inherent in the subject or to develop recommendations and strategies on the subject which will be of concrete assistance to this Church or to study or make recommendations concerning the subject.

(5) Recommends concurrence, with or without amendment, with House of Deputies Message.

(6) Recommends non-concurrence with House of Deputies Message.

(c) Each report shall be dated, signed by the Chair or Secretary of the Committee, and transmitted to the office of the Secretary of the House, who shall endorse thereon the date of receipt thereof. If there is a minority position in the Committee and a minority spokesperson requests a minority report, the Chair shall include the same in the report.

Report to be signed.

Any resolution which involves an amendment to the Constitution or Canons shall be referred to the appropriate Legislative or Special Committee for action and simultaneously to the Committee on Constitution or the Committee on Canons, as the case may be, and such Committee shall make certain that the Resolution is in proper constitutional or canonical form, achieves consistency and clarity in the Constitution or Canons, and includes all amendments necessary to effect the proposed change, and shall promptly communicate its recommendations to the Legislative or Special Committee. In such case the Committee shall neither concern itself with, nor report on, the substance of the matter referred to it, but whenever requested to do so by the Presiding Officer of the House, the Committee shall in its report to the House make recommendations as to substance.

Amendments to Constitution or Canons to be in proper form.

Review by Program, Budget and Finance.

(d) Before final consideration, by the House, the Joint Standing Committee on Program, Budget and Finance (PB&F) shall have been informed by the Committee considering any proposed action which, if adopted by General Convention, would require an appropriation of funds and PB&F shall have acknowledged receipt of such information by endorsement on the committee report or by other appropriate means. Implementation of any such resolution is subject to funding in the budget.

Reports of Interim Committees.

XIV Reports of Committees appointed to sit during the recess, if not acted upon at once, shall, when presented, be made the Order of the Day for a time fixed. Printed Committee Reports which have been delivered to, and circulated among, the members of the House of Bishops, in advance of the making of such Reports upon the floor of the House, shall be presented by title and the Chair or Committee member presenting said Report shall be allowed five minutes for summarizing the same, which time may be extended only by a two-thirds vote of those present and voting.

Questions of order.

XV All questions of order shall be decided by the Chair without debate, but appeal may be taken from such decision. The decision of the Chair shall stand unless overruled by a two-thirds vote of those present and voting. On such appeal, no member shall speak more than once without express leave of the House.

Amendments.

XVI Amendments shall be considered in the order in which they are moved. When a proposed amendment is under consideration, a motion to amend the same may be made. No after-amendment to such second amendment shall be in order, but a substitute for the whole matter may be received. No proposition on a subject differing from the one under consideration shall be received under color of a substitute.

Reconsideration.

XVII A Question being once determined shall stand as the judgment of the House, and shall not be again drawn into debate during the same session of the House, except with the consent of a two-thirds vote of those present and voting. A motion to reconsider can be made only on the day the vote was taken, or on the next succeeding legislative day, and must be made and seconded by those who voted with the majority.

Time limit on new business.

XVIII Except by a two-thirds vote of those present and voting, no new business shall be introduced for the consideration of the House after the second day of the Session. All matters originating in this House requiring concurrent action by both houses shall be considered before the last legislative day except for Resolutions of Privilege and Courtesy.

Circulate Resolutions in advance.

XIX Except by a two-thirds vote of those present and voting, no member of the House may introduce a Resolution at a special meeting unless the Resolution has been circulated thirty days in advance to the members. This rule shall not be construed in any way to prevent a Committee of the House from introducing Resolutions at special meetings.

Messages to the House of Deputies.

XX All Resolutions which are to be communicated to the House of Deputies, unless they contain information of action incomplete in this House, or be temporarily withheld by order of this House at the time of their passage, shall be transmitted to the House of Deputies as soon as conveniently may be, under the direction of the Presiding Officer of the House.

XXI Committees from the House of Deputies shall be admitted immediately. Messages from the House of Deputies shall be handed by the Secretary of this House to the Presiding Officer, to be laid before the House as early as may be convenient. However, consideration of such Message shall be subject to a motion for the appointment of a Committee of Conference as hereinafter provided in these Rules. All such Messages communicating any legislative action on the part of the House of Deputies shall, without debate, be referred to the proper Committee, unless, without debate, the House shall decide to consider such Messages without such reference. When the consideration of such Message shall have been begun, it shall continue to be the Order of the Day until final action thereon.

Messages from the House of Deputies.

The final action of this House upon any Message from the House of Deputies shall be by vote upon the question "Shall this House concur in the action of the House of Deputies as communicated in their Message No. _____?" Messages requiring no action by the House may be received by Title.

XXII If, during the consideration by this House of any action taken by the House of Deputies, a motion is made stating the position of this House and requesting a Committee of Conference, such motion shall have precedence and be put to a vote without debate, and if passed by a majority of the members of this House then present, a Committee of Conference shall be appointed. A Committee of Conference shall also be in order, with or without motion, (1) in cases where the House of Deputies has concurred, with amendments, in action taken by this House, or (2) in cases where this House has concurred, with amendments, in action taken by the House of Deputies. When a Committee of Conference has been appointed, final action upon the matter under consideration shall be deferred until the Committee of Conference shall have reported to this House; Provided, such report shall be made no later than the next business day or within one hour after the convening of the last meeting of this House in Convention assembled, whichever event shall first occur. Further, the Chair of any Standing or other Committee shall have full authority, either alone or with members of the Committee, to confer with the Chair of the cognate Committee of the House of Deputies.

Committee of Conference.

XXIII Two Bishops may be appointed by the Presiding Officer to act with the Secretary in preparing daily reports of the action of this House, and furnishing them, at their discretion, to the public press.

Daily reports.

XXIV Any Bishop of a Church in the Anglican Communion who is in exile from a Diocese, or is without membership in a House of Bishops because the Diocese is temporarily in an extra-provincial status, and who is resident in any jurisdiction in this Church, or any other Bishop of a Church in the Anglican Communion who has resigned his or her position

Collegial members.

in that Church, who has made his or her primary residence in any jurisdiction in this Church may be admitted to this House as a collegial member. Such membership may be extended to such a Bishop by a two-thirds vote of those present and voting on each Bishop, taken by secret ballot if requested by at least six members of the House, considered by the members of the House present at any regularly called meeting, and shall continue until such time as the collegial member removes from the jurisdiction of this Church, or until such time as it is withdrawn by a like vote. Such collegial member shall be assigned a seat, and have a voice, in this House. No vote shall be accorded such collegial member, in keeping with the Constitution of this Church.

Nominations for collegial membership.

The Committee on Privilege and Courtesy must receive, one month in advance of any meeting of this House, nominations for collegial membership in this House, said nomination to be made only by the Bishop in whose jurisdiction the proposed collegial member resides. The nominations for collegial membership shall be circulated in writing to the members of the House before the nominations shall be presented to the House.

Honorary members.

Any Bishop of an extra-provincial Diocese which originated in the Church or any Bishop of this Church who removed from the jurisdiction of this Church to the jurisdiction of a Church in the Anglican Communion may be continued in relationship to this House as an honorary member. Thirty days prior to each stated or called meeting of the House such honorary members shall give written notice of their intention to be present to the Presiding Officer of this House. Seat and voice shall then be accorded such honorary members, upon the nomination to the House by the Presiding Officer. No vote shall be accorded the honorary member.

Bishops admitted to honorary and collegial seats in the House shall at all times be entitled to be present except when the House is in Executive Session. At such a call, the Secretary shall ask the guests to leave the House.

Nonvoting membership.

XXV Any Bishop of this Church who resigns a position for reasons other than those specified in Article I.2 of the Constitution, but whose resignation is not for reasons related to the Bishop's moral character, may, on motion and by a majority vote, be accorded non-voting membership in the House. Until further contrary action by the House, any such non-voting member shall have the right to seat and voice at all meetings, the right to serve on committees, and all other rights of membership except that of voting on any matter.

Advisory Committee.

XXVI There shall be an Advisory Committee, composed of Bishops who are the Presidents or Vice-Presidents of each Province, which will act as advisory council to the Presiding Bishop between meetings of the House of Bishops. The Committee shall elect its own officers.

Committee on Pastoral.

XXVII The Committee on the Bishop's Pastoral shall be a Standing Committee of the House, composed of persons eminently qualified for the task, and empowered to enlist additional assistance, with the consent of the Presiding Bishop, as may seem wise. The Committee shall make a Report at each Session of the House.

XXVIII Additions and amendments to, or suspension or repeal of these rules shall require a two-thirds vote of those present and voting.

Amendment of rules.

XXIX These rules shall be in force in subsequent Sessions of this House unless otherwise ordered.

XXX Except when in conflict with the Constitution or Canons, or any Rule herein contained, the latest edition of Robert's Rules of Order shall govern the interpretation of these rules, and the parliamentary procedures to be followed in this House.

Robert's Rules apply.

THE PRESIDING BISHOP

I On the day following the Joint Session to which the Joint Nominating Committee has reported pursuant to Canon I.2, the House of Bishops shall meet in executive session in a church to discuss the nominees presented at the Joint Session, and to elect a Presiding Bishop from among those nominees.

Election.

II The House of Bishops should remain within the confines of the church where the election has been held, until word has been received of the action of the House of Deputies.

Awaiting confirmation from Deputies.

MISSIONARY BISHOPS

I When a vacancy occurs or is about to occur in the Missionary Episcopate, it shall be the duty of the Presiding Bishop to investigate the situation existing in the Diocese, to consult with those persons in the field and at home best fitted to advise as to the conditions in the Diocese, and to submit to the members of the House such information as the Presiding Bishop may secure.

Vacant episcopate.

II Before any vacancy in the Missionary Episcopate is to be considered or filled at any Meeting of the House, notice to this effect shall be given in the call of such Meeting. The ballot for the election to any such vacancy shall not, without unanimous consent, be taken at a Special Meeting until at least the first day, nor at a Meeting of the General Convention until at least the second day, after nominations have been made to the House. In the event of the occurrence of a vacancy in a Missionary Diocese, or the resignation of a Missionary Bishop, between the issuance of the call for a Special Meeting of the House of Bishops and the meeting thereof, the House, by a two-thirds vote of those present and voting, shall be competent to fill such vacancy, or to act upon such resignation.

Notice of election in call for Meeting.

III Further proceedings for the election of a Missionary Bishop shall be as follows:

(1) In the case of each vacancy to be filled, a special Joint Nominating Committee shall be appointed. The Committee shall be composed of three persons from the jurisdiction concerned, chosen by its Council of Advice or in some other manner as ordered by the Presiding Bishop, and three members of this House appointed by the Presiding Bishop. The Joint Nominating Committee shall elect its

Joint Nominating Committee.

own officers and shall nominate three persons for the vacancy. Three weeks before the Meeting of the House these names shall be sent in confidence to each Bishop.

Presiding Bishop may nominate.

(2) The Presiding Bishop may, in the exercise of discretion, make nominations for such vacancies.

Nominations from floor.

(3) At the Meeting of the House, the names of the persons proposed by the Joint Nominating Committee shall be formally placed in nomination, and opportunity shall also be given for nominations from the floor.

Information about nominees.

(4) The Joint Nominating Committees and the Bishops making nominations, and other having knowledge of the persons nominated, shall give to the Committee on Domestic Missions or the Committee on Overseas Missions, as the case may be, full information regarding the nominees, and such Committee, having secured further information as may be possible, shall report to the House in Executive Session such further information concerning the intellectual, moral, and physical qualifications of the persons nominated, with dates of birth, graduation, and specific statements as to theological attainment, proficiency in languages, and any specialty in sacred duties to which such persons may have devoted themselves. Questions may be asked and other information given by the Bishops.

Executive Session.

(5) All nominations for vacant Missionary Dioceses shall be made in Executive Session. The names of the nominees shall be made known to the public only after the election.

Declination.

(6) In the case of a declination, another election can be held from the same names without further formality than renomination; but if new names are introduced, the order prescribed above shall be repeated.

Translation to another Diocese.

(7) In the case of the proposed transfer of a Bishop in charge of a Missionary Diocese to another Diocese, action shall be as in the case of the election of Missionary Bishops.

Confidentiality.

(8) All proceedings in Executive Session shall be held strictly confidential. In the case of elections held in Executive Session and to be confirmed by the House of Deputies or by the Standing Committees of the Church, the names of those elected shall not be made known until they are published by the House of Deputies, or until they are ordered to be sent to the Standing Committees.

STANDING ORDERS

Ordination and consecration of Bishops.

I *Whereas,* by provisions of Canon III.11.1(a) and (b), and Canon III.17.2(d), the Presiding Bishop is empowered to take order for the ordination and consecration of Diocesan and Missionary Bishops, either in the Presiding Bishop's own person or by commission issued to three Bishops; *It is hereby ordered,* that, in all cases of Episcopal consecrations, the place for the same shall be designated only with the consent of the Ecclesiastical Authority in whose Diocese or Jurisdiction such proposed place is; that the Bishop-elect shall have the right to designate the Preacher and the two Bishops by whom the Bishop-elect is to be presented; and that, in the absence of the Presiding Bishop, the Senior Bishop by consecration who is present shall preside, unless some other Bishop shall have been designated by the Presiding Bishop.

II Seniority among the Bishops is according to the date of the consecration of each Bishop.

III The House of Bishops shall assemble on every morning during the period of the General Convention, except the Lord's Day, for business, unless adjournment beyond that morning has been ordered by the vote of the House.

Daily sessions at General Convention.

IV Two or more of the Bishops shall be appointed at each General Convention to take charge, together with the Secretary of the House of Bishops, of the Journal of its proceedings, and to see that the whole, or such parts of it as the House may direct, be entered in its proper place in the Journal of the General Convention.

Committee on Journal.

V The Secretary of the House of Bishops shall keep a permanent record of the members and officers of the House from the beginning, and shall record therein the names of the Bishops who are or have been members of this House, the date and place of their consecration, the names of their consecrators, together with the date of the termination, by death, resignation, or otherwise, of the membership of such Bishops as have ceased to have seats in this House, all of which facts shall be recorded only upon official notification, for which it shall be the duty of the Secretary to call upon such persons as may be competent to furnish the same. The said record shall be the official Register of this House, and the roll of the House communicate the same to the House, as its official roll, as soon as the Presiding Officer shall have taken the chair. Such roll shall be subject to change only by vote of the House.

Official Register.

VI In making up the list of the Bishops who have retained their constituted rights to seats in this House, the Secretary is instructed to leave the name of any Bishop resigned in the place which the Bishop occupies in the order of consecration, with the addition of the word "Bishop," which shall be considered as the sufficient title of such resigned Bishop.

Resigned Bishop.

VII In the event of the loss by any Bishop of a seat in the House of Bishops, with the consequent omission of the Bishop's name from the roll, and a subsequent return to the House, the Bishop's name shall be entered on the roll at the place corresponding with the time of such return.

Restored Bishop.

VIII At every meeting of the House of Bishops a seat for the Chair of the Committee on Dispatch of Business shall be assigned near the front of the House.

Chair of Dispatch.

IX At every meeting of the House of Bishops seats on the platform shall be assigned to such Bishops present as have formerly held the office of Presiding Bishop, and at every service of the General Convention such Bishops as have formerly held the office of Presiding Bishop shall be assigned places immediately in front of the Chaplain of the Presiding Bishop.

Former Presiding Bishops.

Definitions.

X Whenever the House shall make a determination under Article I.2 of the Constitution that a resigned Bishop shall or shall not retain a seat and vote in the House, the following understanding of the intent of the pertinent terms of that provision of the Constitution shall apply:

(a) "advanced age" shall mean at least 62 years of age;

(b) "bodily infirmity" shall mean either a condition for which one is eligible for disability retirement benefits from the Church Pension Fund or Social Security Administration, or a physical or mental impairment that a physician or psychiatrist (approved by the Presiding Bishop) certifies would likely result in eligibility for such disability retirement benefits should the Bishop continue in active episcopal ministry;

(c) "office created by the General Convention" shall mean a ministry funded by the General Convention Budget and approved by the Presiding Bishop; and

(d) "mission strategy" shall mean a strategy that would allow the election of an indigenous member of the clergy of a non-domestic diocese as Bishop, or that would allow a diocese to implement a new mission strategy as determined by the Presiding Bishop, or that would allow a transition in episcopal leadership after a Diocesan Bishop or Bishop Suffragan has served 10 or more years in either or both of those offices.

STANDING RESOLUTIONS

Resolutions for for resigning Bishops.

I *Resolved*, That the Standing Committee on the Resignation of Bishops be requested to prepare a Resolution taking note of the service of each Bishop whose resignation is being accepted, such Resolution to be presented to the House of Bishops along with the recommendation on the resignation. Where a resignation is accepted between Meetings of the House, such Resolution shall be presented at the next Meeting.

Memorial messages.

II *Resolved*, That the Presiding Bishop be requested to appoint, on each occasion, a Committee of three or more Bishops to prepare, on behalf of the House of Bishops, and send to the family of each Bishop who dies, a Memorial Message, such Committee to represent the House of Bishops at the funeral, where it is practical for them to attend.

Conveners of Commissions.

III *Resolved*, That, within six months after the adjournment of each General Convention, the Secretary of the House of Bishops shall communicate with the Bishop named as Convener of each Commission appointed during the preceding General Convention, and inquire whether the Commission has convened and organized, keeping a record of the replies received.

RULES OF ORDER
HOUSE OF DEPUTIES

I The Holy Scriptures

1. As an indication of our humble dependence upon the Word and Spirit of God, and following the example of primitive Councils, a copy of the Holy Scriptures shall always be reverently placed in view at the meetings of this House. This rule is to be carried into effect under the supervision of the President and Secretary of the House.

Placement of Holy Scriptures.

II Opening of the Daily Session

2. The daily sessions of the House shall be opened with prayer, and prayer for Missions shall be had daily at noon.

Daily Devotions.

3. The President having taken the Chair, the roll of members shall be called whenever so ordered, without debate, by a majority of those present.

Roll call.

4. Unless otherwise ordered by majority vote, the Minutes of the preceding day's session shall not be read; but, in lieu thereof, the same shall be certified by a Committee on Certification of the Minutes consisting of three Presbyters and three Lay Persons appointed by the President. This Committee shall meet daily, for the purpose of reviewing the Minutes, with the Secretary of the House, by arrangement, prior to the hour of assembly, and said meeting shall be open to any member of this House who may desire to attend.

Certification of Minutes.

III Order of Business

5 (a) The Daily Order of Business shall be as follows:

Daily order of business.

- **(i)** Opening Prayer.
- **(ii)** Report on the Certification of the Minutes, or Reading of the Journal.
- **(iii)** Communications from the President.
- **(iv)** 1. Report of Committee on Elections.
  2. Report of Committee on Dispatch of Business (The President may also recognize the Committee on Dispatch of Business for further reports, as required, at any time.)
- **(v)** Reports of other Legislative Committees, in numerical order, as given in Rule 7.
- **(vi)** Reports of Special Committees.
- **(vii)** Reports of Joint Committees and Joint Commissions in the following order:
  - (1) Joint Committee on Program, Budget and Finance.
  - (2) Other Joint Committees.
  - (3) Joint Commissions.
- **(viii)** Introduction of Resolutions.
- **(ix)** Business on the Calendar.

Interruption of Daily Order.

(b) The President may interrupt the Daily Order of Business for Messages from the House of Bishops, Noonday Prayers, or Special Orders. If the Daily Order is not completed during the day, the President may, on the following day, after Items I to IV inclusive, resume the order where it was interrupted the previous day.

Calendar of Business.

6. The Secretary shall keep a Calendar of Business, on which shall be placed, in the order of their presentation, the subjects being briefly indicated, Orders of the Day, reports of Committees, Resolutions which lie over, and other matters undisposed of.

Consent Calendar.

The Secretary shall also keep a Consent Calendar, which shall be published daily and distributed to the members before the convening of the House on each legislative day, and designate it as a separate calendar. Matters shall be listed on the Consent Calendar in separate groupings according to the date that they have been placed thereon. All matters to which amendments have been proposed by a Committee shall be so designated. No debate is in order regarding any matter appearing on the Consent Calendar. However, the President shall allow a reasonable time for questions from the floor and answers to those questions. No amendment other than an amendment contained in a Committee report is in order regarding any matter on the Consent Calendar. Any amendments contained in Committee reports on such matters shall be deemed adopted unless the matter is objected to and removed from the Consent Calendar. Immediately prior to a vote on the first matter on the Consent Calendar the President shall call to the attention of the members the fact that the next vote will be on the first matter pending on the Consent Calendar. Matters appearing on the Consent Calendar shall be taken up immediately following the noon recess of the next legislative day following their placement on the Consent Calendar, or otherwise by unanimous consent or by adoption of a special order of business. A matter may be placed on the Consent Calendar by report of a Legislative Committee, if the Committee vote to report the matter with a recommendation for adoption, with or without amendments, or for discharge, or referral to a Joint or Standing Commission, or for rejection was by three fourths of the members present and if the Committee recommends placement of the matter on the Consent Calendar. Prior to a vote on final passage of any matter appearing on the Consent Calendar, it shall be removed from the Consent Calendar if (1) any three Lay or Clerical deputations, or (2) the sponsor of the matter, or (3) the Committee on Dispatch of Business files with the Secretary written objections to the presence of the matter on the Consent Calendar. Any matter so removed may not be placed thereafter on the Consent Calendar but shall be restored to the Daily Calendar. Any matter removed from the Consent Calendar, to which amendments have been proposed by a Committee, shall stand on the Daily Calendar in its original, unamended form, and amendments shall be treated as if the matter had never been on the Consent Calendar.

IV Legislative Committees

7. Not later than 90 days in advance of the opening date of the Convention, the President may appoint the following Legislative Committees, and such other committees as may be deemed necessary, and shall designate the Chair, Vice-Chair, and Secretary thereof,

President may appoint Legislative Committees.

(1) Dispatch of Business.
(2) Certification of Minutes.
(3) Rules of Order, of which the President shall be Chair, *ex officio*.
(4) Constitution.
(5) Canons.
(6) Structure,
(7) Consecration of Bishops
(8) World Mission.
(9) National and International Concerns
(10) Social and Urban Affairs
(11) Church in Small Communities
(12) Evangelism
(13) Prayer Book, Liturgy and Church Music.
(14) Ministry.
(15) Education
(16) Church Pension Fund.
(17) Stewardship and Development.
(18) Ecumenical Relations
(19) Communications
(20) Miscellaneous Resolutions
(21) Privilege and Courtesy
(22) Committees and Commissions
(23) Credentials
(24) Sergeant-at-Arms

In addition, the President shall appoint Legislative Committees on Admission of New Dioceses if such legislation will be presented to the Convention.

8. The President may appoint Study Committees related to work of the Executive Council, and such Special Committees as the President deems desirable or as may be ordered by the House.

Other Committees.

9. The size of all Committees, unless otherwise noted, shall be at the discretion of the President; *Provided,* that, when the number of members equals or exceeds the number of Provinces, there shall normally be at least one member from each Province. The President shall be a member, *ex officio*, of all Committees.

Size of Committees.

10. A list of the members of the Legislative, Study, and Special Committees shall be prepared and distributed to the House as soon as may be after appointment.

Committee lists to be distributed.

Committees meeting in advance.

11. Such Committees as are so instructed by the President shall convene in advance of the opening of Convention to consider matters referred to them.

Assigned room and meeting time.

12 (a) The Secretary shall arrange a permanent Committee room and a regular time for meeting of each Legislative or Special Committee and shall publish and post a chart indicating the arrangements.

Quorum.

(b) A majority of any Committee shall constitute a quorum, but the question of the presence of a quorum in Committee shall not be raised on the consideration of a Committee report or recommendation in the House unless the same question was raised in Committee.

When Chair fails to act.

(c) In case of the failure of the Chair of any Committee to call a meeting of the Committee, or to call up for consideration a matter referred to it, then a majority of the members of the Committee shall have the right to call a meeting of the Committee or to require such consideration, as the case may be.

Prior notice of hearings.

(d) No hearing by a Committee shall be held upon any matter before it unless notice of the time and place of hearing and the matter to be heard is posted no later than at least four hours before the matter is scheduled to be heard. Each day the Chair or the Secretary of each Committee shall deliver to the Secretary of the House (at the office of the Secretary of the House) a written notice signed by the Chair or by the Secretary. Such notice shall state the time (both date and hour) and the place of the proposed hearing and shall identify by number (and *Blue Book* page reference, if available) the proposition or propositions to be considered at the next session of the Committee. The Secretary shall post a copy of each notice received on a bulletin board at or near the chamber and easily accessible to the members of the House and to the public. If the notice contains a request that the notice be read to the House prior to adjournment, the Secretary shall do so.

Testimony before Committee.

(e) No person not a member of a Committee shall be permitted to testify before that Committee until they register by signing a witness slip upon which they state their names, their identifications (*e.g.* Bishop, Deputy and Diocese, and, if Visitor, their addresses and organizations, if any, represented) and the particular proposal to which their testimony is to be addressed. The person testifying shall be subject to such time limitations as may be imposed by the Chair.

Record to be kept.

(f) The Chair of each Committee shall keep, or cause to be kept, a record in which there shall be collected or entered:

(1) The time and place of each hearing, and of each meeting of the Committee, and the matters considered at the meeting.
(2) The attendance of Committee members at each meeting.
(3) The name and identification of each person appearing before the Committee and the proposition upon which each person spoke.

Meetings in conference or executive session.

(g) Except as provided herein, every Committee meeting shall be open to the public. However, the Chair may convene the Committee in conference, during which time the public may remain but may not participate in the Committee deliberations. Upon a two-thirds majority vote of Committee members present, a Committee may go into executive session if the matter to be considered in executive session has first been scheduled for hearing and heard in open session, and interested persons have been given an opportunity to be heard.

(h) At the conclusion of each meeting of a Committee, its Chair shall prepare, or cause to be prepared on forms provided for the purpose, a separate report with regard to each matter upon which the Committee took final action during the meeting. Each such report shall be in the following alternative form:

Committee Chair to prepare a report from the alternatives:

(1) Recommends adoption, with or without amendments, in which case the question shall be on the adoption of the Resolution, or the Resolution as amended.

Adoption.

(2) Recommends rejection, with or without reasons, in which case the question shall be on the adoption of the Resolution, notwithstanding the recommendation of the Committee for rejection.

Rejection.

(3) Recommends that it be discharged from further consideration of the Resolution because

Discharge from consideration.

(i) the matter is not within the scope of the Committee's function, in which case it may recommend referral to an appropriate Committee;

(ii) the matter has already been dealt with by action of the House at this meeting of the General Convention; or

(iii) the matter is covered by a Resolution of a prior General Convention; or

(iv) for other reasons.

(4) Recommends referral to a Standing Commission of the General Convention to study the theological, ethical and pastoral questions inherent in the subject or to develop recommendations and strategies on the subject which will be of concrete assistance to this Church or to study or make recommendations concerning the subject.

Referral.

(5) Recommends concurrence with or without amendment with House of Bishops Message.

Concurrence.

(6) Recommends non-concurrence with House of Bishops Message.

Nonconcurrence.

Each report shall be dated, signed by the Chair or Secretary of the Committee, and transmitted to the office of the Secretary of the House, who shall endorse thereon the date of receipt thereof. If there is a minority position in the Committee and a minority spokesperson requests a minority report, the Chair shall include the same in the report.

Reports to be signed.

13. Reports of all Committees shall be submitted to the House by the Secretary of the House. At the time of the announcement of the report of a Committee, its Chair, or a member thereof designated by the Chair, shall be available and prepared to explain the report or the recommendation of the Committee. Printed reports of Committees dealing with matters other

Reports to be submitted to the Secretary of the House.

than pending proposals, and requiring no action by the House, and which have been delivered to members of the House in advance, shall be presented by title, except that the spokesperson for the report, upon request, shall be allowed five minutes for summarizing the same.

Resolutions to amend Constitution or Canons.

14. Any Resolution which involves an amendment to the Constitution or Canons, shall be referred by the President to the appropriate Legislative or Special Committee for action and simultaneously to the Committee on the Constitution or the Committee on Canons, as the case may be, and such Committee shall make certain that the Resolution is in proper constitutional or canonical form, achieves consistency and clarity in the Constitution or Canons, and includes all amendments necessary to effect the proposed change, and shall promptly communicate its recommendations to the Legislative or Special Committee. In such case the Committee shall neither concern itself with, nor report on, the substance of the matter referred to it, but whenever requested to do so by the Presiding Officer of the House, the Committee shall in its reports to the House make recommendations as to substance. The Committee on the Constitution and the Committee on Canons, when acting on a matter first heard in another Committee, shall not be required to give the notice required by Rule 12(d). No such resolution shall be placed on the Calendar until such Committee shall have approved it in proper constitutional or canonical form.

Requests for appropriations to Committee on Program, Budget and Finance.

15. Before final consideration by the House, the Joint Standing Committee on Program, Budget and Finance (PB&F) shall have been informed by the Committee considering any proposed action which, if adopted by General Convention, would require an appropriation of funds and PB&F shall have acknowledged receipt of such information by endorsement on the committee report or by other appropriate means. Implementation of any such resolution is subject to funding in the budget.

Dispatch of Business to set order when Committees are ready.

16. The Committee on Dispatch of Business, when in its opinion it is advisable, may provide that no Report of a Commission or Joint Committee, or of any Committee of this House to which any part of such Report has been referred, be made the order of business, until the reports of all Committees to which any part of such Report has been referred be ready to report thereon.

Exceptions to Rules 12 and 13.

Proviso.

17. The provisions of Rules 12 and 13 shall not apply to Committees having procedural matters only, including, but not limited to, the Committee on Elections, Committee on Certification of Minutes, Committee on Dispatch of Business; *Provided, however* the meetings of such Committees shall be open to Bishops, Deputies, and Visitors, except that, on a two-thirds majority vote of Committee members present, the Committee may go into executive session.

Memorial Roll.

18. The Secretary shall prepare a Memorial Roll listing the names, Dioceses or Missionary Dioceses, dates of birth and death, and time of service in the General Convention, of all deceased members of the current or any preceding General Convention of whom memorials shall not theretofore have been made; and, after suitable devotions arranged by the Chaplain, such Memorial Roll shall be received by the House standing.

V Commissions and Joint Committees

19 (a) No Report of a Commission or a Joint Committee containing Resolutions, that has been printed and distributed to the members of this House at least three weeks before the meeting of the Convention, shall be read at length to the House, but the Chair or a member of that Committee or Commission may make an oral summary.

Oral summary.

(b) If there be a minority report of such Commission or Joint Committee, a member of such minority shall be afforded an opportunity to make an oral summary on the floor of the House.

20 (a) Every Report of a Commission or Joint Committee shall be referred to the appropriate Legislative Committee of this House, if there be one; but, if not, to a Special Committee of this House. The House may at any time refer any Report or Resolution to the Committee on the Constitution to draft a constitutional amendment or to the Committee on Canons to draft a canon or amendment to the Canons which will carry into effect, if enacted, the Report or Resolution so referred.

Referrals to appropriate Committees.

VI Resolutions and Memorials

21 (a) All Resolutions requiring concurrent legislative action shall contain the phrase, "*Resolved*, the House of ________ concurring," and shall be in such form that, when adopted by concurrent action of the House of Bishops or the House of Deputies pursuant to the Constitution and Canons, it shall constitute action of the General Convention.

In proper form.

(b) Resolutions may be introduced only by:

Submitting resolutions.

(1) Deputies.
(2) Dioceses.
(3) Provinces.
(4) Standing Commissions.
(5) Standing, Joint, and Legislative Committees.
(6) The Executive Council.
(7) Other Boards and Agencies created by and required to report to the General Convention.
(8) The House of Bishops by Messages.

(c) All resolutions of Deputies shall be proposed by one Deputy and be endorsed by not less than two additional Deputies. Individual Deputies shall be limited to proposing not more than three resolutions.

Endorsement.

(d) Except for Resolutions contained in Messages from the House of Bishops, Resolutions to be introduced must be in writing, filed with the Secretary of the House of Deputies, bearing a brief descriptive title and the name and Diocese of the Deputy or the name of the Commission, Committee or other organization presenting the same. In all cases where a Resolution seeks to amend a Canon or a Title of the Canons the form of Resolution submitted shall set out the enactment in the form prescribed by Canon V.1, shall include with a dash overstrike on each letter any words

Resolutions to be in writing.

In case of Canonical amendment.

that are deleted by the amendment and shall underline any words which are added by the amendment; provided that if the amendment of an entire Title is to be covered by one enactment under Canon V.1.4, the deleted text and the underlining of the new text need not be included but the proponent shall make adequate written explanation of the changes. The Secretary shall prepare a concise digest of each Resolution (including identification of the sponsor). The Secretary shall also provide each Deputy and Bishop with a copy of such digest and of each Resolution; shall provide each Legislative Committee to which the Resolution is referred a sufficient number of copies; and shall retain on file in the office of the Secretary additional copies for review by any Deputy or Bishop.

Prefiled Resolutions.

(e) Any such Resolutions received by the Secretary of the House of Deputies at least ninety (90) days prior to the opening date of the Convention shall be referred to the proper Legislative Committee or Special Committee Chair at least sixty (60) days prior to the opening date of Convention. The Secretary shall acknowledge receipt of all such Resolutions to the proposer.

Referral to be made to one Committee.

(f) Each Resolution shall be referred by the President to one appropriate Legislative Committee for action, or if, in the opinion of the President, there be no appropriate Committee, then to a Special Committee; or, in the discretion of the President, it shall be placed on the Calendar. Upon a vote of two-thirds of the members present, the House may consider immediately any Resolution. Each Resolution which involves an amendment to the Constitution or to the Canons shall be referred to the appropriate Legislative Committee on Constitution or on Canons pursuant to Rule 14;

Proviso.

Provided, however, that the substance of any such Resolution may be considered by the House, sitting as a Committee of the Whole, prior to referral to, or report of, such appropriate Committee.

(g) The President may refer any Resolution, for information only, to an appropriate Legislative Committee other than it has been referred to for action or as to form. Consideration by such Committee shall not be required prior to action thereon by the House. The Resolution shall not be the subject of a report to the floor from such Committee.

Procedural Resolutions.

(h) Procedural Resolutions offered for the immediate action of the House shall be considered at once, unless objection be made or reference be requested, in which event the provisions of Rule 21(e) shall apply.

Memorials.

22 (a) All Memorials shall contain the substance of the phrase, "The (*organization*) memorializes the General Convention to . . . ," and shall be in such form as to urge action by the General Convention on a Resolution already introduced or on any other matter on which the General Convention is requested to take action. The inclusion in a Memorial of a suggested form of Resolution shall not have the effect of requiring that the Memorial be given the status of a Resolution as defined in Rule 21.

(b) Memorials must be in writing, filed in duplicate with the Secretary of the House of Deputies, bearing a brief descriptive title and the identification of the person or organization filing the same. The Secretary shall prepare a concise digest of each Memorial (including identification of the sponsor) which digest shall be distributed to all Deputies and Bishops. The Secretary shall also provide each Legislative Committee to which the Memorial is referred a sufficient number of copies, and shall retain on file in the office of the Secretary additional copies for review by any Deputy or Bishop.

(c) Each Memorial shall be referred by the President to one or more appropriate Legislative Committees for information. Such Committee may consider such Memorial and submit to the floor a Resolution embodying the substance of such Memorial, but the Memorial itself shall not be the subject of a report from the Committee to which it is referred.

Memorials referred for information only.

23. The President, or the House, by a majority vote, may at any time refer any Resolution to a Special Committee on Drafting, appointed or to be appointed by the President, for the purpose of putting in proper language the substance of the matter so referred. Any Deputy desiring to introduce a Resolution, and any Legislative or Special Committee to which a Resolution has been referred, may request assistance in the proper drafting or redrafting of the substance of any matter.

Committee on Drafting.

24. Except by a vote of two-thirds of the members present, no new business requiring concurrent action shall be introduced in this House after the second legislative day of its session, and no matter which originated in this House and which requires concurrent action by both Houses shall be considered by the House during the last two legislative days.

Time limit on concurrent Resolutions.

25. Any Resolution not reported to the House by the third legislative day after its being referred to a Committee may be recalled by a two-thirds vote of the members present, and thereupon shall be placed upon the Calendar, unless the motion to recall include a provision that the question be taken up for consideration immediately upon the recall.

VII Motions in Order of Precedence

26. The following motions shall have priority in the order listed. The mover

Motions with priority.

- cannot interrupt a member who has the floor;
- must be recognized; and
- the motion must be seconded.

Motions are subject to the following further rules:

(a) To Adjourn or Recess

(1) Not debatable, if unqualified.
(2) Not amendable.
(3) Cannot be laid on table.
(4) May be renewed after progress.
(5) Majority vote.
(6) The motion to adjourn shall always be in order, except that it shall not be offered when another member has the floor.

(b) To Adjourn to Time Certain

(1) Debatable, as to the time, for two minutes to each speaker.

(2) Amendable as to the time.
(3) Cannot be laid on table.
(4) May be renewed after progress.
(5) Majority vote.

(c) To Lay on Table or to Table

(1) Not debatable.
(2) Not amendable.
(3) Cannot be laid on table.
(4) May be renewed after progress.
(5) Majority vote.

(d) To Vote Immediately or at Time Certain, or to Extend Debate

(1) Not debatable.
(2) Amendable, as to time, if a time specified.
(3) Cannot be laid on table.
(4) May be renewed after progress.
(5) Two-thirds majority to vote.
(6) When applied to a Substitute, covers main Question also, unless otherwise specified.
(7) At time fixed for vote to be taken, no motion shall be in order except to adjourn.

(e) To Postpone to a Time Certain

(1) Debatable for two minutes to each speaker.
(2) Amendable as to time.
(3) May be laid on table.
(4) May be renewed after progress.
(5) Majority vote.
(6) When applied to a Substitute, covers main Question also, unless otherwise specified.

(f) To Commit or Recommit to any Committee

(1) Debatable, except as to a Legislative Committee.
(2) Amendable as to the Committee to which to be sent.
(3) May be laid on table.
(4) May be renewed after progress.
(5) Majority vote.

(g) To Amend or to Substitute

(1) Amendments and Substitutions are debatable only when main Question is debatable.
(2) One Amendment may be made to each independent or seperable portion of a Resolution; and the right to amend extends only to one Amendment of that Amendment and to a Substitute and one Amendment thereto.
(3) A Substitute and its Amendment may be laid on table, but cannot be otherwise voted on until original matter is perfected.
(4) May not be renewed.
(5) Majority vote.
(6) Amendments and Substitutes must be germane.
(7) Amendments and Substitutes may be withdrawn by maker, with consent of the seconder, before decision is had thereon.

(8) If Amendment or Substitute is laid on table the effect is the same as if it had not been offered.

(9) Neither the Substitute nor its Amendment shall be voted on (except to lay on table) until the original matter is perfected, and when the Original Question and Substitute are both perfected, the vote comes first on the adoption of the Substitute or the Substitute as amended.

(10) When a Substitute is pending, the motion to postpone indefinitely shall not be in order; but, unless otherwise therein provided, the motions (i) to postpone to a certain time, (ii) to commit or to recommit, (iii) to take a vote immediately or at a certain time, or (iv) to extend limits of debate, shall cover both the Substitute and the main Question.

(11) No action on an Amendment or Substitute changes the status of the original Question. The original Resolution, as so amended, then remains the Question before the House.

(h) To Postpone Indefinitely

(1) Debatable, including main Question.
(2) Not amendable.
(3) May be laid on table.
(4) May not be renewed.
(5) Majority vote.

VIII Motions Without Order of Precedence

27. The following motions have no order of priority, but are subject to the following rules:

Motions without order or priority.

(a) Appeal from Decision of Chair

(1) Must be made immediately after decision. Mover need not be recognized, but requires a second.
(2) Debatable for two minutes by each speaker, each speaking once.
(3) Not amendable.
(4) May be laid on table.
(5) Majority vote. A tie vote sustains Chair.
(6) Cannot be renewed.

(b) To Take from Table

(1) Mover must be recognized and requires a second.
(2) Not debatable.
(3) Not amendable.
(4) Cannot be laid on table.
(5) Majority vote.
(6) May be renewed after progress.

(c) To Recall from Committee

(1) Mover may be recognized.
(2) Debatable.
(3) Amendable as to whether to be considered or placed on Calendar.

(4) May be laid on table.
(5) Two-thirds majority vote.
(6) May be renewed after progress.

(d) To Create Special Order of Day for a Particular Time

(1) Mover must be recognized and requires a second.
(2) Debatable.
(3) Amendable as to time.
(4) Cannot be laid on table.
(5) Two-thirds majority vote.
(6) May be renewed after progress.

(e) Call for Order of the Day

(1) Mover may interrupt a member who has the floor and is not required to be recognized or to have a second.
(2) Not debatable.
(3) Not amendable.
(4) Cannot be laid on table.
(5) No vote required, but two-thirds majority vote is necessary to suspend general or special order.
(6) May be renewed after progress.

(f) To Suspend the Rules or Take Up Business Out of Order

(1) Mover must be recognized and requires a second.
(2) Debatable; two minutes to each speaker.
(3) Not amendable.
(4) Cannot be laid on table.
(5) Two-thirds majority vote.
(6) Cannot be reconsidered or renewed.

(g) To Divide the Question

(1) May be made without being recognized and even though another member has the floor. When the voting is by Dioceses and Orders, the request for division must be made by the entire Clerical or Lay representation from any Diocese.
(2) Not debatable.
(3) Cannot be amended.
(4) Cannot be laid on table.
(5) Majority vote, if vote required.
(6) Can be reconsidered.
(7) If the Question under debate contains several distinct propositions, which are independent of each other, at the request of any member the same shall be divided and a separate vote shall be taken, but the motion to strike out and to insert shall be indivisible.
(8) If the propositions relate to the same subject, and yet each part can stand alone, they may be divided only on a regular motion and vote.

(h) Objection to Consideration

(1) If objection made before debate is begun, the mover may interrupt a member who has the floor and is not required to be recognized or to have a second.

(2) Not debatable.
(3) Not amendable.
(4) Cannot be laid on table, but yields to all privileged motions.
(5) Two-thirds majority vote.
(6) Negative, but not affirmative, vote may be reconsidered.

IX Reconsideration

28. Neither a Question once determined, nor any Question of like import, shall be drawn again into debate or presented for action again during the same Convention, except upon the adoption of a motion to reconsider the action previously taken on such Question.

Motion to reconsider.

29. All motions to reconsider shall be made and seconded on the day the vote is taken on the matter sought to be reconsidered, or on the next succeeding day on which the House shall be in session.

To be made on same or next day.

30. The effect of a motion to reconsider, if carried, is to restore the matter reconsidered to its status immediately prior to the original vote upon it.

Effect of motion.

31 (a) In all Questions decided numerically, the motion to reconsider must be made by one Deputy, and seconded by another, who voted in the majority; or, in case of equal division, by those who voted in the negative. In case of a vote by orders, where there is a concurrence of both Orders, the motion shall be made by a majority of a Deputation from any Diocese of either Order voting in the majority; and, in case of a nonconcurrence of Orders, the motion shall come from a majority of a Deputation of that Order from a Diocese which gave the majority in the negative. In either case, a motion to reconsider may be seconded by a majority of any Deputation of either side, without regard to its previous vote.

Who may move and second.

(b) Motions to reconsider are subject to the following further rules:

Rules governing motion to reconsider.

(1) Mover must be recognized and requires a second.
(2) Debatable when motion to be reconsidered is debatable.
(3) Not amendable.
(4) May be tabled.
(5) Two-thirds majority vote.
(6) Cannot be reconsidered.
(7) No Question can be twice reconsidered unless it was materially amended after its first reconsideration.

X Decorum and Debate

32. When the President shall be in the Chair, no member shall address the House or make any motion until after recognition by the President, except to make a parliamentary inquiry, a point of order, or a motion not requiring recognition.

Recognition by Chair.

33. No member shall address the President while any other member has the floor; except to present a parliamentary inquiry, a point of order, or a question of privilege touching the character of the House or of one or more of its members.

Rights of member who has floor.

Speaking to the House.

34. When any member is about to speak or to deliver any matter to the House, he shall, with due respect, address himself to the President, state his name and his Diocese, and confine himself strictly to the point of debate.

On private discourse.

35. While the President is putting any Question, the members shall continue in their seats, and shall not hold any private discourse.

President to leave Chair before members are excused.

36. When the House is about to rise, every member shall keep his seat until the President leaves the Chair. Before putting to a vote a motion to adjourn, the President may make any communication to the House, or may cause any notice to be read by the Secretary.

Limits on debate.

37. Except by leave of the House, no member shall speak more than twice in the same debate, nor longer than three minutes at one time. The total time of debate on any Resolution or Message shall be a maximum of thirty minutes.

38. No applause shall be permitted during any session of the House or of the Committee of the Whole.

Question of order.

39. All questions of order shall be decided by the President, without debate, but any member may appeal from such decision, as provided in Rule 27(a). On such appeal the vote shall be upon the Question, "Shall the decision of the Chair be sustained?"

XI Voting

Members must vote.

40 (a) Unless excused by the House, every member who shall be in the House when any Question is put must vote on a division.

When late vote may be recorded.

(b) Any member absent from the House when a vote is taken, but coming in before the final announcement of the vote on any Question, may vote thereon, if then permitted by the President, but not otherwise.

Vote by Dioceses and Orders.

Poll of Deputation.

41. The vote upon any Question shall be taken by Dioceses and Orders whenever required by the Constitution or by Canon, or whenever required by the Clerical or Lay representation from three or more Dioceses, before the voting begins. Whenever a vote shall be taken by Dioceses and Orders (except in the case of elections), the vote of each Order in each Diocese shall be stated by one member in each Order as "Aye" or "No" or "Divided". If desired by the entire Deputation from any Diocese that the Deputation be polled, the vote of the individual Deputies representing that Diocese shall be stated and recorded, or if by ballot or electronic means shall be recorded. Such record shall be made, also, in respect of the individual members of every Deputation, if so ordered, without debate, by a majority of the House. In lieu of a roll call, a vote by Dioceses and Orders may be taken by such electronic or mechanical means as may be provided, or by written ballots of each Order, each such ballot to be signed by the Chairman, or, in the Chairman's absence, by another member of the Deputation in the Order for which the ballot is cast; and, if the vote of a Deputation be divided, it may indicate the individual names of the Deputies and their votes on the Question. The results of all votes by Orders, whether by voice vote, by ballot, or by electronic means, shall be posted.

42. Whenever a vote shall be taken by Orders (except in the case of elections), the Secretary of the House of Deputies shall audibly announce in cases where the prevailing side is less than a two-thirds majority of either order, the nay and divided votes in each Order in each Diocese before announcing the result to the House, and the vote in each Order in each Diocese so announced shall be corrected before, but not after, the final announcement of the vote of the House.

Verification of votes before announcement of results.

43. Unless otherwise expressly provided, any Rule requiring a two-thirds majority shall be construed to mean the affirmative vote of two-thirds of the members of the House present and voting. Whenever a Vote by Orders is called for on a proposition requiring a two-thirds vote under these Rules of Order, if not expressly prohibited by constitutional requirements, the proposition shall prevail if it received a majority of votes cast in each Order.

Definition of two-thirds majority.

44. The election of President, Vice-President, or Secretary of the House, or of Treasurer of the General Convention, shall be by individual secret ballot; though, by unanimous consent and direction of the House, a single ballot may be cast by an officer of the House in its behalf.

Election of Officers by individual secret ballot.

XII Messages from the House of Bishops

45. Messages from the House of Bishops shall be handed by the Secretary of this House to the President, to be laid before the House as early as may be convenient. All such Messages communicating any legislative action on the part of the House of Bishops shall be referred, without debate, to the proper committee, unless, without debate, the House shall decide to consider such Message without such reference. The report of the Committee upon any Message so referred shall be entitled to consideration as of the date and priority of the original receipt of such Message. The question of its immediate consideration, to be decided by two-thirds vote as soon as the report is presented.

Procedure.

46. When, either without reference or after reference and report, the consideration of such Message shall have begun, it shall continue to be the Order of the Day until final action thereon, and shall not be subject to any motion to postpone or to lay on the table. However, consideration of such Message shall be subject to a motion for the appointment of a Committee of Conference, as hereinafter provided in this Rule 48.

Messages not subject to motion to postpone or lay on table.

Exception.

47. The final action of the House upon such Message shall be by vote upon the Question, "Shall this House concur in the action of the House of Bishops as communicated by their Message No. ___?" If amendments have been adopted, then shall be added the further words, "as amended." Upon the submission of such Question, all votes in the affirmative shall be counted in favor of such concurrence.

Form of final action.

Committee of Conference.

48. If, during the consideration by this House of any action taken by the House of Bishops, a motion is made stating the position of this House and requesting a Committee of Conference, such motion shall have precedence and be put to vote without debate, and, if passed by a majority of the members of this House then present, a Committee of Conference shall be appointed. A Committee of Conference also shall be in order, with or without motion, (1) in cases where the House of Bishops has concurred, with amendments, in action by this House, or (2) in cases where this House has concurred, with amendments, in action taken by the House of Bishops. When a Committee of Conference has been ordered, final action upon the matter under consideration shall be deferred until the Committee on Conference shall have reported to this House; *Provided*, that such report shall be made not later than the next business day, or within one hour after the convening of the last session of this House in Convention assembled, whichever event shall first occur.

Report of.

Report of Committee debatable.

49. The report of the Committee of Conference shall be subject to debate and to amendment in the House. Action of the House shall be by vote upon the Question, "Shall the House adopt as its action the report of the Committee of Conference?" or, if amended, " . . . the report of the Committee of Conference, as amended?"

Procedures if House of Bishops has taken prior action.

50. In the event that the House of Bishops shall have taken final action on the report of the Committee of Conference prior to its consideration by this House, the Message from the House of Bishops conveying the result of its action shall be considered by this House in all respects as an original Message from the House of Bishops.

Authority of Chair to confer.

51. The Chair of any Legislative or Special Committee shall have full authority, either alone or with members of the Committee, to confer with the Chair of any Committee of the House of Bishops having duties and responsibilities the same as, or similar to, those of the Committee of the House of Deputies of which the person is Chair.

XIII Committee of the Whole

52. Whenever so ordered by a vote of a majority of the members present, the House may go into the Committee of the Whole for the consideration of any matter.

President to name Chair.

53. The President shall designate some member of the House to act as Chair of the Committee of the Whole, which, when in session, shall be governed by these Rules, as adapted by the Chair, subject to appeal to the Committee, and also to the following provisions: rise and report to the House shall take precedence.

Motion to rise and report.

(a) A motion to rise and to report to the House, with or without request for leave to sit again, may be made at any time, shall take precedence over all other motions, and shall be decided without debate by majority vote. No such motion shall be renewed until after further proceedings shall have been had in the Committee of the Whole.

(b) A motion that a vote upon any pending proposition be taken immediately or at some designated time may be made and be disposed of by majority vote, without debate, at any time; but, as before provided, a motion to rise and report to the House shall take precedence.

Other rules.

(c) No motion to lay on the table shall be entertained.

(d) The Committee of the Whole cannot alter the text of a Resolution referred to it, but may adopt and report amendments for action by the House.

54. No debate shall be allowed in the House on any motion to permit the Committee of the Whole to sit again regarding the same subject matter. Requests for such permission shall take precedence over all other business, and the motion thereof shall be put to vote immediately, without reference.

Motion to sit on the same subject not debatable.

XIV Election of a Bishop

55. When considering the election of a Bishop, the approval of the Candidate's testimonials, or assent to the Candidate's consecration, and when acting upon the election of the Presiding Bishop, the House shall sit as soon as practicable after the receipt of official notification from the House of Bishops of such elections.

To sit as soon as practicable.

56. The confirmation of the Presiding Bishop shall be by individual secret ballot, unless otherwise ordered by vote of the House, or unless a vote by Orders be required by the entire Clerical or Lay representation from any Diocese before the balloting begins.

Individual secret ballot.

57. Confidential notifications from the House of Bishops of the election by them of a Presiding Bishop or of any other Bishop shall be referred immediately, without reading, to the Committee on the Consecration of Bishops, which shall make report thereon to such session of the House.

Immediate referral.

XV General Regulations

58. Unless a member have leave from the President or be unable to attend, no member shall be absent himself from the service of the House.

Absence.

59. Seats upon the platform shall be occupied by officers of the House of Deputies, designated members of the Committee on Dispatch of Business, and such other persons as may be invited by the President or authorized by vote of the House.

Platform seating.

60 (a) No one shall be admitted to the floor except members and officers of this House, and except that two Ordained Persons, and two Lay Persons who are duly authorized representatives of the Episcopal Church in Liberia, and like representatives of the Episcopal Church in Navajoland, shall have seat and voice in a designated section on the floor of the House. In addition, up to 18 youth (not more than two youth from each Province) who are duly authorized representatives known as the Official Youth Presence, shall have seat and voice in a designated section on the floor of the House.

Admission to floor.

Seating for special guests.

(b) Alternate Deputies and former members of the House; the Presidents of Church colleges and Deans of Church seminaries; the President, Vice-Presidents, Secretary, Treasurer, and elected Members of the Executive Council; and the Directors and Associate Directors of the Departments and General Divisions of the Executive Council may be seated in a section reserved for Special Guests, except during Executive Sessions.

Alternate Deputies.

(c) Alternate Deputies may not sit or vote with their Deputations, unless and until certified by the Committee on Credentials as a substitute for a Deputy.

Privilege of speaking.

(d) The President of this House may further grant to any designated representative of any of the Departments and General Divisions of the Executive Council the privilege of speaking, on the same footing as a member of the House, on any matter pertaining to the work of the representative's Department or General Division which is under discussion by the House.

Voting by President and Vice-President. Proviso.

61. When not occupying the Chair as presiding officer, the President and Vice-President, if duly elected Deputies, may sit with their Deputations and vote, both individually and in votes by Orders; *Provided, however,* that in an individual vote the presiding officer, whether or not an elected Deputy, may vote only in case the presiding officer's vote is necessary to break a tie.

Relinquishing Chair.

62 (a) The President may relinquish the Chair to the Vice-President, the Secretary, or any member, for any session or portion thereof, and may resume the Chair at any time, except during progress of debate. Likewise, the Vice-President, while presiding, shall have the same right to relinquish and resume the Chair.

Absence of officers.

(b) In the event of the absence of the President at the opening of any session, the Vice-President shall assume the Chair; and if both be absent, the Secretary shall assume the Chair and conduct the election of a Chair *pro tem*, who shall relinquish the Chair upon the return of the President or the Vice-President.

Appointment of Chaplain.

63. The President may appoint a Chaplain from among the Deputies. The President may delegate to the Chaplain Opening Prayers or other devotions or may call upon the Chaplain for special prayers at any time the President deems appropriate.

Distinguished visitors and others.

64. The President may invite a distinguished visitor to speak for not more than ten minutes, or may extend the privileges of the floor to a representative of a Church agency, although not a Deputy, to speak for not more than five minutes to a report of that agency.

Priority of appointed sessions.

65. Except with the assent of three-fourths of the members present, the House shall not accept any invitation, or participate in any exercises, which shall involve suspension, interruption, or abridgment of its regularly appointed sessions.

Distribution of printed matter.

66. Except when otherwise ordered by majority vote of the House, no books, pamphlets, or other printed matter shall be distributed in the House, or be placed on the seats or desks of the Deputies, without the express permission of the President; but this prohibition shall not apply to reports of Committees, or to any papers or other documents present to and accepted by the House or printed by its authority.

67. No smoking shall be permitted in the House chamber. When the House is in session, no one shall use communications devices, including, but not limited to, wireless telephones and pagers, while in the House chamber, except as approved by the President.

Decorum in the House chamber.

XVI Unanimous Consent

68. By unanimous consent, any action may be taken that is not in contravention of any provision of the Constitution or the Canons.

Rule of unanimity.

XVII Rules in Force

69. At the meetings of the House of Deputies, the Rules and the Orders of the previous meeting shall be in force until they are amended or repealed by the House.

Rules and Orders of previous meeting.

XVIII Amendments

70. These Rules may be amended at any time by a two-thirds majority vote of the members present, but only after the proposed amendment has been introduced in the House, has been referred to the Committee on Rules, and the report of such Committee has been made to the House. The proposed amendment shall be subject to debate and amendment before a vote is taken.

Amendment of Rules by two-thirds majority vote.

XIX Robert's Rules of Order

71. Except when in conflict with the Constitution or Canons, or any Rule herein contained, the latest edition of Robert's Rules of Order shall govern the interpretation of these Rules and the procedure to be followed.

STANDING ORDERS

I. Prior to the meeting of each General Convention, the Secretary of the House of Deputies shall determine, by lot, the seats to be occupied by the Deputation from each Diocese.

Seating of Deputations.

II. The names of Deputies who have not registered in the manner designated by the Secretary, shall be noted as absent in the List of Members, as printed in the Journal.

Recording of attendance in Journal.

III. Proper notice boards shall be provided in a prominent place in the chamber of the House of Deputies or in the lobby, upon which the Secretary shall cause to be posted notices of all the meetings of Committees and Commissions of the House.

Notice boards.

IV. At all times when the House is in session, the National and Church flags shall be flown on the platform.

Flags.

Sergeant-at-Arms.

V. There shall be a Sergeant-at-Arms, a member of the House of Deputies appointed by the President, and such assistants as are required. Their duties, under the direction of the President or presiding officer, shall be:

(a) To maintain order and decorum in the House.

(b) To exclude from the floor of the House those not entitled to seats thereon.

(c) To exclude non-members and visitors when the House is in Executive Session.

(d) To escort distinguished visitors, and to perform such other ceremonial duties as may be assigned by the President or presiding officer.

JOINT RULES OF ORDER OF THE HOUSE OF BISHOPS AND THE HOUSE OF DEPUTIES

I Joint Standing Committees and Joint Legislative Committees

Composition

1. By Joint Rule or Joint Resolution the House of Bishops and the House of Deputies may authorize or direct the appointment of Joint Legislative Committees and Joint Committees.

May authorize by Joint Rule.

2 (a) The Joint Rule may specify the size and composition and shall specify the duties of each Committee. The membership of such Committees shall be limited to Bishops having vote in the House of Bishops, members of the House of Deputies, and such *ex officiis* members as may be provided in the Joint Rule creating such a Committee.

Membership.

(b) The terms of all members of Joint Standing Committees shall be equal to the interval between the regular meeting of the General Convention preceding their appointment and the adjournment of the succeeding regular meeting of the General Convention and until their successors are appointed; *Except,* that any Clerical or Lay member who has not been elected as a Deputy to the succeeding General Convention by the 31st day of January in the year of the said Convention shall be replaced on the Joint Standing Committee by the President of the House of Deputies, such appointment to be for the unexpired term of the former member. Any other vacancy, by death, change of status, resignation, or any other cause, shall be filled by appointment by the Presiding Officer of the appropriate House, and such appointments, likewise, shall be for the unexpired terms. The terms of all members of Joint Legislative Committees shall be only from the time of appointment until the adjournment of the first regular meeting of the General Convention following their appointment.

Terms.

Replacing any member not re-elected a Deputy.

(c) The Presiding Bishop shall appoint the Episcopal members and the President of the House of Deputies the Lay and Clerical members of Joint Standing Committees as soon as practicable after the adjournment of the General Convention, and of Joint Legislative Committees not later than sixty (60) days in advance of each General Convention. Vacancies shall be filled in similar manner.

Appointments.

(d) The Presiding Bishop, in respect of Bishops, and the President of the House of Deputies, in respect of Clergy and Lay Persons, may appoint members and staff of the Executive Council, or other experts, as consultants to any such Committee, to assist in the performance of its function. Notice of such appointment shall be given to the Secretaries of both Houses. Each such Committee shall have power to constitute subcommittees and engage the services of consultants and coordinators necessary to the carrying on of its work.

Consultants and sub-committees.

(e) The Presiding Bishop and the President of the House of Deputies shall be members *ex officiis* of every such Committee, with the right, but no obligation, to attend meetings, and with seat and vote in the deliberations thereof, and shall receive their minutes and an annual report of their

Ex officiis members.

activities; *Provided*, that the said presiding officers may appoint personal representatives to attend meetings in their stead, but without vote.

Notification of appointments.

(f) The Executive Officer of the General Convention, shall, not later than the month of January following the meeting of the General Convention, notify the members of the respective Houses of their appointments upon Joint Committees and their duty to present Reports to the next Convention. One year prior to opening day of the Convention, the Executive Officer of the General Convention shall remind the Chairs and the Secretaries of all Joint Committees of this duty.

Officers appointed.

(g) Except as otherwise provided, the Presiding Bishop and the President of the House of Deputies shall designate a Chair and Vice-Chair, or Co-Chairs, of such Committees. Each such Committee shall elect its own Secretary.

Referrals.

(h) It shall be the privilege of either House to refer to such a Committee any matter relating to the subject for which it was appointed; but neither House shall have the power, without the consent of the other, to instruct such Committees as to any particular line of action.

Duties.

(i) All such Committees shall perform all of the duties with respect to their work that are imposed on Standing Commissions by Canon I.1.2(i) through (m).

II Joint Standing Committee on Program, Budget, and Finance

Membership.

10 (a) There shall be a Joint Standing Committee on Program, Budget, and Finance, consisting of 27 persons being members of the General Convention (one Bishop, and two members of the House of Deputies, either Lay or Clerical, from each Province), who shall be appointed not later than the fifteenth day of December following each regular Meeting of the General Convention, the Bishops to be appointed by the Presiding Bishop, the Deputies by the President of the House of Deputies.

Ex officiis members.

The Secretary and the Treasurer of the General Convention and the Treasurer of the Executive Council shall be members *ex officiis*, without vote.

Advisers.

The Joint Standing Committee may appoint advisers, from time to time, as its funds warrant, to assist the Joint Standing Committee with its work.

Officers elected.

(b) Organization. The Joint Standing Committee shall elect its Chair from its membership, and such other officers as needed.

Organized in Sections.

The Joint Standing Committee shall be organized in Sections, which shall conform to the major subdivisions of the Budget, as well as Sections on Funding and Presentation, the size and composition of the several Sections to be determined by the Joint Standing Committee.

The Chairs of each Section shall be elected by the Joint Standing Committee; the several Sections shall elect their own Secretaries from among their own membership.

The Joint Standing Committee may refer to a Section any of the duties imposed upon it by this rule; *Provided, however,* that final action on Budget shall be taken only by the full Committee, either in meeting assembled or by a vote by mail.

(c) During the interim between regular Meetings of the General Convention, the Joint Standing Committee shall act in an advisory capacity to the officers of the General Convention and to the Executive Council, holding such meetings as may be deemed necessary for the purpose.

Committee to advise officers of Convention.

Meetings of the Joint Standing Committee shall be called by the Chair, or upon the request of any five members thereof.

Call to meeting.

In respect of the Budget for the Episcopal Church, the Joint Standing Committee shall have the power to consider, and either by a vote by mail, or in meeting assembled, to make such adjustments therein, or additions thereto, as it shall deem to be necessary or expedient, and which, in its judgment, available funds and anticipated income will warrant; and it shall likewise have the power to adjust the annual askings of Dioceses within the limit established by the General Convention.

Adjustments to Budget and annual askings.

With regard to the General Church Program, the Joint Standing Committee shall:

Preparing and reporting on General Church Program.

(i) Meet and consult with the Executive Council, or its Administration and Finance Committee, on adjustments to the program priorities, and on alternate income generating resources;
(ii) Receive from the Executive Council, not less than four months prior to the meeting of General Convention, the proposed General Church Program for the upcoming triennium, including a proposed detailed Budget for the year next following that of such Convention;
(iii) Meet in such places as it shall determine, sufficiently in advance of the next General Convention to expedite its work.
(iv) Conduct hearings upon such proposed Program and Budget; and
(v) Consider such proposed Program and Budget and report thereon to the next succeeding General Convention.

(d) Not later than the third day prior to the adjournment of each regular meeting of the General Convention, the Joint Standing Committee shall report to a Joint Session, pursuant to Canon, a proposed Budget for the Episcopal Church for the ensuing Convention period, subject to the approval of the said Budgets subject also to increase, reduction, or elimination of items, based on open hearings held during the General Convention and by subsequent concurrent action by the House of Deputies and the House of Bishops.

Committee to propose a Budget at Joint Session.

11. Two members of the Joint Standing Committee shall be appointed by the Chair of the Joint Standing Committee on Program, Budget and Finance to the Audit Committee of the Executive Council. The Audit Committee shall report annually to the Joint Standing Committee, which shall report to the General Convention.

Audit Committee.

The Joint Standing Committee shall present the reports of its action on audit to the General Convention at each regular meeting thereof.

III Proposals for Legislative Consideration

12. Each proposal for legislative consideration, however addressed to the General Convention or to either House thereof, received prior to a date in

Resolutions to be referred.

advance of the Convention agreed upon by the Presiding Bishop and the President of the House of Deputies, shall be referred by mail to the proper Standing Committee or Special Committee of the appropriate House, the Presiding Bishop making the referrals to the Committees of the House of Bishops and the President of the House of Deputies making the referrals to the Committees of that House.

Resolutions to be in proper form.

13. Each proposal for legislative consideration which includes the language of a proposed addition to or amendment of an existing Constitutional or Canonical provision shall be drawn, insofar as may reasonably be possible, (1) so as to indicate in Roman type the portion, if any, of the existing Constitutional or Canonical provision proposed to be retained, (2) so as to indicate in italic or underlined type the new language proposed to be inserted or added, and (3) so as to indicate, by Roman type which has been stricken through, manually or otherwise, the language of the existing Constitutional or Canonical provision proposed to be eliminated. Each such proposal calling for action shall designate the individual or body for communication and implementation, but if no such designation is included in the resolution as adopted, it shall be referred to the Office of the Secretary of General Convention for communication and implementation.

Implementation of actions.

Report or study materials must be readily available.

No proposal for legislative consideration which approves, endorses, adopts, or rejects a report, study, or other document that is not generally known by the members of the House or readily available may be considered by the General Convention unless such material is first distributed to both Houses. It is the responsibility of the proposer to provide the necessary copies to the Secretary of each House.

House of initial action.

14 (a) By joint action, the Presiding Bishop and the President of the House of Deputies may determine that one House shall be assigned responsibility for initiating legislation in respect of any such proposals (and any other proposals germane thereto introduced in either House prior to the close of the third legislative day), in which event, reference in that House shall be *for action* and reference in the other House shall be *for information.* No legislative action with regard to any proposal referred for information shall be initiated on the floor of the House to which it has been so referred until the close of the third legislative day.

Exception.

All restrictions hereby imposed with regard to any proposal referred for information shall expire at the close of the third legislative day.

Nothing herein shall affect the right of any Committee of either House to deliberate with regard to any proposal referred for information.

(b) Resolutions not reported by a legislative committee or not acted upon by both Houses shall have no further force or effect following the adjournment of the General Convention at which they are introduced.

IV Supplemental Money Bills

Referral required.

15. Whenever, in either House, after the adoption of the Budget for the Episcopal Church, a resolution is introduced calling for the expenditure of any moneys (or containing implied funding), it shall be referred to the Joint Standing Committee on Program, Budget, and Finance for consideration and recommendation back to the General Convention, or to the Executive Council if the General Convention fails to act.

V Summary of General Convention Action

16. The Secretary of the House of Deputies, being the Secretary of the General Convention, shall, with the cooperation of the Secretary of the House of Bishops, and of such Bishops as may be appointed by the Presiding Officer of the House of Bishops, prepare a summary of the actions of the General Convention of particular interest to the Congregations of the Church, and make the same available to the Congregations, through the Ministers-in-charge thereof, and to the Lay Deputies; such summary to be sent to the Clergy along with the Pastoral Letter put forth by the House of Bishops, and to be made available to all Deputies on the last day of the Convention, along with such Pastoral Letter, if feasible to do so, or within thirty days thereafter.

Secretary to prepare a summary within 30 days of Convention.

Pastoral Letter.

VI Joint Standing Committee on Planning and Arrangements

17 (a) There shall be a Joint Standing Committee on Planning and Arrangements for the General Convention, which shall have responsibility between Conventions for the matters indicated by its title. The Committee shall be composed, *ex officio*, of the Executive Officer of the General Convention, the Vice-Presidents, Secretaries, and Chairs of the Committee on the Dispatch of Business of the two Houses, the Treasurer of the General Convention, the President and First Vice-President of the Episcopal Church Women, the General Convention Manager and one Presbyter or Deacon and one Lay Person appointed by the President of the House of Deputies. In the case of a General Convention for which a meeting site has been selected, the Committee shall also include the Bishop and the General Chairman of Arrangements of the local Committee of the Dioceses in which that General Convention shall be held.

Membership.

(b) It shall be the duty of the Committee to consult with the Presidents of the two Houses, the Chairs of the Joint and Standing Committees and Commissions, Boards and Agencies of the General Convention, the Executive Council, and such other representative bodies as it may deem necessary, in the study and determination, prior to any meeting of the General Convention, of the arrangements for, and the nature of, the Agenda thereof, to be recommended by it to the General Convention for such meeting.

Prepare agenda for Convention.

(c) It shall be the further duty of the Committee to take such action as may be provided by Canon for the selection of sites for meetings of the General Convention.

Select sites.

(d) The Committee shall have an Executive Committee composed of the Presidents of the two Houses, the Chair of the Committee, the Executive Officer of the General Convention, the Treasurer of the General Convention, and the General Convention Manager.

Executive Committee.

VII Joint Standing Committee on Nominations

18. There shall be a Joint Standing Committee on Nominations, which shall submit nominations for the election of:

Charge.

(a) Trustees of The Church Pension Fund, serving as the Joint Committee referred to in Canon I.8.2.
(b) Members of the Executive Council under Canon I.4.1(c).
(c) The Secretary of the House of Deputies and the Treasurer of the General Convention under Canon I.1.1(j).
(d) Trustees of the General Theological Seminary.
(e) General Board of Examining Chaplains.

Membership.

19. The Joint Standing Committee on Nominations shall be composed of three Bishops, three Presbyters, and six Lay Persons.

Solicit recommendations.

20. The said Committee is instructed to solicit recommendations from interested organizations and individuals, to be considered by them for inclusion among their nominees.

Nomination procedures.

21. Except for the Secretary and the Treasurer of the General Convention, the said Committee is instructed to nominate a number, equal to at least twice the number of vacancies, which shall be broadly representative of the constituency of this Church; to prepare biographical sketches of all nominees; and to include such nominations and sketches in the *Blue Book*, or otherwise to circulate them among Bishops and Deputies well in advance of the meeting of the next succeeding General Convention; this procedure, however, not to preclude further nominations from the floor in the appropriate House of the General Convention.

VIII Joint Legislative Committee on Committees and Commissions

22. There shall be a Legislative Committee to be designated the Joint Committee on Committees and Commissions to which shall be referred all Resolutions relating to the creation, continuation, merger or other changes in Standing Committees and Commissions, Boards and other Agencies of the Church.

IX Task Forces of the General Convention

May be established by Convention.

23. By concurrent action, the General Convention may from time to time establish Task Forces of the General Convention to consider and make recommendations to the General Convention on specific subjects of major importance to the Church and its ministry and mission requiring special attention and competence not otherwise provided for in the Canons and/or Joint Rules, or as shall be otherwise determined by the General Convention to require the appointment of such a Task Force. The Resolution shall specify the size and composition, the clear and express duties assigned, the time for completion of the work assigned and the amount and source of the funding of each such Task Force. No Task Force shall be continued beyond the time for completion of the work assigned except by a concurrent vote of two-thirds of the members present and voting in each of the Houses. Unless otherwise specifically provided in the establishing Resolution, the Presiding Bishop shall appoint the Episcopal members and the President of the House of Deputies shall appoint the Priests and Deacons

Convention to specify membership, duties, and funding.

Appointments.

and the Lay Persons. Such Resolution may, but need not, provide for the service of Executive Council staff and other experts as consultants and co-ordinators for the Task Force.

Consultants.

X Rules in Force

24. At the meetings of the House of Bishops and the House of Deputies, the Joint Rules of the previous Convention shall be in force, until they be amended or repealed by concurrent action of the two Houses and after their reports thereon.

The General Convention
Minneapolis, July 30 – August 8, 2003
Index of Resolutions Amending the Constitution, Canons, and Rules of Order

A009	Amend Canon I.4.2(b)	Term of Office of Executive Council Members
A040	Amend Canon I.1.2(n)(6)	Standing Commission on Liturgy and Music
A042	Amend Canon I.1.9	Treasurer of the General Convention
A044	Amend Canon I.17.1(c)	Affirmation of Faith and Reception of Adult Members
A045	Amend Canon I.17.2	Definition of Communicants
A046	Amend Canon III.22.1(e)	Election of Bishops
A047	Amend Canon IV.14.13	Disqualification in Ecclesiastical Proceedings
A048	Amend Canon IV.4.16(d)	Sentencing if Respondent Fails to Appear
A049	Amend Canon IV.2(A)(2)	Sentencing of Priests and Deacons
A050	Amend Canon IV.2.(B)(10)	Sentencing of Bishops
A051	Amend Canons IV.4-6, 14-15	Repository for Proceedings of Ecclesiastical Courts
A072	Amend Canon I.6.1	Annual Parochial Reports
A111	Amend Title III Canons	Revision of Title III Canons
A124	Amend Canon I.1.2(n)	Standing Commission on Health
A141	Amend Canon I.9.1	Admission of Puerto Rico to PECUSA
A144	Amend Canon I.1.14	Guidelines for General Convention Site Selection
B011	Amend HB Rules	Voting Procedures in House of Bishops
B012	Amend HB Rule XXIV– General Rules	Admission to the House of Bishops
B013	Amend HB Rule II– First Day	Election of Secretary of House of Bishops
B014	Amend HB Rule VI–First Day	Election of Vice-Chair of House of Bishops
B015	Add HB Rule X–Standing Orders	Definitions Pertaining to Retired Bishops
D010	Amend Canon I.1.2(n)(5)	Standing Commission on Ecumenical and Interreligious Relations
D027	Amend Constitution Article II.1	Election of Bishops [Second Reading]
D044	Amend Joint Rule 18.(c)	Membership of Joint Standing Committee on Nominations
D062	Amend Constitution Article IX	Trial Court of Bishops [Second Reading]
D067	Amend Canon II.2	Bible Translations
D069	Add Canon I.1.2(n)(12)	Standing Commission on Episcopal Church Communication
D072	Amend Canon III.22.1 and Canon III.22.3(a)	Election of Bishops

References to the Constitution are made to the article (Art.) number. The Canons are referenced by title, canon, section, and subsection number. Rules of Order are identified for the houses of Bishops (RHB), Deputies (RHD) and Joint Rules (JR). Send corrections to: research@episcopalarchives.org.

- A -

- B -

- C -

- D -

- H -

- L -

Offenses and Charges

- P -

- T -

- U -

- V -

-W -

- Y -

Constitution and Canons CD-ROM Instructions

System Requirements

Windows

- Microsoft® Windows® 95/98/NT/Me/2000/XP
- CD-ROM drive

Macintosh

- Mac OS software version 9.0 or later
- CD-ROM drive

Windows Users...

1. Insert the *Constitution and Canons CD-ROM* into your CD-ROM drive.
2. If you do not already have Adobe Acrobat Reader installed on your computer:
   Open *My Computer*, double-click on your CD-ROM drive, double-click on the folder named **Windows**, then double-click on the folder named **Acrobat Reader**, then double-click on the folder named **Installer** (this is for all versions of Windows), then double-click on the icon for **Setup.exe**. This begins installation for Acrobat Reader.
3. Open *My Computer*, double-click on your CD-ROM drive, double-click on **CC2003**, then double-click on the **CandC2003.pdf** document. This will open the Constitution and Canons document.
4. For help using Acrobat Reader, select Reader Guide under the Help menu.

Macintosh Users...

1. Insert the *Constitution and Canons CD-ROM* into your CD-ROM drive.
2. If you do not already have Adobe Acrobat Reader installed on your computer:
   Open the folder for OS 9 or OS X, depending on which version of the Mac OS you are using. Open the folder named **Acrobat Reader** and double-click the **Acrobat Reader** installer icon. Follow the instructions on your screen.
3. After installation of Acrobat Reader is complete, double-click on the **CandC2003.pdf** document. This will open the Constitution and Canons document.
4. For help using Acrobat Reader, select Reader Guide under the Help menu.

Note to Windows users: If you copy the Constitution and Canons PDF file to your hard drive from the CD-ROM, be sure to copy the index.pdx file and the index folder to the same folder as the Constitutions and Canons PDF. This file and folder add to the searching capabilities of Acrobat Reader.

Note also: *Constitution and Canons* is a heavily formatted technical document. If you are performing a COPY/PASTE, choosing *copy as graphics* may help to retain the formatting, while *copying as text* will not.